Single Payer Healthcare Reform

"In this passionate and timely study, Lindy Hern brings together decades of personal involvement in the campaign for national health insurance with a scholar's immersion in social movement theory. This work should be read by all interested in the history of the campaign for Medicare for All, and by all looking to understand movements for social change."

—Gerald Friedman, Professor of Economics at the
University of Massachusetts Amherst, USA

"To date, no one has taken on the monumental task of documenting the healthcare justice movement in a thorough, comprehensive way. Yet Hern not only does so in her book, she also participates in the movement for single-payer, working for Medicare for All coverage for every person. Hern demonstrates her wide breadth of knowledge in her well-researched and well written book. Never before has the single-payer community of activists had such a rich accounting of the people who are driving the movement ever closer to the day when every person in America has access to truly high quality care without financial barriers."

—Donna Smith, Advisory Board Chair and former Executive
Director of *Progressive Democrats of America*, former National Organizer
for *National Nurses United*, and star of the *Michael Moore film SiCKO*

"Single-payer health care was kept on the nation's agenda for decades by the organizing and the protests of thousands of dedicated citizen-activists. Lindy Hern's inspiring analysis of the making of grass-roots history provides us with a democratic vision of America to last through troubled times."

—Clarence Y. H. Lo, Emeritus Professor of Sociology at the *University
of Missouri, USA,* and author of *Small Property Versus Big Government:
Social Origins of the Property Tax Revolt*

Lindy S. F. Hern

Single Payer Healthcare Reform

Grassroots Mobilization and the Turn Against
Establishment Politics in the Medicare for All
Movement

Lindy S. F. Hern
Department of Sociology
University of Hawaii at Hilo
Hilo, HI, USA

ISBN 978-3-030-42766-5   ISBN 978-3-030-42764-1   (eBook)
https://doi.org/10.1007/978-3-030-42764-1

This Palgrave Macmillan imprint is published by the registered company Springer Nature Switzerland AG.
The registered company address is: Gewerbestrasse 11, 6330 Cham, Switzerland

Dedicated to Julia Lamborn and Marilyn Clement
Two of the Rocks on Which the Single Payer Movement was Built

Preface: "Onward to Single Payer"

One of my mentors—Mary Jo—once asked me, "when will you be finished with this project?" At that point in the spring of 2010, I had already been "in the field" working with the Single Payer Movement for almost six years. I had just defended my dissertation proposal and was preparing to start the process of writing a dissertation, which would eventually be defended in the spring of 2012. Now, here I am, almost ten years later, finishing a book about the movement that includes an additional decade of data about the process of mobilization in support of the creation of a system that would guarantee quality healthcare for all through a healthcare system financed by the state.

When Mary Jo asked me that question, I knew that she expected a different answer than the one that I gave her. Typically, field research takes place over a set period of time—a researcher may spend months in the field, but years? Decades? Surely not. At that point in 2010 I had already spent more time in the field than was typical of most field research projects. So, I knew that she was expecting me to tell her that I would stop "collecting data" and just focus on writing at a point in the not so distant future. But, I couldn't do that because I was in the field of the Single Payer Movement, not just as a researcher, not just as a sociologist, but also as an activist committed to doing what I could to move our great but imperfect nation toward the creation of a just healthcare system. So, my answer to Mary Jo was simple—"I'll be finished when we have a single-payer healthcare system in the United States." And, that answer is just as true today as it was on that day almost ten years ago. But, the completion of the project with that end point in mind may just be closer than we know.

We are currently in an era in which the rise of right-wing authoritarian politics threatens to dismantle the progress that we have made as a society to move toward a truly just system that protects and empowers all of its members. Yet, it is also a time when movements for progressive change, including the Single Payer Movement, have seen an influx of support and greater opportunities for mobilization. When I first started this project no one, except for a very select few, knew what I was talking about when I mentioned single-payer and even fewer thought that it was a worthwhile project due to the seeming lack of importance of what was then a marginalized movement. But I was concerned about issues of inequality and understood that the creation of a universal healthcare system was a necessary step to address this problem. I had learned from my research on the subject that single-payer was probably the best way to achieve universal coverage given the particularities of our political, economic, and cultural context. I also had a feeling that there was something special about what was happening within the Single Payer Movement at that time, and I wanted to figure out what that special thing was. Witnessing the movement grow in both recognition and participation as it moved from an extremely marginalized position to a central position within American politics has been both a challenging and rewarding experience.

This book is my humble attempt to explain how the movement continued to mobilize in the face of failure in order to create more opportunity to achieve single-payer, even when progress toward the goals of the movement seemed impossible for so many years. I think that this explanation is valuable for multiple audiences including—but not limited to—academics who attempt to understand politics, social change, and/or social movements through research and critical thinking; political actors who enact social change inside the halls of government; activists who work for social change from the outside those halls; and a general public that is concerned about progressive policy reform, including though not limited to issues related to healthcare. For this reason, I have tried to write the book in such a way that it would be both interesting and accessible to these multiple audiences. I hope that I have succeeded in this endeavor and look forward to future discussion with you, the reader, about this and other related issues.

Hilo, HI   Lindy S. F. Hern

ACKNOWLEDGEMENTS

There are many people to whom I owe my thanks and appreciation. First, I would like to thank Dr. Clarence Lo who was my PhD advisor until 2012 and has continued to be a mentor since then. I first began to work with Dr. Lo in the spring of 2004. This book is actually the summation of a process that started in his graduate seminar on social movements that spring. Even following my graduation, Dr. Lo continued to be an enthusiastic mentor and reviewer on occasion. Many of the ideas developed here bloomed initially as Dr. Lo listened to my ideas, read my written work, and gave me excellent detailed feedback. During the final stages of writing this book, when I found myself in a rather disconnected cave of writing fatigue, Dr. Lo took a break from retirement to review chapters of this book for me and gave me feedback that brought enthusiasm back into the process. Dr. Joan Hermsen was one of the most important mentors for my intellectual development and has been a source of support. Her criticism, as well as her encouragement, on this and other work, has helped me to become a better scholar and activist. I will forever be grateful for that. Dr. Victoria Johnson introduced me to historical sociology, which was so important to the development of this project driven by the analysis of historical processes. I owe much to Dr. Mary Jo Neitz. It was in her seminars that I had my awakening as a feminist scholar and developed many of the methodological tools that are so important to my research. Dr. Marjorie Sable's interest in and support for my work has also been very important for my development as a scholar of social movements for healthcare reform. Dr. Andrew Twaddle played a central role in my development as a scholar of social movements for healthcare reform. Dr. Mike Hirsch, my undergraduate advisor, has continued to be a supportive and attentive mentor throughout my academic career. Dr. Jaber Gubrium first introduced me to narrative analysis in his seminar on "Narrative and Identity" and I thank him for this. Dr. Ken Benson was influential in the development of my thinking about organizations. I met Dr. Aldon Morris through my work with the Association for Applied and Clinical Sociology and he became a mentor to me in the last three or four years. He has reviewed materials for me and encouraged my development as a scholar—even though we have only met in person once at the 2015 AACS conference in Montgomery, Alabama, where he gave the keynote address.

I'd also like to thank my newer colleagues at the University of Hawaii at Hilo. With them I have found a professional home that has been supportive of my ongoing research. Specifically, I'd like to thank Dr. Marilyn Brown and Dr. Noelie Rodriguez for their interest in my work and their support through conversation and written review. I'd also like to thank Dr. Thom Curtis for engaging in amicable debate about healthcare politics with me, and Dr. Alton Okinaka for seeing the value of my work to the Hawaiian context. Drs SuMi Lee, Sarah Marusek, Celia Bardwell Jones, Yolisa Duley, Kerri Inglis, Amy Gregg, Michael Bitter, and Katie Young have also been sources of support and comradery. Finally, I would like to thank Dr. Susan Brown for her enthusiasm for my work and for giving me the opportunity to apply it within my teaching during her time as Dean of the College of Arts and Sciences at UH-Hilo.

Several others have been helpful during this process. Many people have reviewed pieces of the puzzle that make up this book. Drs Colin Suchland, Kathy Stolley, and Frances Fox Piven (who I met at a single-payer conference) have reviewed portions of the content presented here. I'd like to thank my editors—Michelle Chen, John Stegner, and especially Rebecca Roberts—for their help during the process of publication, which was new to me. Several activists have also given me feedback—Donna Smith, Rita Valenti, Don Bechler, Mimi Signor, and Lisa Patrick-Mudd have been especially responsive. It was important to me that this also be a book for activists, so their review comments were invaluable. A few research assistants also helped me organize data for components of this text—I thank Megan Floyd for her meticulous work in digitally archiving my historical data and Kanoelani Dodd for coding newspaper articles. Although Remi Nakaza McKay did not assist me on this project, her assistance on other projects freed up time for me to focus on this project. I'd also like to thank my librarian friend Jill Mahoney for helping me with library resources when needed and Dr. Steve Barnard for his advice on the book publication process.

I would like to thank my family and friends. It is also important to me that this book is accessible to a general audience, so comments, criticisms, and questions from this community were key. My folks, Kyle and Marie Hern, have been my constant source of support and unconditional love since birth. Without their presence in my life, none of this would have been possible. When I was in a writing hole they offered to read chapters for me and give me feedback to pull me out of it. My dad, Kyle, was fond of reminding me to "just get done what you can get done today," which got me through some rough moments. My mom was always ready to jump in with clerical assistance—such as indexing—when needed. She was also happy to listen to me read chapters out loud—even through cross pacific phone calls—because it helped me in my process. My cousins, Sara Page and Kelly Hunolt, provided support and places to stay as I conducted my research around the country. My siblings—Jon, Nathan, and Melissa—and grandparents—Bill, Lucille, Lawrence, and Kate—were also constant sources of support and love. Jennifer Lux has also been a consistent source of support even when our politics weren't in agreement. Dr. Brooke Williams and Dr. Kathleen Krueger have always been available for a supportive phone conversation over vast distances as we started our academic careers on opposite sides of the country. Portia King, Derek Evans, and Jon Huffman have also been ready to give feedback or positive affirmation when needed. Finally, Matthew Humphrey was my day-to-day source of support for many years first in Missouri, then in Indiana, and finally in Hawaii.

I would like to thank the activists who have been so important in and supportive of my research. Many of them make appearances in this text and I thank them all. I would like to specifically thank Mimi Signor, Mary Jane Schutzius, Donna Smith, Katie Robbins, Cindy Young, Lisa Patrick Mudd, and Stephanie Nakajima. Mimi has been a consistent source of expert and experiential knowledge of the healthcare system since the early days of this project in 2004 and she has always been willing to act as a sound board for my ideas. Mary Jane allowed me to utilize her immaculately kept files for the historical portion of my research and connected me with others who kept similar files. Donna brought enthusiasm and light to my research, as well as a writer's critical eye. I thank Katie, Cindy, Lisa, and Stephanie for several conversations during which we discussed many of the issues presented here. Roger Signor, Ben Day, Mark Dudzic, Gerald

Friedman, Walter Tsou, Lee Kramer, and John Lozier have also all been important sounding boards at some point over the years for my ideas presented in this text.

Finally, I would like to dedicate this book to Marilyn Clement and Julia Lamborn. Until her death in 2009, Marilyn was one of the many rocks on which the contemporary Single Payer Movement was built. She welcomed me into the Healthcare NOW community with open arms and was consistently supportive of my research. Julia was also foundational to the Single Payer Movement, especially in Missouri, and to the early years of my project. Julia introduced me to the world of single-payer and without her fierce support of single-payer and of my research, this study may have never even begun. Her death left a hole in the movement but her earlier actions made sure that this hole would not remain empty. They will forever be remembered and will forever be missed. As they would say, "Onward to Single Payer".

CONTENTS

List of Figures

LIST OF TABLES

CHAPTER 1

"A Single Prayer for Single Payer": Opportunity and Narrative Practice in the Single Payer Movement

I'd like to tell you a story. I'd like to tell you a story about ants. You see, there was this community of ants. It was a normal community, like any other community, with ants going about their little ant business. Some ants were teachers, some ants were janitors, some ants were doctors, and yes, one ant was the President. Although a few enjoyed abundance in this community, many more suffered due to their lack of access to the basic resources needed for living. One day, a small segment of this ant community determined that they could solve this problem if they could only climb to the tippy top of the tallest building, (which was really just a table leg), because in that place there were enough resources for the entire ant community. If they could only get to the top. So, they decided to climb. Most of the ant community did not notice the mission of this segment of the ant community until they were high enough to be visible above the hustle and bustle of the rest. Once they did notice, after first ignoring them in the hopes that this minor annoyance would just go away, they began to laugh saying "You silly ants! You are too weak. You are too small. And that building is far too tall for you to ever possibly be able to get to the top! Come back down and perhaps we will give you a scrap to eat." Although it was difficult, most of the climbing ants chose to ignore this, but some did go back down to the floor with hopes of coming to a compromise. As time went on, and the ants got higher and higher, the laughter of the ants on the ground turned to jeers of anger. "You idiots" they said, "how could you possibly expect to reach the tippy top when you are SO WEAK, you are SO SMALL, and that building is far too TALL. You might as well come back down, you must be tired, and just look at the sweet things we are eating down here!" And indeed, many of the climbing ants were tired, and began to believe that they were too weak to go on. Some dropped back

© The Author(s) 2020
L. S. F. Hern, *Single Payer Healthcare Reform*,
https://doi.org/10.1007/978-3-030-42764-1_1

1

down to the floor in defeat, waiting for the scraps that would supposedly quell their hunger for the time being. As time went on, and the ants got higher and higher, more and more of the climbing ants fell, succumbing to the jeers of the ants on the floor. But, one little ant, the littlest ant indeed, kept climbing. Even as the others screamed "you are TOO WEAK, you are TOO SMALL, and the building is far, far, far TOO TALL" the little ant kept climbing. Eventually, the tiny tired ant reached the tippy top of the tallest building, which was really just a table leg, proving to the others that it could be done, even by a DEAF little ant like her.

I first heard the story of the ants when Mimi Signor addressed the attendees of the 2009 Healthcare NOW national strategy meeting in St. Louis, Missouri, and then again as she accepted the Paul Wellstone Award for Community Activism on behalf of Missourians for Single Payer (MoSP) at the 2010 meeting of the Association for Applied and Clinical Sociology. As the legislative chair and vice president of MoSP, Mimi knew how the little ants were feeling as she accepted this award over a year after she had first told this story to a conference hall full of activists attempting to redirect the healthcare reform debate that was raging in D.C. at that time. She later explained to me that she had told the story just as much for Julia, then president of MoSP (who was also there to accept the award), as she had told it for the crowd of sociologists from the Association for Applied and Clinical Sociology (which was giving the award). This storytelling took place in October of 2010, after the passage of the Patient Protection and Affordable Care Act, now commonly referred to as the Affordable Care Act (ACA), or more simply as "Obamacare," and on the eve of a mid-term election that would likely return power to the Republican Party. In other words, during a time in which the chances of successfully achieving their goal of single-payer healthcare seemed very bleak.

I decided to start with the telling of this story because it not only symbolically summarized for Mimi the story of the Single Payer Movement (SPM) or because it illustrates the relationship between opportunity and action, but also because it draws attention to the important role that narrative story-telling plays in the SPM. In the story, the little ant is met with an impossible task but succeeds anyway because the little ant ignored all of those saying that the goal was impossible. The SPM is a collection of activists and organizations that have continued to mobilize even within a context in which the dominant narrative was that their goal of creating a single-payer healthcare system in the United States was impossible. They continued to act with the belief that "It always seems impossible until it's done."[1]

I will examine the role that narrative plays in the lives of grassroots social movements and the ways in which narrative practice can result in grassroots mobilization that can change political realities. Academic literature dealing with healthcare reform primarily forms a state-centered account of periods in which healthcare reform is a primary focus within the political sphere of federal-level policy change. Popular writing about healthcare reform typically focuses on federal-level actors participating in this process when there is movement toward healthcare reform at the federal level. Reading this, one might conclude that mobilization for healthcare reform occurs only when political leaders decide that the time is ripe for it. I will show instead that the movement for universal health care, and indeed the SPM, has a relatively long history that transcends specific presidents, periods, or political epochs and is as connected to factors that lie outside of the political realm as it is to factors that lie within it.

I completed the writing of this book during a time period in which the United States was at a crossroads. The heavy stone of progress that had been slowly rolling toward a truly just and inclusive society that would protect the rights of all groups of people had almost been pushed to the "tippy top" of the hill of social justice. For centuries, groups of individuals with shared ideas about social change had taken on the task to expand a democratic system of rights to more groups of people. The expansion of civil rights to previously excluded populations during the twentieth century represented progress toward the goal of creating a society that would justly support the "life, liberty, and pursuit of happiness" of all members, just as the abolition of institutionalized slavery had 100 or so years before. It seemed that a bit more effort could push that heavy stone of progress over the summit of the hill and start it rolling down the other side—quickly moving as an unstoppable force toward a society that would protect the social and human rights of everyone in all areas, including health care. At the same time, the rise of anti-establishment politics that resulted in a wave of grassroots organizing for progressive social change on the left also resulted in the rise of radical right-wing populism, which led to the election of Donald Trump. This wave of authoritarian politics threatens to not only halt the forward momentum of the heavy stone of social justice but to also force it back down the slope with a retraction of the rights

[1] Senator Bernie Sanders (D-VT), Rally in Detroit Michigan, 10/27/2019.

secured over the past 200 years—turning the fight for a socially just society into a Sisyphean tale of progression and regression. The analysis presented here, of one progressive social movement, sheds some light onto how we arrived at this crucial point in our collective history. As I finish this book there is anger, fear, and despair over the efforts to roll back rights in the areas of reproductive choice, immigration, and LGBTQ civil liberties among others. Yet, there is also powerful hope that we can and will continue to move forward as a community by pushing that stone down the path that will lead us to a truly just society that not only protects the rights of all but also provides a framework in which all people have the support and opportunities needed to achieve their goals. How did we get to this point? And how do progressive movements continue to produce hope that a brighter future is possible even in a context of such uncertainty? How does a social movement that has experienced so many years of failure with its primary goal not achieved, continue to mobilize in order to produce the lesser social changes that will create a path toward its ultimate goal? In this analysis of the past thirty years of the SPM, I will develop answers to these questions.

A SINGLE PRAYER FOR SINGLE PAYER

When I first began my work with the SPM, there was a great deal of confusion about the term "single payer." At one of my early field trips—to the annual meeting of an organization called Missourians for Single Payer (MoSP)—in November of 2004, the hotel at which the meeting was taking place had enthusiastically welcomed meeting attendees on their front marque saying "Welcome Missourians for Single **Prayer**." The then President of the organization, Julia, remarked that the sign was partially right—that they did have one prayer for one thing—creating a single-**payer** system (SPS) in Missouri and beyond. I also recall being at a national meeting of single-payer activists a few years later, in the fall of 2007, in Chicago. At breakfast, assuming that those assembled were supportive of the goals of the meeting, I asked a young woman at my table how she thought that the movement would achieve the goal of creating a single-payer system in the United States. She responded with "You know, I really think that something needs to change, but I just don't think that single people should be paying for health care for everyone." I explained to her that in a single-payer system, everyone, not just singles, would pay into the same health assurance system through taxes (instead of premiums, co-pays, and deductibles) which would finance the health care of everyone in the country. In the early years of this field study, confusion over the term single-payer often resulted in debates within activist circles about whether they should use the term at all—especially in organizational names. Activists often shared the sentiment that "the name is hard to understand for people, you know they don't understand what single-payer means."[2]

This confusion was understandable, while healthcare reform debates in the 1970s did include support for movement toward a Canadian style system, the term single-payer didn't arise as a conceptual framework for an already existing form of healthcare system until the early 1990s.[3] Indeed, single-payer is a relatively new umbrella term for a system in which health care is financed by one entity—although this entity is typically the state, not singles. Until quite recently, the term was often met with little recognition when used outside of specific circles. Yet, activists within the movement remained committed to using the term. At one meeting of MoSP in 2004, when discussing the refusal of political actors to use the term single-payer, Julia explained that "for a long time no one would say the words women's rights either, but it gradually worked into the discussion and I think the same thing will happen with single-payer."[4] I have been impressed to see the term, or terms used as synonyms (such as Medicare for All), become commonly used in multiple circles, including mainstream political debates. Although usage of the term and awareness of its meaning has grown, there is still confusion about exactly what a single-payer system is—even within academic circles. At a meeting in 2014, seven years after my breakfast conversation, Pam explained the confusion over the term saying "when I talk about single-payer healthcare, now people are thinking its single parent healthcare! We need to use enhanced Medicare for All or something."[5] In order to clarify the concept and how it is used within the movement, I will briefly describe what a single-payer healthcare system is and how it differs from other types of systems around the world. I will

[2] Bob Interview, November 20th, 2004.

[3] Tuohy, Carolyn Hughes. 2009. "Single Payers, Multiple Systems: The Scope and Limits of Subnational Variation under a Federal Health Policy Framework" Journal of Health Politics, Policy, and Law Vol. 34 No.4.

[4] Fieldnotes, Missourians for Single Payer Meeting, September 2004.

[5] Fieldnotes, One Payer States National Meeting, 2014.

also explain the reasons why activists support single-payer. But before I discuss the "what" and "why" of single-payer, it is important to first explain the "who" of the SPM, as they are the focus of this book.

WHO IS SINGLE PAYER: JULIA'S STORY

I first met Julia on a warm sunny day in the spring of 2004. I had done some research to find out what was going on with healthcare reform in the state of Missouri as part of a class project for a graduate seminar on social movements. I was interested in the issue of healthcare reform due to my concern about overcoming poverty and other forms of inequality. I learned from the work of scholars such as William Julius Wilson that creating a universal healthcare system was a necessary step in overcoming the root causes of poverty and socioeconomic, as well as racial, inequality.[6] I first met Julia, who was then the President of MoSP at a truck stop about halfway between Columbia Missouri where I was located and St. Louis Missouri where she lived, worked, and fought for single-payer healthcare reform. I was immediately struck by her strong and stern demeanor. As we started talking, her sincere and compassionate attitude toward others also became obvious. We talked about my newness to the world of single-payer and also my desire to understand what was happening with healthcare reform in Missouri. I explained to Julia that I would like to work with her and with MoSP so that I could develop a better understanding of the process of healthcare reform. She was a bit cautious with me at first, initially calling me her stalker because I would follow her around everywhere and she wasn't sure about my intentions.[7] Over the years I got to know Julia very well. I learned that both her feminist awakening and one of her earliest indicators of the problems within the American healthcare system happened when she was in her early 30s. In her 50s, she told me the story saying,

> So, the point came that I was thirty years old, and I decided that I wanted to have a tubal ligation. And in order to have one, my husband had to sign the release form. And that made me very angry. Because I could not go and

---

[6] See Wilson, William Julius. 1987. The Truly Disadvantaged: The Inner City, The Underclass, and Public Policy. University of Chicago Press, Chicago IL.

[7] For a more in-depth discussion of this process see also Hern, Lindy. (2016) "From Stalker to Board Member: Navigating the Borderland of Scholar Activism in the Movement for Single Payer Health Care Reform." *Journal of Applied Social Science.*

have a tubal ligation. It was like I didn't have enough sense to make up my own mind. Somebody else was controlling my body. Somebody who didn't even know anything about me.[8]

It wasn't until several years later, when she was struggling to cover the cost of health insurance for her employees, that she decided to try to change the laws that determined the characteristics of this system. As the owner of a small oil recycling business in St. Louis Missouri, it was important to Julia and her husband that they provide health insurance for their employees. Every year their costs would go up and their coverage would go down—to the point that it was hurting their ability to stay in business. There was a contradiction between their belief that they should provide health insurance for their employees and their need to maintain a profitable business. So, Julia started doing research to see what other options were there. She spent quite a long time just studying and researching healthcare systems and policies around the world until she finally concluded that a single-payer system would be the best form of healthcare financing system for the United States. At that point, in the mid-1990s, she decided to start working for single-payer healthcare reform. Eventually she became the president of MoSP. Over the next 10 years I worked with Julia to better understand the process that activists around the country were undertaking in order to move the United States toward a more just healthcare system. I spent time with her and many other single-payer activists at meetings, at rallies, in interviews, on conference calls, and in many other ways—working on this issue.

Julia was the type of person who kept a couple of dollars and a pair of gloves in her car just in case she came upon someone who needed those things. She was also the type of person who wouldn't take any "bullshit" from anyone and who would stand up for what she believed was right. She was both kind and compassionate, as well as stern and strong. Julia would tell me "I'm going to keep working for single-payer. I know that I might not see it in my lifetime, but I sure as hell hope that you'll see it in yours." And until the day that she died in 2013 she worked—through sickness, through health, through anything that life threw at her, for the rest of her life—she worked to build support for a single-payer system in the United States.

[8] Julia Interview—October, 2005.

I'm starting with the description of who is single-payer and not what is single-payer, because ultimately this is not a story about policy. Yes, policy is important as it is often the social change outcome of social movements, but policy change does not just happen. The story of policy change is ultimately a story about people—people who work to make a change happen because they care about the lives of others. People who work to create hope for themselves, for each other, and for the larger society so that something different is possible. People who will not stop pushing the heavy stone of progress until change is made. In order to understand the what, the why, or the how, you must understand the people who are behind all of those things. Julia is just one person out of thousands that have been working on this issue for decades. But she is one person who made a difference. There are numerous activists who will play a role in the following pages—but many others will go unnamed. And there are organizations that have also worked for years to change the scope of what is possible and to make this particular social change a reality.

The SPM is made up of not only people but it is also made up of organizations. Some organizations are going to come to the forefront of my analysis because I was embedded within them and through them I had an inclusive view of what was happening with healthcare reform. Until recently, these organizations were marginalized within the larger Movement for Healthcare Reform. I have learned from the epistemology of standpoint theory that if you are trying to really understand something, then you should start the process from the bottom up and not from the top down.[9] If you are building knowledge from positions of power and privilege, then you are not understanding the whole picture. Those in positions of power and privilege do not have to see the whole picture in order to successfully achieve their goals. So, the organizations that are centered in this analysis are grassroots single-payer organizations that were marginalized from the centers of political power. For example, I started my work with MoSP which is a state-based organization born in the early 1990s. Later, I began working with Healthcare NOW which is a national organization that was formed around a specific piece of single-payer legislation—H.R. 676—in the early 2000s. Connected to these organizations is a network of other groups that will also be discussed and analyzed for the role that they play in the story of the SPM.

[9] Smith, Dorothy. 1999. Writing the Social: Critique, Theory, and Investigations. Toronto, ON: University of Toronto Press.

Table 1.1 Typology of single-payer organizations

	Professional organizations	Political organizations	Cultural organizations	Grassroots organizations
Single issue	Physicians for a National Health Program Labor Campaign for Single Payer Business for Medicare for All Unions for Single Payer	Medicare for All Caucus	Healthy Artists Initiative	Healthcare NOW Missourians for Single Payer Single-Payer Action Health Over Profit for Everyone One Payer States
Multi issue	National Nurses United American Medical Student Association American College of Physicians	Progressive Democrats of America Democratic Socialists of America Justice Democrats Progressive Caucus	Presbyterian and United Methodist Churches Unitarian Universalist Association Church Women United	Public Citizen Our Revolution NOW Gray Panthers Raging Grannies Code Pink MoveOn

This is not an exhaustive list of single-payer organizations—there are others that will be discussed in the following chapters.

A typology of organizations involved in the SPM relies on several dimensions (see Table 1.1). The first dimension is whether the organization is focused on one single issue or on multiple issues. Until relatively recently, organizations focused solely on creating a single-payer healthcare system in the United States were few and far between. While there was an increase in the numbers of this type of organization in the early 1990s, an abeyance period[10] following the failure of healthcare reform during the Clinton presidency resulted in the death of many single-payer organizations or in the shifting focus of single-payer healthcare organizations that survived the era. From the early 2000s to the current era, the SPM once

[10] Abeyance refers to a period of decreased activity in which a social movement or social movement organization experiences less participation or grassroot mobilization and more centralization of, or emphasis on, shared values and identity within a smaller group of participants. For a more in-depth discussion of abeyance, see also: Sawyers, Traci M. and David S. Meyer "Missed Opportunities: Social Movement Abeyance and Public Policy" Social Problems, Volume 46, Issue 2, 1 May 1999, Pages 187–206.

again saw an increase in the number of organizations focusing on single-payer. These shifts are tied to changes within the context in which the movement exists, discussed in the following chapters. There are other organizations that support the shift toward a single-payer system along with many other goals. These multi-issue organizations that have multiple goals are better able to survive negative shifts in the context but are also more likely to shift focus away from the single-payer. They are not as equipped to put the bulk of their resources toward a specific goal as single-issue organizations are.

Another important dimension is related to the typical membership within the organization. Professional organizations are tied to a membership base within a specific profession or group of professions—this includes unions, social movement organizations (SMOs), and advocacy groups oriented toward a specific profession. For example, the Physicians for a National Health Program (PNHP) was formed in 1987 specifically to support the creation of a single-payer system in the United States. PNHP is classified as a single-issue professional organization. The National Nurses United (NNU), an example of a multi-issue professional organization, is the largest nurses' union in the United States and works on multiple issues, including a central focus on supporting Medicare for All. Professional organizations often contribute financially to movement activities and organizations in addition to contributing to change by using their professional expertise. Some, such as NNU, also contribute significantly to grassroots mobilization efforts by putting "boots on the ground." Political organizations have a membership that is tied to a particular political party or ideology. These organizations are more likely to be multi-issue but can include subsections of larger political organizations or parties. For example, the Medicare for All Caucus within the U.S. House of Representatives is a single-issue political organization inside of the political sphere, while the Progressive Democrats of America is a multi-issue political organization that is outside of institutionalized political structures. Cultural organizations are grounded in a membership that is tied to specific cultural practices or systems of belief. For example, some religious organizations that are not overtly political, such as the Presbyterian Church (USA) and the United Methodist Church (USA), have passed resolutions to support the creation of a single-payer system. Cultural organizations, especially those of the religious type, have played an extensive role in both progressive and conservative social movements. For example, the role that southern black churches played during the Civil Rights Movement of the 1950s and 1960s was key to the success of that movement.[11] Finally, and most importantly for the analysis presented here, there are grassroots organizations. Unlike the other organizational types that have some larger unifying characteristic beyond the goals of the movement—such as profession, political party, or cultural affiliation—participants in grassroots organizations come together in order to promote a specific goal or set of goals. They do not necessarily share anything in common other than the support of a specific goal. These organizations are outside of any institutionalized system of power and instead build their power from the bottom up. They are often marginalized from traditional systems of power, and thus must learn to navigate each system in order to gain influence or support.

Grassroots organizations don't just differ based on their single vs. multi issue status but also based on their organizational form and national vs. state focus (see Table 1.2). National organizations have a membership that is nation-wide, while state organizations focus on building their membership within specific states. While both types of organizations can support national or state level healthcare reform, state organizations are more likely to support state-level policy changes than national organizations, which are typically focused on changes to national policy.

Organizations also differ based on organizational form which is rooted in the way that decisions are made within the organization. Participatory democratic organizations value collective decision making with minimal to no hierarchy. While many grassroots organizations start in this way, it becomes difficult to maintain as the organization grows in size—the

Table 1.2 Typology of single-payer grassroots organizations

	Participatory democratic organizations	Centralized organizations	Professionalized organizations
State level	Healthcare for All Hawaii	Missourians for Single Payer	Healthcare for All Oregon
National level	Red Berets for Medicare for All	Health Over Profit for Everyone (HOPE)	Healthcare NOW

This is not an exhaustive listing of single-payer organizations

[11] See McAdam, Doug. 1982/1999. Political Process and the Development of Black Insurgency. 1930–1970. Second Edition. Chicago: University of Chicago Press and Morris, Aldon. (1984). The Origins of the Civil Rights Movement. New York: The Free Press.

difference between coming to a consensus within an organization of 10 people vs. an organization of 100 people is significant. With a growth in size, a hierarchy typically develops to facilitate decision making within the organization. Organizational decision making becomes more centralized with a hierarchy typically involving a board of directors and an executive committee of some sort. A key feature of centralized organizations is that the hierarchy is still made up of volunteers. This differs from professionalized organizations in which there is a paid staff that takes care of the day-to-day activities and decision making of the organization. While professionalized organizations have been praised for their efficiency,[12] they have also been critiqued for their lack of grassroots participation and collective decision making as membership is increasingly based on financial contributions rather than on direct participation.[13] This form of membership can leave out those who are not able to financially contribute to the organization, which can mean that those who would benefit from the initial goals of the organization are locked out of the decision-making process. Professionalized organizations have also been critiqued for becoming too invested in self-perpetuation, because jobs depend on the sustainability of the organization which will no longer exist once the organizational goals are achieved. Organizations must carefully develop management forms that are both efficient and oriented toward achieving the original goals in order to be successful.

During the course of my field study I was embedded primarily within one centralized state-level organization—Missourians for Single Payer (MoSP)—and one professionalized national-level organization—Healthcare NOW. I also became more loosely embedded within a participatory state-level organization—Healthcare for All Hawaii—after moving to the state. Each of these organizations is oriented toward one goal—achieving a single-payer system at the state or federal level. I will discuss each of these organizations in greater detail in the following chapters. Many other organizations fitting all of the types described (some are listed in the non-exhaustive tables above) also play a role in my analysis due their

---

[12] McAdam, Doug, John D. McCarthy, and Mayer N. Zald (1996). Comparative Perspectives on Social Movements: Political Opportunities, Mobilizing Structures, Cultural Framings Ed. By Doug McAdam, Cambridge University Press.

[13] Piven, Frances Fox, and Richard Cloward. 1977. Poor People's Movements: Why They Succeed, How They Fail. New York: Vintage Books.

intersection with these grassroots organizations. All of these organizations have fought for years to make this change happen. So, what exactly is it that they are fighting for?

What Is Single Payer?

The term "universal health care" refers to a healthcare system that covers everyone within a particular nation or state. It is not synonymous with single-payer, but at times the terms are used interchangeably. This can be confusing because not all universal systems are the same. If you examine universal healthcare systems around the world, they can be categorized primarily into three forms—multi-payer, single-payer, and socialized medicine. The United States is the only high-income OECD nation without some form of universal system. It is better to think of these forms as places on a fluid continuum rather than as concrete and rigidly defined types. There is much variation within each form and some overlap between forms. Systems may have some characteristics of a particular form, but not all (Fig. 1.1).

The first form is a universal multi-payer system. In this type of system, healthcare facilities and healthcare insurance are both public and privately operated and financed. This type of system is more likely to be found in continental Europe—in countries with a strong history of non-competing social insurance tied to trades (guilds, employers, etc.).[14] Universality in these systems is based on everyone having guaranteed access to an insurance provider, typically through a non-profit social insurer. If the United States maintained the current system but added a "public option" that would cover everyone who was not already covered by private insurance, Medicare, or Medicaid, then this would ideally create a universal multi-payer system. However, because the system would lack the historical legacy of non-profit social insurance and would maintain for-profit private insurers, it would function differently from the current universal multi-payer systems operating around the world today, which are highly regulated by state interventions. On the other end of the continuum of universal health care are socialized systems in which the state both owns and operates most medical facilities. This type of system in its ideal type is

[14] Oliver, Adam. 2009 "The Single-Payer Option: A Reconsideration" *Journal of Health Politics, Policy, and Law* Vol. 34 No.4.

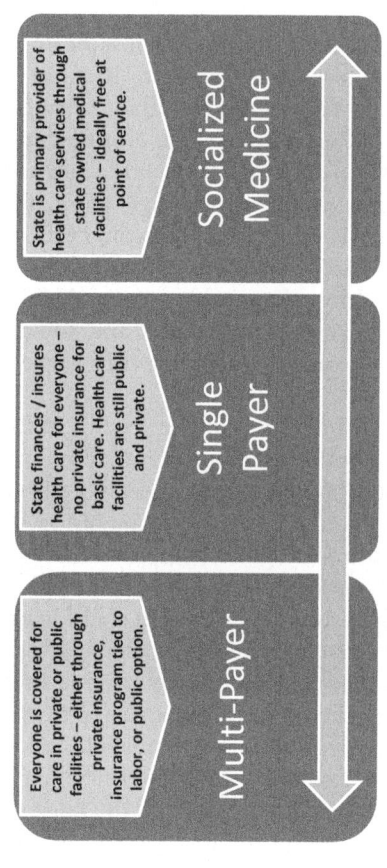

Fig. 1.1 Continuum of universal healthcare systems

totally, publicly funded and operated. These systems are not prevalent in the capitalist world economy, but one primary example is the National Health Service that operates in the United Kingdom. While the UK system is often referred to as a "single-payer" system, it is not an ideal type single-payer system nor is it what single-payer activists in the United State are seeking to achieve. Even though there is one payer that guarantees financial coverage for care, and that coverage is funded primarily through taxation—similar to a single-payer system—the NHS goes an extra step and requires most medical facilities to be public as well. Notably, the NHS was established after infrastructure in the United Kingdom was devastated during the Second World War. Those rebuilding the infrastructure following the war made developing a healthcare system that would cover everyone and be free at the point of service a key factor in this process, which resulted in the NHS. Although the NHS has been successfully fulfilling its intended function for decades, it has also been challenged, underfunded, and more privatization has been pushed into the system.[15] Also, even though the key indicators of success within this system, such as cost, health, and patient satisfaction, are typically better than those of the United States system, it is often used in the healthcare reform debate as a specter of "socialized medicine" designed to drive away support from options such as single-payer, which in its ideal type, is not socialized medicine.

In the middle of the continuum are single-payer systems. Single-payer systems blend public and private facilities but ideally finance all basic medical care from a single entity—typically the state.[16] All insurance operates based on sharing risk—a group of people pay into a risk pool with the expectation that care will be covered by the shared resources in that pool.[17] Single-payer creates one risk pool because everyone in the system pays into the same fund, typically through taxes. Many single-payer systems have governing bodies at multiple levels that make decisions for the system— meaning that not all decisions for the system are made at the federal level;

[15] Webster, Charles. 2002. National Health Service: A Political History Oxford University Press.

[16] Tuohy, Carolyn Hughes. 2009. "Single Payers, Multiple Systems: The Scope and Limits of Subnational Variation under a Federal Health Policy Framework" *Journal of Health Politics, Policy, and Law* Vol. 34 No.4.

[17] Chen, Anthony, and Margaret Weir. 2009. "The Long Shadow of the Past: Risk Pooling and the Political Development of Health Care Reform in the States" *Journal of Health Politics, Policy, and Law* Vol. 34 No.5.

some decisions are made at the state or even the local level.[18] This results in a lot of variation between, and even within, single-payer systems. The key distinction between single-payer and other types of systems is that health care is primarily publicly financed while facilities are both publicly and privately operated. This distinguishes single-payer systems from both "socialized" medicine in which the state both pays for medical care and owns most medical facilities and multi-payer systems in which there are multiple financers. Single-payer systems operate all around the world, with primary examples existing in Sweden, Taiwan, and Canada.

Even within systems that fit each of these forms, there is much variation, which makes direct comparison between systems difficult. Studies have focused on several metrics when comparing universal systems. These include cost containment, patient satisfaction, and measurable health outcomes. There is minimal difference in these metrics when comparing universal systems, but there is some evidence that shows single-payer systems are more effective in relation to cost containment than other universal models. However, when comparing universal systems with the non-universal system in the United States it is clear that "the difference between the performance of any of these countries and the United States is enormous and persistent."[19]

Although the United States healthcare system has a few internal programs that reflect some characteristics of these three forms of universal systems, it falls far short from being a universal system. Traditional Medicare, prior to or excluding Medicare Advantage Plans, is reflective of a single-payer system that is paid for through a federal financier.[20] The Veterans Administration facilities are reflective of a socialized system in which the state owns and operates the facilities—the success of these facilities depends heavily on how vigorously they are funded by the state. The programs within the Affordable Care Act, which was enacted relatively recently in 2010, represent an effort to move the United States toward a universal multi-payer system. The lack of a public option in the final policy, as well as other issues, resulted in the ACA falling far short of creating a truly universal system. Additional measures taken in the first years of the

[18] Oliver, Adam. 2009 "The Single-Payer Option: A Reconsideration" *Journal of Health Politics, Policy, and Law* Vol. 34 No.4.

[19] Glied, Sherry. 2009. "Single Payer as a Financing Mechanism" *Journal of Health Politics, Policy, and Law* Vol. 34 No.4 p. 614.

[20] Oberlander, Jonathon. 2016. "The Virtues and Vices of Single-Payer Health Care" New England *Journal of Medicine* 374:15.

Trump administration undercut aspects of the ACA. These retractions, such as a reduction in enforcement of the individual mandate, have resulted in an increase in the number of uninsured—in 2017, there were 25.6 (7.9 %) million people who had not had health insurance at any point during the year and in 2018 this number was 27.5 million (8.5%).[21] Much time and effort has been invested in moving the United States toward a universal system through programs or policies, yet, the country still lags behind other nations of similar economic and political caliber.

The United States has a system that is built upon both public and private financing, as well as both public and private provision, of health care. In 2017, roughly 37 percent of health care was already paid for via public programs such as Medicare and Medicaid, while 34 percent was financed through private health insurance.[22] Most Americans garner health insurance as an employee benefit, with around 60 percent of the non-elderly population getting their health insurance in this way.[23] Although the Affordable Care Act did initially increase the number of insured in the United States, challenges to the programs and policies enacted by the ACA have resulted in a reduction of the insured. The United States is once again experiencing an increase in the number of uninsured.[24] In part, because of the failure of these policies to push the United States to a truly universal system, single-payer activists argue that incremental measures are no longer an option, and that only a radical change to create a SPS will result in a genuinely universal system.

[21] Berchick, Edward., Jessica C. Barnett, and Rachel D Upton "Health Insurance Coverage in the United States: 2018" United States Census Bureau Report Number P60-267 (RV) 11/08/2019 https://www.census.gov/library/publications/2019/demo/p60-267.html.

[22] Centers for Medicare and Medicaid Services. "National Health Expenditures 2017 Highlights" Retrieved from: https://www.cms.gov/Research-Statistics-Data-and-Systems/Statistics-Trends-and-Reports/NationalHealthExpendData/Downloads/highlights.pdf.

[23] Lee, Chris. 2019. "Coverage at Work: The Share of Nonelderly Americans with Employer-Based Insurance Rose Modestly in Recent Years, but Has Declined Markedly Over the Long Term" Kaiser Family Foundation. Retrieved at: https://www.kff.org/health-reform/press-release/coverage-at-work-the-share-of-nonelderly-americans-with-employer-based-insurance-rose-modestly-in-recent-years-but-has-declined-markedly-over-the-long-term/.

[24] Ibid.

WHY SINGLE PAYER?

Activists support single-payer for many reasons. Not only have incremental measures failed to achieve a truly universal system, but the argument that a SPS would not only be better for the United States than the current non-universal system, but that it would also be a better option than the other forms of universal systems is supported by the evidence from other countries. Activists stress that they support the single-payer option because not only would it result in universal access but it would also do this in a more affordable way which will include more comprehensive coverage and more choice. And contrary to the political infeasibility narrative which concludes that radical healthcare reform is not possible, single-payer activists argue that it is possible, perhaps even more so than other forms of universal care.

Universal Access

While many past attempts at healthcare reform focused on universal health insurance, single-payer activists focus on universal healthcare access—or healthcare assurance—rather than on universal health insurance. One reason for this is that having insurance does not always mean having access to care nor does it mean that one can afford the care even when it is accessible. With the rising cost of premiums (the amount paid on a regular basis to have a healthcare insurance plan) and copays (the amount paid at the point of service), as well as increasing deductibles (the amount that you must pay out of pocket before your insurance coverage begins) have become prohibitive to individuals needing access to care even when they have health "insurance."[25] Single-payer activists support a system in which there are no roadblocks to accessing care. A common chant at SPM events is "Everybody In! Nobody Out!" While a narrative of "long wait lines" is often used to discredit single-payer systems, as well as other forms of universal systems, this narrative does not involve a holistic understanding of the experiences of patients in those systems or take into account the differing dynamics that may result in a wait within each system. For example, while wait times in universal systems are typically based on the urgency of the care needed and many of these countries have a "wait time guarantee"

---

[25] Almgren, G. 2018. Health Care Politics, Policy, and Services: A Social Justice Analysis (3rd ed.). New York, NY: Springer Publishing Company, LLC.

that works to limit the length of waiting that occurs for needed care, wait times in the United States are often related to other factors, such as the ability to pay, which can have negative consequences—especially when urgent care is needed.[26] Patients in single-payer systems also indicate that they are satisfied with their care, although rates of satisfaction may be marginally higher in other types of universal systems.[27]

Affordable

A major point of support for single-payer activists is that single-payer would cost less for most patients. While health care within the current system in the United States is paid for through a complex system of premiums, copays, deductibles, and other out-of-pocket expenses, most single-payer systems, including those being proposed through legislation in the United States, are funded through a progressive tax system (rather than premiums or deductibles) and result in minimal to no costs at the point of service. The Sanders Bill (S 1129) for example, removes almost all costs at the point of service. Although individuals may be paying more in taxes, middle-income Americans would be spending less than they spend on health care in the current system even with tax increases.[28] This would also address the fact that roughly 60–65 percent of bankruptcies in the United States are related to unpaid medical debt[29]—which applies to both insured as well as uninsured patients. Single-payer activists are also quick to point out that single-payer is not only more affordable for patients but it is also more affordable for the nation as a whole. They emphasize that it will "decrease the overall cost of healthcare and the money Americans spend on healthcare."[30] While the United States spends around 18 percent of GDP on health care, nations with single-payer spend much less. For example, the neighbor to the north—Canada—spends just around 11 per-

[26] Viberg, Nina. Birger C. Forsberg, Michael Borowitz, and Roger Molin. 2013. "International comparisons of waiting times in health care—Limitations and prospects" Health Policy 112: 53–61.

[27] Glied, Sherry. 2009. "Single Payer as a Financing Mechanism" *Journal of Health Politics, Policy, and Law* Vol. 34 No.4.

[28] Oberlander, Jonathon. 2016. "The Virtues and Vices of Single-Payer Health Care" New England Journal of Medicine 374:15.

[29] Himmelstein DU, Thorne D, Warren E, Woolhandler S. 2009. Medical bankruptcy in the United States, 2007: results of a national study. Am J Med. 2009;122(8):741–746.

[30] Activist, Health Care Now Conference Call, August 2012.

cent of GDP on health care through a single-payer system.[31] The difference in expense comes not only from the exorbitant and increasing costs for care in our largely private and for profit system but also from the administrative overhead and waste that occurs when healthcare facilities must battle with health insurance companies to get treatment covered—with administrative costs[32] within the commercial health insurance sector typically exceeding those in the public sector by 7–11 percent.[33]

The profit motive that pervades the American healthcare industry not only results in higher costs due to profit-driven motivations but it can also result in less care provision for patients who are determined by institutional actors to be less profitable, even within the nonprofit sector. This has resulted in a "medical arms race" in which healthcare providers compete for profitable patients. All of this serves to increase costs while reducing care.[34] Even conservative studies have shown that a single-payer system would result in a lower national expenditure than the current system.[35] Some single-payer opponents argue that while single-payer might cost less, it would do so at the expense of quality health care, in part due to the predicted reduction in the salaries of healthcare professionals. However, research on single-payer systems around the world has shown that there may be an initial increase in the income of healthcare professionals as they will be more assured of payment without as much administrative waste occurring. Also, while physicians in the United States do earn more on average than physicians in single-payer systems, physicians in those systems are still among the highest paid professionals in that context.[36] Single-payer supporters argue that while these systems are more affordable, they also provide more comprehensive benefits that result in better health outcomes.

[31] Canadian Institute for Health Information. "Health Spending" Accessed via: https://www.cihi.ca/en/health-spending.

[32] Almgren, G. 2018. Health Care Politics, Policy, and Services: A Social Justice Analysis (3rd ed.). New York, NY: Springer Publishing Company, LLC. Pg. 241.

[33] Oliver, Adam. 2009. "The Single-Payer Option: A Reconsideration" Journal of Health Politics, Policy, and Law Vol. 34 No.4.

[34] Cunningham, Peter J., Gloria J. Bazzoli, and Aaron Katz. 2008. "Caught in The Competitive Crossfire: Safety-Net Providers Balance Margin and Mission In A Profit-Driven Health Care Market" Health Affairs. Vol. 27.

[35] Blahous, Charles. 2018. "The Costs of a National Single-Payer Healthcare System" Mercatus Working Paper, Mercatus Center at George Mason University, Arlington VA.

[36] Duffin, Jacalyn 2011 "The Impact of Single-payer health care on physician income in Canada" American Journal of Public Health Vol. 101 No. 7.

Comprehensive

Single-payer supporters also argue that not only are costs lower in a single-payer system but also that within these systems coverage is more comprehensive. This conclusion is founded upon a couple of different factors. First, a single-payer system ideally cuts out the middleman—insurance companies—that often tell medical professionals what services or treatments they can or cannot provide for their patients. If you have ever seen a doctor who prescribed a specific medication or treatment but were then told by your insurance company that they would not cover that medication or treatment, then you have experienced this first hand. In an ideal single-payer system there is no middleman at the point of service and decisions about care are between the patient and their healthcare professional. While the governing bodies within the single-payer system might make decisions about how much the system will pay for specific treatments or medications, they do not play a role in decisions made about patient treatment at the point of service.[37] This is not only ideal, but it is how single-payer systems around the world currently operate. The conclusion that cutting out the middleman will not only result in more cost savings at the point of service due to the reduction of administrative overhead is tied to this conclusion that more autonomy and choice for both patients and providers exists in single-payer systems.[38] The second key factor in this argument is that single-payer systems cover the costs of more forms of care than other types of systems and that this comprehensive care is tied to better health outcomes. "Compared to the US system, the Canadian system has lower costs, more services, universal access to health care without financial barriers, and superior health status. Canadians and Germans have longer life expectancies and lower infant mortality rates than do US residents."[39] Single-payer proponents have incorporated this ideal for comprehensive care into their proposed policy changes. The single-payer bills promoted by single-payer activists during the 2019/2020 legislative session—most notably S. 1129 and H.R. 1384—the Medicare for All Acts—cover some forms of health care that are not always covered by

---

[37] Tuohy, Carolyn Hughes. 1999. "Dynamics of a Changing Health Sphere: The United States, Britain, and Canada" Health Affairs 18(3).

[38] Ridic, Goran. Suzanne Gleason, and Ognjen Ridic. 2012. "Comparisons of Health Care Systems in the United States, Germany, and Canada. Materia Socio Medica—*Journal of the Academy of Medical Sciences of Bosnia and Herzegovenia* 24(2): 112–120.

[39] Ibid.

private insurance or by the current Medicare system—such as dental, vision, and long-term care. The conclusion emphasized here is that not only will the new single-payer system cover everyone and be more affordable but it will also cover more types of care than both the current private insurance market and the existing Medicare system put together.

Choice

One of the key messages that the other side uses is that we need to preserve choice and competition. Ask them, how much choice do you really have? Most of us don't have a lot of choice—it's not you that makes the decision. It's your employer. What you do have in a single-payer system is a choice of provider and isn't that the most important thing? They want to make you think that the current system gives you choice, but you don't have choice.[40]

As discussed in the previous section, the autonomy of healthcare providers, or the liberty for doctors to choose which treatments or medications to prescribe, is an important element of choice that is ideally greater within a single-payer system.[41] But perhaps just as important is the choice that patients have in who will be providing those services. Single-payer systems do eliminate choice of insurer, but greater choice of provider is a benefit of single-payer systems.[42] Single-payer activists emphasize that while "most private plans restrict what doctors, other caregivers, or hospital you can use, under a Medicare for All system, patients have a choice, and the provider is assured a fair reimbursement."[43] While the choice of providers for many patients today is typically limited by their PPO or HMO networks, in an ideal type single-payer system, there would be no limitations due to closed networks. Healthcare providers would not need membership in a network in order to provide care to a patient. While single-payer systems often do rely heavily on primary care and referrals to specialists, the choice of primary care physician or specialist is primarily in

---

[40] Fieldnotes: Wendell Potter, One Payer States / Healthcare NOW National Strategy Meeting, Philadelphia PA, June 2012.

[41] Tuohy, Carolyn Hughes. 1999. "Dynamics of a Changing Health Sphere: The United States, Britain, and Canada" Health Affairs 18(3).

[42] Duffin, Jacalyn 2011 "The impact of single-payer health care on physician income in Canada" *American Journal of Public Health* Vol. 101 No. 7.

[43] Campaign for a Health California Flier distributed before Medicare's 49th birthday in 2014 "Why is a Medicare for ALL program the way to finish the job that the Affordable Care Act started.

the hands of the patient and their primary care provider within an ideal type single-payer system. The issue of health insurance is also tied to employment opportunities due to the fact that most Americans have healthcare insurance through their employers.[44] This can result in a situation of "job lock," in which individuals lose the autonomy to make a decision about changing jobs due to the possibility that this may also result in them losing access to health care.[45] This lack of employment mobility, or choice in employment, is another significant flaw in the current system that would ideally not exist in a single-payer system in which access to health care would not be tied to employment.

It's Possible

Finally, while some single-payer activists would support any form of universal health care and may even prefer a more extreme form of socialized medicine, they have decided to focus on single-payer because it is defined as the type of system that is the most possible to achieve in the United States. In relation to a national health services, or socialized medicine, single-payer is the more conservative option due to the fact that it results in less structural change because it maintains private facilities. The creation of a single-payer system would be less radical and less disruptive of the current medical infrastructure than the creation of a truly socialized system. Single-payer activists have also decided that single-payer is a more possible option than a multi-payer system not in spite of but because of the entrenched power of private insurance companies within our current system. According to this logic, one must get rid of private health insurance that is primarily rooted in a profit-making ethos in order to create a just healthcare system primarily rooted in a health-promoting ethos because including profit in healthcare financing creates an adverse incentive to not provide care. This is a fatal flaw within the current system. Those activists who have studied the development of universal systems around the world also recognize that the historical and situational reality of the U.S. healthcare system more closely aligns to other countries, such

[44] Berchick, Edward., Jessica C. Barnett, and Rachel D Upton "Health Insurance Coverage in the United States: 2018" United States Census Bureau Report Number P60-267 (RV) 11/08/2019.

[45] Almgren, G. (2018). Health Care Politics, Policy, and Services: A Social Justice Analysis (3rd ed.). New York, NY: Springer Publishing Company, LLC.

as Canada, that have successfully transitioned to a single-payer system, than to countries, such as those in continental Europe, that have achieved successful multi-payer systems.[46] While some healthcare reform activists argue that incremental reforms, such as the creation of a public option, are more possible than the more extensive structural change required for a single-payer system, single-payer activists argue that incrementalism often results in taking two steps forward and at least one step back, which means that they will not result in a truly universal system. At times, incremental reforms entrench problematic aspects of the current healthcare system. For example, the creation of Medicare Part D in 2003 strengthened the autonomy of pharmaceutical companies and thus their power within the system by restricting the ability of the federal government to negotiate the price of drugs. Implementing a "public option" is a popular incremental reform because it would maintain the "choice" to participate in the private insurance market while creating a publicly funded insurance system that is ideally available to all. The public option is also critiqued for the negative consequences that it could have. Single-payer supporters have argued that it would,

> be worse for us. It is going to cost us more and it is going to divide the country in such a way that the for-profit private insurance companies will game the system, so they get the healthiest people on their plan. The sickest people go to the government plan. And because they're (private insurance) still in the marketplace they're still driving up costs. Notice that the public option, Medicare buy in, all of those things, none of those have any way to bring down costs. The question to every candidate out there should not be just to the Medicare for all folks—why does your plan cost what it does—it should be to everyone to say how are you bringing down costs and how are you universally covering everyone.[47]

Jill Quadagno has called the entrenchment of the private insurance industry through incremental policy changes the "ironic outcome of health care reform."[48] Single-payer activists argue that because private insurance com-

[46] See Esping-Andersen. Gosta. 1990. The Three Worlds of Welfare State Capitalism. Princeton Univ. Press.

[47] Representation Pramila Jayapal (D-WA), sponsor of HB 1384—Medicare for all Act of 2019, on the Van Jones Show, CNN, November 2019—find it here, https://twitter.com/VanJones68/status/1197593147423051779.

[48] Quadagno, Jill. 2005. One Nation Uninsured: Why the U.S. Has No National Health Insurance New York: Oxford University Press.

panies have both so much power in and negative consequences for the current system, a new socially just system can only be created through the complete removal of the for-profit insurance industry. So, although the medical industrial complex (insurance, pharmaceuticals, and for-profit care facilities) represents a strong front against progressive reform and are often used by single-payer detractors as evidence of the impossibility of creating a single-payer system, single-payer activists argue that a universal and socially just system is only possible if private insurance is removed from the equation. Activists also look to indicators within their environment that can be interpreted as opportunities for progressive social change and use these to develop arguments that a change to a single-payer healthcare system is realistic. They work to make the supposedly impossible possible—but how?

Healthcare Reform in the Environment of Opportunity

In the remainder of this book, I analyze the "how" of the Single Payer Movement over the last three decades. Through this research, I have developed a theoretical framework that addresses the relationship between grassroots mobilization, narrative, and opportunity. I call this framework the *Environment of Opportunity Model*. This model is grounded in the data I have collected but previous theorizing on social movement activity was also foundational. Particularly relevant are the concepts developed by political process theorists such as Doug McAdam[49] and scholars who were influential in the "cultural turn" in social movements theorizing, such as James Jasper[50] and Francesca Polletta.[51] While this model instructs the analysis to pay attention to structure, at its core it is an interactionist model grounded in developing conclusions about how social movement actors understand and adapt to aspects of the context in which they exist.

At the center of this model are *social movement actors*—a term which encapsulates both individuals and organizations working within a social

[49] See McAdam, Doug. 1982/1999. Political Process and the Development of Black Insurgency. 1930–1970. Second Edition. Chicago: University of Chicago Press.

[50] See Jasper, James M. (1997). The Art of Moral Protest: Culture, Biography, and Creativity in Social Movements. Chicago, IL: University of Chicago Press.

[51] See Polletta, Francesca. (2006). It Was Like a Fever: Story Telling in Protest and Politics Chicago, IL: University of Chicago Press.

movement. The environment in which social movement actors exist involves a complex interaction between multiple kinds of opportunity for social change. I find that the opportunity for reform is understood by social movement actors through an interpretive process in which a shared definition of conditions in the environment, including material concrete factors, is developed. Activists build understandings about the opportunities for mobilization that are available to them and develop ways in which they can realistically act on those opportunities through the process of telling stories about their specific historically situated context. I call this process *narrative practice*. The narrative practice of social movement actors encourages specific forms of *grassroots mobilization* oriented toward various types of opportunity. The particular forms of grassroots mobilization that social movement actors undertake are oriented toward mobilizing differing forms of support. This means that the process of *movement building* is impacted by both the environment of opportunity and the narrative practice through which social movement actors interpret it. Movement building is necessary for a social movement to achieve the goal of *social change*. Social change, both minor and significant, results in shifts within the *environment of opportunity*. This is visualized below in circular form because it is not a unilinear process, rather it is an interactive cycle that is ongoing (Fig. 1.2).

Social movement actors create a shared understanding of their context through narrative practice. By centralizing the analysis of narrative practice, I move beyond a standard frame analysis of meaning-making within social movements. Frames have been defined as the "action-oriented sets of beliefs and meanings that inspire and legitimate the activities and campaigns of a social movement organization."[52] While some attention has been paid to how frames are produced, my analysis centers this process of production through a focus on the narrative practice of social movement actors. This narrative practice is foundational in the creation of frames or collective action frameworks. Collective action frameworks are systems of meaning that diagnose a problem, define a prognosis or a solution to that problem, and motivate action through the creation of a collective

---

[52] Benford, Robert D., and David A. Snow. 2000. "Framing Processes and Social Movements: An overview and Assessment." *Annual Review of Sociology* 26(1): 611–639, pg. 614.

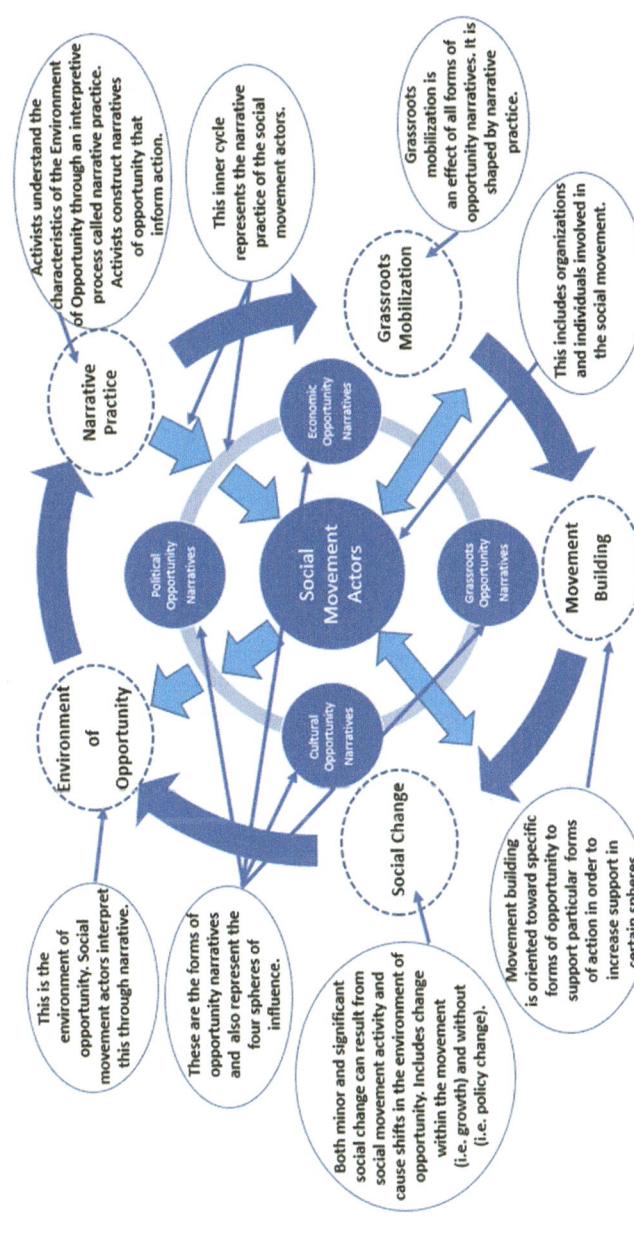

Fig. 1.2 The environment of opportunity model

identity.[53] Scholars have also found that the motivational aspect of framing often relies on an "us vs. them" understanding through which "enemies" are defined.[54] An analysis of narrative allows for the in-depth examination of how activists develop the diagnostic and prognostic conclusions within particular historical contexts, as well as how the antagonist (the them of the narrative practice) is defined in contradiction to the protagonist of the social movement narrative—otherwise understood as the "us" that is working to enact social change. In this way, my conceptualization of narrative practice is both complementary to and builds upon the dominant theoretical focus on framing processes.

Activists continually construct narratives in order to understand even the most minute changes in the environment of opportunity. While the concept of framing allows for some analytical focus on the discursive process that results in a master frame or collective action frameworks,[55] more often frames are analyzed as a static and ahistorical tool that impacts social movement activities. While frames can become relatively concrete as "mutually reinforcing constraints,"[56] narratives are the product of the ongoing process of interpretive practice. They are thus fluid and include an ongoing participatory process of interpretation. Whereas frames may take on a "social marketing" form, narratives are necessarily participatory and more akin to the "participatory communication model" of framing.[57] Narrative practice occurs as an ongoing process behind the framing strategy, it is a key element in the creation of frames.[58] However, unlike the framing process, prescribing an outcome is not an integral element of narrative practice. Rather, the end of the narrative may remain ambiguous or

[53] Whooley, Owen. 2004. "Locating Master frames in History: An Analysis of the Religious Master frame of the Abolition Movement and its Influence on Movement Trajectory" Journal of Historical Sociology. 17(4).

[54] Knight, Graham, and Josh Greenberg. (2011). Talk of the Enemy: Adversarial Framing and Climate Change Discourse. Social Movement Studies 10(4): 323–340.

[55] McCammon, Holly. (2012). "Explaining Frame Variation: More Moderate and Radical Demands for Women's Citizenship in the U.S. Women's Jury Movements." Social Problems 59 (1): 43–69.

[56] Miceli, Melinda S. (2005). "Morality Politics vs. Identity Politics: Framing Processes and Competition Among Christian Right and Gay Social Movement Organizations." Sociological Forum 20 (4): 589–612.

[57] Ryan, Charlotte and William A. Gamson. 2006. "The Art of Reframing Political Debate" Contexts. 5(1): 13–18.

[58] Olsen, Kristine A. (2014). Telling Our Stories: Narrative and Framing in the Movement for Same-Sex Marriage. Social Movement Studies. 13(2): 248–266.

predictive, and this can increase its mobilization potential.[59] Social movement actors must become "cognitively liberated"[60] with an awareness of the opportunity that exists for social change and how to pragmatically act on these opportunities.[61] Narrative practice is oriented toward the everyday process of interpreting the environment of opportunity and making decisions about strategy, as well as tactics, in response to continually changing opportunities.

Social movement actors exist within a particular context in which they must develop strategy and tactics that adapt their efforts to opportunities for change.[62] This context includes many "spheres of influence,"[63] rooted in different discourses and opportunity frameworks or structures.[64] Rather than conceptualizing opportunity as a rigid *structure* that can create opportunities for political action, I conceptualize opportunity as the outcome of an interpretive process through which activists make decisions about mobilization. In this analysis, I focus on how social movement actors within the Single Payer Movement (SPM) have interpreted the

---

[59] Polletta, Francesca. (2006). It Was Like a Fever: Story Telling in Protest and Politics Chicago, IL: University of Chicago Press.

[60] The concept of cognitive liberation is typically attributed to Doug McAdam as found in his influential work on the Civil Rights Movement, but the conceptual process through which individuals become aware of opportunity and realize their collective power to act on it was previously discussed in "Poor People's Movements" by Frances Fox Piven and Richard Cloward.

Piven, Frances Fox and Richard Cloward. 1977. Poor People's Movements: Why They Succeed, How They Fail. New York: Vintage Books.

McAdam, Doug. 1982/1999. Political Process and the Development of Black Insurgency. 1930–1970. Second Edition. Chicago: University of Chicago Press.

[61] See Hern, Lindy S. F. (2012). "Everybody In and Nobody Out: Opportunities, Narrative, and the Radical Flank in the Movement for Single-Payer Health Care Reform." PhD thesis, University of Missouri Library Systems (Order No. 3530875)—for a more detailed discussion of pragmatic liberation.

[62] See also: Coddou, Marion. (2015). "An Institutional Approach to Collective Action: Evidence from Faith-Based Latino Mobilization in the 2006 Immigrant Rights Protests" Social Problems 63(1): 127–150; Lo, Clarence Y.H. and Michael Schwartz. Eds. (1998). Social Policy and the Conservative Agenda. Oxford, England: Blackwell Publishers; Rohlinger, Deana A. (2006). "Friends and Foes: Media, Politics, and Tactics in the Abortion War." Social Problems 53(4): 537–561.

[63] Massey, Douglas S., and Stefanie Brodmann. (2014). Spheres of Influence: The Social Ecology of Racial and Class Inequality. Russell Sage Foundation.

[64] Meyer, David S. (2004). Protest and Political Opportunities. Annual Review of Sociology 30: 125–145.

opportunity for political mobilization that can exist within the political, cultural, economic, and grassroots spheres.

Through my grounded analysis of this movement, I came to understand that single-payer activists often acted based on definitions of opportunity outside of the political realm. Within theory and research dealing with social movements, focus has primarily been placed on political opportunity,[65] but other forms of opportunity, such as cultural[66] and economic,[67] have also been considered. Political opportunity has been primarily defined as the concrete institutional factors that plays a role in political action, such as the structure of the political system, the openness of the policy process to political outsiders, the possibility for and type of state repression, and the presence of elite political allies or adversaries.[68] Rather than political opportunity being conceptualized as the structural opportunity *for* any and all political mobilization—an idea that can result in the concept becoming a sponge[69] that attempts to explain all political action—I conceptualize political opportunity as the product of the narrative practice through which activists assess the likelihood that mobilization directed toward the political sphere of influence will be successful. This opens the analysis to a focus on other forms of opportunity that can also affect mobilization within social movements.

Challenges to political power often occur outside of the political sphere, especially in the case of healthcare reform.[70] Scholars have further developed the concept of opportunity by focusing on economic[71] and cultural

[65] Goodwin, Jeff and James M. Jasper. (1999). "Caught in the Winding, Snarling Vine: The Structural Bias of Political Process Theory" Sociological Forum Vol. 14(1): 27–54.

[66] Wahlström, Mattias. (2011). Taking Control or Losing Control? Activist Narratives of Provocation and Collective Violence. Social Movement Studies 10(4): 367–385.

[67] Luders, Joseph. (2006). The Economics of Movement Success: Business Responses to Civil Rights Mobilization. The American Journal of Sociology 111 (4): 963–998.

[68] Williams, Gregory P. 2010 "When Opportunity Knocks: Social Movements in the Soviet Union and Russian Federation." Social Movement Studies 9 (4): 443–460.

[69] Gamson, William A. and David S. Meyer. (1996). "Framing Political Opportunity." Comparative Perspectives on Social Movements: Political Opportunities, Mobilizing Structures, Cultural Framings Ed. By Doug McAdam, John D. McCarthy and Mayer N. Zald Cambridge University Press.

[70] Banaszak-Holl, Jane C., Sandra R. Levitsky, and Mayer N. Zald. 2010. Social Movements and the Transformation of American Health Care. New York, NY: Oxford University Press.

[71] Mintz, Beth. 1995. "Business Participation in Health Care Policy Reform: Factors Contributing to Collective Action Within the Business Community" Social Problems 42 (3): 408–428; Mintz, Beth, and Donald Palmer. 2000. "Business and Health Care Policy Reform in the 1980s: The 50 States." Social Problems 47 (3): 327–359.

opportunity.[72] Economic opportunity primarily includes the structure of the economic system, the stability of the economic system, and the presence of elite economic allies or adversaries (e.g. businesses, unions, and professional organizations) that can be affected by the disruptive potential of social movements.[73] The status of each of these economic factors is tied to the historical period and must be defined by social movement participants through narrative practice. Economic actors, in the forms of professional organizations such as unions, are often important sources of economic support for the activities of grassroots social movement actors. Scholars have primarily focused on cultural opportunity in relation to dominant ideological frameworks, democratic political culture, discursive opportunity, and the relationship between activists and media elites.[74] Although these are important factors, in this analysis, I primarily consider the ways in which social movement actors are able to adapt their narrative practice to changes in the dominant forms of material culture in order to mobilize. Cultural opportunity may be interpreted as more open to progressive goals when democratized cultural forms are available. For example, the internet became a form of cultural opportunity for mobilization when it became widely available to grassroots actors as a democratized form of communication.[75]

[72] Wahlstrom, M. and Peterson A. 2006. "Between the State and the Market: Expanding the Concept of Political Opportunity Structure" Acta Sociologica, 49 (4).

[73] King, Brayden G. 2011. "The Tactical Disruptiveness of Social Movements: Sources of Market and Mediated Disruption in Corporate Boycotts." Social Problems. 58(4): 491–517.

[74] Jasper, James M. (1997). The Art of Moral Protest: Culture, Biography, and Creativity in Social Movements. Chicago, IL: University of Chicago Press.; Johnson, Victoria. (2008). How Many Machine Guns Does It Take To Cook One Meal?: The Seattle and San Francisco General Strikes Seattle. WA: University of Washington Press; Lo, Clarence Y. H. 1990. Small Property versus Big Government: Social Origins of the Property Tax Revolt, Expanded and Updated edition. Berkeley: University of California Press; Sobieraj, Sarah. 2010. "Reporting Conventions: Journalists, Activists, and the Thorny Struggle for Political Visibility." Social Problems. 57(4): 505–528.

[75] Carty, Victoria. (2010). New Information Communication Technologies and Grassroots Mobilization. Information, Communication & Society 13(2): 155–173; Cogburn, Derrick and Fatima K. Espinoza-Vasquez. (2011). From Networked Nominee to Networked nation: Examining the Impact of Web 2.0 and Social Media on Political Participation and Civic Engagement in the 2008 Obama Campaign. Journal of Political Marketing 10(1–2): 189–213; Earl, Jennifer and Katrina Kimport. (2009). Societies and Digital Protest: Fan Activism and Other Nonpolitical Protest Online. Sociological Theory. 27(3): 220–243; Vasi, Ion and Edward T. Walker, John S. Johnson, and Hui Fen Tan. (2015). "No Fracking Way!" Documentary Film, Discursive Opportunity, and Local Opposition against Hydraulic

In addition to political, economic, and cultural opportunity, I found through grounded analysis that *grassroots opportunity* also exists and may become a focus of narrative practice. While previous research has primarily focused on "mobilizing structures" which are "those collective vehicles, informal as well as formal, through which people mobilize and engage in collective action,"[76] as positive aspects of the grassroots environment, I have found that there are additional conditions that can be interpreted as grassroots opportunity for the mobilization of the public. These conditions are

1. The existence of active interest and participation of members, non-members, and new members in a social movement or social movement organization (SMO).
2. A popular public definition of grassroots mobilization as a legitimate outlet for political action.
3. The availability of grassroots resources, such as existing mobilizing structures, which can be used to facilitate the mobilization of public support.

Although social movement scholars have recognized the importance of mobilizing structures, or indigenous organizations, to emergent mobilization efforts, these structures are often incorporated into the conceptualization of political opportunity.[77] In this analysis of the SPM, I conceptualize grassroots opportunity as distinct from the other three forms of opportunity—meaning that grassroots opportunity can be perceived as positive, even when other forms of opportunity are defined in negative ways. Positive constructions of grassroots opportunity can encourage mobilization even when other forms of opportunity are negatively defined through narrative practice.

There is a distinction between "grassroots opportunity" and "grassroots mobilization." Grassroots mobilization is used here as an umbrella

Fracturing in the United States, 2010 to 2013" American Sociological Review 80 (5): 934–959.

[76] McAdam, Doug. 1996. "Conceptual origins, current problems, future directions." Comparative Perspectives on Social Movements: Political Opportunities, Mobilizing Structures, Cultural Framings Ed. By Doug McAdam, John D. McCarthy and Mayer N. Zald Cambridge University Press. PG. 3.

[77] Morris, Aldon. (1984). The Origins of the Civil Rights Movement. New York: The Free Press.

term for any grassroots group activity that is oriented toward social change. While grassroots mobilization is a possible effect of all types of opportunity, the form of grassroots mobilization that is developed is also dependent upon how social movement actors narratively construct those opportunities. If social movement actors focus their narrative practice on perceived opportunities in the political sphere, then they will likely orient their grassroots mobilization efforts toward mobilizing the support of political actors (i.e. politicians) through conventional forms of political action. On the contrary, if social movement actors perceive a lack of opportunity in the political sphere, but significant opportunity in the grassroots (public) sphere, then they will focus on grassroots mobilization efforts oriented toward increasing public support for their goals. This applies to all other spheres of opportunity, such as cultural and economic, as well. The ways in which these opportunity spheres intersect can also impact the development of opportunity narratives and affect the specific form of grassroots mobilization that occurs. Activists are able to "keep on keepin on." even during time periods in which there is less likelihood that their goals will be supported in the political sphere by focusing on other forms of opportunity. This process can encourage some activists to remain committed to more radical goals, while others shift to a position of compromise.[78]

The specific forms of grassroots mobilization that develop affect how social movement actors engage in movement building. If the focus of the narrative practice is on political opportunity and the grassroots mobilization efforts are oriented toward mobilizing support within the political sphere, then social movement actors will be more likely to focus on a movement-building model that is rooted in engagement with institutionalized politics. The orientation here is to build a movement with the infrastructure to push political actors to support specific policy goals. This orientation works better if there are more people involved in the actions of the social movement but is not dependent upon massive actions involving large numbers of people. A movement-building period focused on the political sphere would encourage activists to build a movement with a constituency that was trained to engage in actions within the political sphere—such as citizen lobbying. On the other hand,

---

[78] See also, Hern, Lindy. 2019. "Resisting 'Politics as Usual': Examining the Rise of Anti-Establishment Politics by Comparing the Narratives of Opportunity Used Within the Single Payer Movement During Two Presidential Eras" *Journal of Historical Sociology*. 1:18.

if narrative practice is oriented toward positive narratives of opportunity in the public sphere—or grassroots opportunity—but political opportunity is defined as negative, then movement building is more likely to be oriented toward building a mass movement that engages in direct action or civil disobedience in order to increase public awareness of and support for the movement. Ideally, this would increase participation in future movement activities. Within the SPM, this movement-building orientation toward building a mass movement of the public became a process through which activists worked to change the environment of opportunity so that the political sphere would be forced to be more open to their goals. The political strategy of the movement transitioned away from concentrating on increasing the support of established political actors toward a focus on creating a "political revolution" that could change the established political framework. This transition was tied to specific definitions of the enemy that developed within the narrative practice of social movement actors through which "politics as usual" became defined as the enemy of single-payer healthcare reform. Any mobilization effort that creates social change—no matter how small—also changes the environment of opportunity in which social movement actors continue to work. The related rise in "anti-establishment" politics in American political discourse was tied to definitions of the "enemy" in the process of social change. This process played a role in creating a larger environment of opportunity in which the movement continues to work to achieve its goals.

THE METHODOLOGY BEHIND STUDYING SUCCESS AND FAILURE WITHIN SOCIAL MOVEMENTS

When I first began my study of social movements as a young graduate student, most of the academic research that I read on the subject focused on figuring out how successful movements, such as the Civil Rights Movement, had achieved that success. This focus on success didn't quite match my interest in studying healthcare reform because at that point in 2004, there had not been successful mobilization for large-scale change within the healthcare system since the 1960s—a period that resulted in the creation of the Medicare and Medicaid systems which continue to provide much needed care to the elderly, disabled, and economically disadvantaged.[79] The materials available at that time that were about the most recent attempt to reform the healthcare system during the Clinton administration of the 1990s, mostly focused on state-centered analysis of the failure of that era.[80] While this form of analysis continues to be important, it left me with lingering questions about what was happening within grassroots mobilization efforts at that time. These mobilization efforts had also failed to achieve significant change and I wanted to better understand how healthcare justice activists worked to overcome that failure in order to continue the process of movement building.

Movement building is a key characteristic of creating a successful social movement. Grassroots activists come together to work for a goal because they are outside of established systems of power. Working for significant change from a disempowered position is a process that is often full of failure. Even movements that are esteemed as examples of successful mobilization efforts, such as the Civil Rights Movement, experienced that success after decades if not centuries of failure.[81] Yet, their continued mobilization over those years of failure indicates that some form of success or progress encouraged continued mobilization. Other movements that were not successful at achieving their primary goals were still integral to creating significant changes to social policy. The Townsend Movement, for example, did not achieve its goal of an Old Age Revolving Pension Plan that required no prior payment into the system, but its mobilization efforts did encourage political leaders of the time to enact comprehensive legislation that created the system of social security that is still so important for the seniors of today.[82] All too often, the years of work undertaken by activists to support their goals is pushed aside as the focus turns to activities that occur during the final years leading into success. Indeed, recent discussions dealing with the rise of Medicare for All to the center of political discourse often focus on the impact of the 2016 campaign of Senator Bernie Sanders (I-VT), while

[79] See, Marmor, Theodore R. 1970. The Politics of Medicare. Aldine De Gruyter, New York. 1970.

[80] See, Skocpol, Theda. 1997. Boomerang: Health Care Reform and the Turn Against Government, W.W. Norton and Company, New York.

[81] See McAdam, Doug. 1982/1999. Political Process and the Development of Black Insurgency. 1930–1970. Second Edition. Chicago: University of Chicago Press.

[82] See Amenta, Edwin. 2008. When Movements Matter: The Townsend Plan and the Rise of Social Security Princeton University Press.

not adequately highlighting the years of mobilization within progressive movements such as the SPM that created the momentum for that campaign.[83] Reductive and narrow definitions of success work against developing a holistic understanding of how social change occurs. Success for social movements is more complex than achieving the primary policy goals of the social movement or gaining entry into the insider polity through changes in the repertoires of contention.[84] Social movement actors also achieve success in more minor ways, such as setting the political agenda or changing culturally based conclusions about a particular idea. This progress in the midst of failure is integral to the continued mobilization that must occur to achieve goals for more significant forms of social change.

While social movement scholarship has often focused on successful social movements after the point of success, my analysis is also unique because it includes an examination of the years of failure experienced by the SPM, within the context of a sometimes-successful larger Movement for Healthcare Reform. To this end, I address the following questions.

How has the Single Payer Movement maintained mobilization potential even when countered by elite opposition with entrenched political power?

How has the Single Payer Movement confronted failure in ways that allowed the movement to continue to grow and achieve lesser forms of success while making progress toward the goal of single payer?

The focus of this book is on activists who did not compromise even when confronted with defeat while supporting a "politically infeasible" goal. Instead they developed actions through which they could change the environment in which they were mobilizing. Central to this analysis of success and failure is a focus on the relationship between the contextual conditions of historical periods and the activities of social movement actors. These substantive concerns are closely linked to my broader conceptual concern dealing with how activists understand opportunity

---

[83] See Oberlander, Jonathon. 2019. "Lessons From the Long and Winding Road to Medicare for All" *American Journal of Public Health* 109(11): 1497–1500 AND Levitt L. 2018. Single-Payer Health Care: Opportunities and Vulnerabilities. JAMA. 319(16):1646–1647.

[84] See Tilly, Charles. 1993. "Contentious Repertoires in Great Britain, 1758–1834" Social Science History 17(2): 253–280.

and how this understanding is tied to specific forms of action. A focus on the process of historical change was made possible through many years spent in the field working with the SPM and through the use of historical data.

I built the analysis presented in the following chapters upon over a decade of ethnographic research involving participant observation, semi-structured interviews, and content analysis of organizational documents, both historical and contemporary. The Clinton era data consists of an extensive collection of content produced by the SPM starting in the late 1980s (e.g. meeting minutes, transcripts, newsletters, fliers, emails, etc. produced by multiple organizations) and oral history interviews with activists who were participants during that era. The Bush, Obama, and Trump era data consists of similar content produced by multiple organizations in the SPM, formal and informal interviews, and field notes from my field participation, which started in 2004. This process resulted in a dataset that currently includes over 100 open-ended interviews, field notes from participation in an average of ten events per year as a participant observer over a 15-year period, and analysis of a significant amount of both hard and digital content produced by the movement over a 30-year period.

Because this project occurred over such a long period of time, the data used to write this book was collected within different institutional contexts with differing Institutional Review Boards[85] that had similar requirements for the conduction of ethical research. In all cases, my project protocol included a form of informed consent that varied depending on the form of data being collected (i.e. interviews vs. field study participation at public events). Because the information presented here deals primarily with public figures, public events, and publicly accessible information that reduces any reasonable expectation of anonymity—I often use the actual names of social movement participants, which is in line with my IRB approved protocol. At times, I was asked either directly, or indirectly, to keep specific information confidential—this information

---

[85] An institutional review board is a group of people that assess the ethical conditions of any research project that involves human subjects in order to make sure that the project will include procedures that will reduce or eliminate in any risk of harm to the participants due to the research project that is greater than already existing risks of everyday life. As a sociologist, my data collection process has been assessed by multiple review boards at the University of Missouri, Manchester University, and the University of Hawaii.

contributes to my analysis but is not directly utilized in the text as presented (i.e. direct quotes). At other times, I refrain from using specific names for other reasons in order to protect the confidentiality of participants, even when there was not an implied or explicit request. I also refrain from using pseudonyms, and instead rely on other forms of identifiers when real names aren't used, to avoid confusion or mistaken identities. For the most part, I have found that the activists involved in the movement want their story to be told and their hard work to be recognized—they are fearless about claiming ownership of their activism.[86]

GOING FORWARD: THE OUTLINE

The remaining chapters of this book are organized chronologically in order to highlight the process of historical change within the environment of opportunity and to better understand its impact on the activities within the SPM. In Chap. 2, I discuss the first wave of the contemporary SPM during the Clinton administration's attempt to reform healthcare policy in the early 1990s. While this period started with a lot of positive momentum, it ultimately ended with the death of healthcare reform at the national level. In Chap. 3, I analyze the death of the national-level SPM during the "Contract with America" period of American politics. In Chap. 4, I discuss important developments that occurred during the George W. Bush Presidency which encouraged a rebirth within the SPM. This rebirth facilitated a second wave within the movement, which is further discussed in Chap. 5, the focus of which is the Obama era of healthcare reform. While the enactment of the Affordable Care Act initially resulted in a downturn of social movement activity, in Chap. 6 I discuss the ways in which single-payer actors adapted to and built upon this new policy context. In Chap. 7, I turn my focus to the rise of anti-establishment politics during the 2016 election cycle and the impact of

[86] For a more extensive discussion of the methods used in this project, see

Hern, Lindy S. F. (2012). "Everybody In and Nobody Out: Opportunities, Narrative, and the Radical Flank in the Movement for Single-Payer Health Care Reform." PhD thesis, University of Missouri Library Systems (Order No. 3530875).

Hern, Lindy. (2016). "Navigating the Borderland of Scholar Activism: Narrative Practice as Applied Sociology in the Movement for Single Payer Health Care Reform" *Journal of Applied Social Science* 10(2): 119–131.

that cycle on the third wave of the SPM which is ongoing during the Trump era. In Chap. 8, I discuss the progress that the SPM has made by examining the growth of support within the political, economic, cultural, and grassroots spheres of influence. Finally, in Chap. 9, I discuss some of the practical lessons that can be learned from this history as well as what may happen as the Single Payer Movement moves forward toward a socially just healthcare system.

CHAPTER 2

"First They Ignore You": The Clinton Era of Healthcare Reform

When I was in Georgia, I was called to go to Little Rock Arkansas, and I knew Bill, knew him pretty well, well I don't know if I want to say that, but I knew him and he uh was going to be there and he had just been elected. So, in November we took a caravan of people into Little Rock to encourage him to go for universal single-payer health care. And not go for the plan that they were going for, which was pretty much telling the insurance companies that we're not going to touch their profits, and by making that promise not to touch their profits I think that from the get go they made a complete tactical error. Uh, unfortunately, he got hit by both sides, the left didn't want his plan and the right didn't want his plan either, it was the wrong place to be in the middle.[1]

The dominant narrative of political opportunity within the mobilization for healthcare reform during the administration of Bill Clinton was that single-payer healthcare was not "politically feasible," yet many single-payer supporters continued to fight for this type of progressive reform during this era. They developed counter-narratives of political feasibility which were co-constructed by political agents important to the movement. These narratives were then used by single-payer activists in their efforts to redefine the political opportunity for single-payer healthcare. The construction of political counter-narratives is a historically specific phenomenon, both inhibited and facilitated by multiple aspects of the environment of opportunity (i.e. aspects of material culture). The chant "First they Ignore You, Then They Laugh at You, Then They Fight You,

---

[1] Interview: Mary, former professional organizer for Grassroots Organizing and Missourians for Single Payer board member—Fall 2004.

© The Author(s) 2020
L. S. F. Hern, *Single Payer Healthcare Reform*,
https://doi.org/10.1007/978-3-030-42764-1_2

41

Then You Win," which is often used by activists in their stories about why it is valuable to "keep on, keepin on" in the midst of much adversity, will also be the rhetorical frame for the following discussion dealing with the narratives of opportunity that arose during a distinct historical period—the Clinton era of healthcare reform.

While there had been several attempts to create a universal healthcare system in the United States prior to the 1990s, none of these attempts had been successful at creating a system that covers everyone. The creation of a universal health insurance system was discussed during the "New Deal" era and President Franklin D. Roosevelt included it in his proposal for a second bill of rights during his state of the union address on January 11, 1944. However, the political process of the time resulted in a universal system of social security that did not include health care.[2] In the 1960s, there was again movement to create a universal system. This era resulted in a program that was limited to support of the elderly—Medicare, as well as the needy—Medicaid—rather than a universal system that would have covered everyone.[3] Just a few years later, in the early 1970s, Senator Ted Kennedy was growing support for his "Health Security Act," which was modeled after the Canadian Medicare system. President Richard Nixon responded to Kennedy's efforts and their popularity by supporting the Comprehensive Health Insurance Plan (CHIP) proposed by Stuart Altman and Peter Fox—which was intended to create a universal system through employer mandates, state-assisted insurance for those in need, and an expanded Medicare system. President Nixon eventually proposed the "National Health Insurance Partnership Act," which was based on the CHIP proposal, with additional support for the development of managed care through Health Maintenance Organizations (HMOs).[4] Though it was squashed through the political process at that time, it is still used as a benchmark example today.[5] Although these attempts to create a Universal

---

[2] Amenta, Edwin. 2006. When Movements Matter: The Townsend Plan & the Rise of Social Security Princeton University Press.

[3] Marmor, Theodore R. 1970. The Politics of Medicare. Aldine De Gruyter, New York. 1970.

[4] Quadagno, Jill. 2005. One Nation Uninsured: Why the U.S. Has No National Health Insurance Oxford University Press, 2005.

[5] Altman S. & Shactman D. (2011). Power, Politics, and Universal Health Care. Amherst, NY:Prometheus Books.

Healthcare system did not use the term "single-payer," which did not exist as a conceptual framework for a pre-existing type of healthcare system until the late 1980s,[6] these periods of movement toward reform were the antecedents to the Single Payer Movement (SPM) that arose during the late 1980s and early 1990s.

In the early 1990s, political focus was once again directed toward the issue of healthcare reform. At the national level, the 1992 Presidential race was dominated by discourse surrounding healthcare reform. Candidate Bill Clinton, then Governor of Arkansas, became an influential political agent in the narrative surrounding healthcare reform. While state-level movements for healthcare reform had begun prior to this election season, the national movement for healthcare reform, and specifically for single-payer healthcare, experienced an upswing in activity, organization, and new membership during the election season and during the first few years following the election of President Clinton. The historical narrative of some activists who were participants during that period indicated that within the first term following the election of President Clinton, the SPM moved into a period of relative inaction and was "dead in the water."[7]

> Well, I really think the Health Security Act diffused single-payer. The Health Security Act was really mega managed care and had very little to do with single-payer. I wasn't a member, but my feeling that I've gotten from people like Myrna and Hy is that a majority felt like they'd been betrayed by the Clintons. And I think that they were.[8]

However, a careful examination of historical documents—including organization minutes, organizational newsletters, and other hard copies of organizational documents—indicated that the movement during this time period was not "dead in the water" but rather constructed new narratives and new strategies for combating the dominant opportunity narrative that defined single-payer as "politically infeasible."

[6] Liu, Jodi L. and Robert H. Brook. "What is Single-Payer Health Care? A Review of Definitions and Proposals in the U.S." Journal of General Internal Medicine 32(7): 822–831.
[7] Myrna Fictenbaum, MoSP Member, interview Dec. 2005.
[8] Roger Signor, MoSP Member, interview Nov. 2004.

"First They Ignore You": Rising Action of Clinton Health Security

When Candidate Bill Clinton first became President Elect Bill Clinton in November of 1992, the narrative regarding the political infeasibility of single-payer healthcare had not yet become dominant. Single-payer supporters were still hopeful that their goals would be listened to and considered. This time period was constructed by single-payer activists as a period of political opportunity during which they could convince the Clinton administration to support single-payer, or at least push the new administration toward the principles of a single-payer system.

> With the election of Governor Clinton, the opportunities for meaningful health care reform become more real. Governor Clinton has expressed his commitment to providing universal, affordable care. However, the shape of the plan he will submit to Congress within 100 days of his inauguration remains unclear. Our **opportunity and challenge** will be to influence President Clinton's health care policy in order to get meaningful reform enacted into law.[9]

While the narrative of political opportunity at this time recognized that President Elect Clinton was not a single-payer supporter, it also encouraged single-payer activists to work to change the debate surrounding the options for healthcare reform. This time period represented an "opportunity and challenge" to force single payer onto the table.

This narrative of political opportunity encouraged the formation of new organizations and new activities that would force single-payer into the political debate over healthcare reform. The United Health Care Action Network (UHCAN) was just one of the organizations formed during this period. Their origin narrative explains that

> In March 1992, the Northeast Ohio Coalition for National Health Care, based in Cleveland, took the lead in organizing the first nationwide conference for single-payer activists. Over 100 leaders from 27 states gathered in

---

[9] Church Women ACT Flier, Church Women United—November 1992.

Washington, D.C. for the event. The conference led to plans for another event in November 1992, also in Washington, D.C. At that meeting 250 leaders from 37 states founded a new national organization—the Universal Health Care Action Network (UHCAN). At that time, offices were established in Cleveland, OH, to symbolize UHCAN's identity as a grassroots center for health care reform advocates.[10]

UHCAN became a central organizing group for developing nation-wide support for single-payer. It formed within a context in which there was political opportunity for healthcare reform, as well as grassroots opportunity for mobilizing the public in support of single-payer healthcare.

Initially, the dominant narrative surrounding healthcare reform was still fairly ambiguous and open to different possibilities. By December of 1992, the directions for healthcare reform were largely limited to four areas—Insurance Reform (Tax Incentive Plans), Employer Mandated Coverage (Play or Pay), Managed Competition, and Publicly Financed Health Care.[11] Single-payer activists explained the "Publicly Financed" option in this way,

> In the past, most of the bills in this category were called "Single Payer" bills, however, paying for health care out of taxes can be joined with a variety of delivery mechanisms. This approach would save a considerable amount of money because of substantial administrative simplifications. According to a 1991 study by the US General Accounting Office (GOA), "the savings in administrative costs would be more than enough to offset the expense of universal coverage". The major criticisms are political. Is the American public willing to pay for health care through higher taxes even if it means overall savings? How far are our elected officials willing to go in advancing a program resolutely opposed by the politically influential insurance industry?[12]

---

[10] United Health Care Action Network. "History: UHCAN's Story, written on the occasion of our 20th anniversary" Posted January 2012. https://uhcan.org/about/history/.

[11] Altman S. & Shactman D. (2011). Power, Politics, and Universal Health Care. Amherst, NY: Prometheus Books.

[12] Inter-Religious Health Care Access Campaign—"Understanding the Different Proposals for National Health Care Reform" December 1992.

This discussion, which took place before Clinton was inaugurated, assumes that a publicly financed healthcare system (i.e. single-payer) is still on the table as an option. In it, the writers begin to address the narrative that single-payer is not politically feasible, even though it would be economically beneficial according to the US General Accounting Office. This narrative encouraged more grassroots mobilization directed toward shaping the healthcare reform debate on Capitol Hill.

A "People's Health CARE-avan" to Little Rock Arkansas that took place in December of 1992 drew over 1000 activists from 32 states. Mary, long-time activist and professional organizer, remembered that "in November we took a caravan of people into Little Rock to encourage him to go for universal single-payer healthcare."[13] At this time, directly following the election of Clinton but before the first "100 days" of his term, single-payer activists were still hopeful that they would have the opportunity to direct the debate toward single-payer, or at least to have a seat at the table.

In the following months, as the dominant narrative for healthcare reform became focused on "managed competition," single-payer activists began to realize that they would not have a seat at the table and would in reality be, for the most part,[14] ignored throughout the process of Clinton healthcare reform. By February of 1993, the focus on managed competition had become dominant within the narrative of political opportunity for healthcare reform. An article entitled "Will Managed Competition Cure Our Ills?" in the February 1993 Church Women United flier explained that

> Although President and Hillary Clinton have not formalized a health care plan, advisors have indicated that it will be some version of managed competition. In the coming months as Hillary Clinton and the health care task force work to develop a national health care plan, they need to hear from us. They are certainly hearing from insurance companies and need to be continually reminded who the reforms are really to benefit.[15]

[13] Mary Hussman Interview—Fall 2004.

[14] A few single-payer leaders, including Dr. David Himmelstein (PNHP) and Senator Paul Wellstone (D-MN), were allowed to meet with the Clinton transition team in early 1993—leading one author to write that single-payer was "no longer on the political fringe" (Priest 1993).

[15] Church Women United Flyer, February 1993.

This flier goes on to urge activists to send letters to Hillary Clinton and the recently established Health Care Task Force, providing an example letter which states,

> Thanks for your commitment to reforming the health care system. Perhaps your greatest challenge is to achieve reform that meets people's needs, not the interests of the health insurance lobby. I strongly urge you to support a health care plan similar to Canada's where everyone has access to all medically necessary care and costs are controlled because the role of private health insurance is drastically reduced. Thank you for considering my concerns.[16]

Although other options for healthcare reform were rejected by the Clinton Administrations' focus on "managed competition," single-payer activists still worked to make a place for themselves at the table. In fact, previously disparate groups of single-payer supporters began to create formalized organizations at this time, such as UCHAN and the newly formed "Missouri Coalition for Single Payer Health Care," which eventually became Missourians for Single Payer (MoSP). These organizations were also able to remain actively engaged in the healthcare reform debate by supporting single-payer bills at the national and state levels.

In the June 1993 meeting minutes of MoSP, this redirection of focus on state and national single-payer bills, rather than on the Clinton reform strategy, is apparent.

> PNHP (Physicians for a National Health Program) has two contacts in Washington DC that meet regularly with Congress, and met earlier with President Clinton's transition team. No representative from Hillary Clinton's Health Care Task Force would meet with PNHP representatives. However, the President and first lady know shortcomings and strengths of Single Payer system. Clintons do not believe they have political will or support for a single payer system … As a statewide organization, however, we can concentrate on passage of the 'Chatfield' bill, which has eleven sponsors for the next legislative session.[17]

[16] Church Women United Flier, February 1993.
[17] MoSP—East meeting minute June 1993.

The narrative told in these meeting minutes explains that single-payer activists, who were now being ignored by the Clinton Health Care Task Force, should redirect their focus to supporting specifically single-payer bills, rather than on trying to shape the Clinton agenda for health-care reform.

At this point, national single-payer organizations, such as UCHAN, also began redirecting their focus to supporting the "American Health Security Act" which was introduced by Senator Paul Wellstone (D-MN), Representative Jim McDermott (D-WA), and Representative John Conyers (D-MI) in March of 1993. By May of 1993, this bill had more co-sponsors in the House and Senate than any previously introduced single-payer bill with **five co-sponsors in the Senate and seventy-four in the House.**[18] Single-payer activists and organizations began using these state and national bills as tools to challenge the dominance of "managed competition" in the debate over healthcare reform.

> The American Health Security Act provides for universal access to comprehensive health care including preventative care, health education, long-term care, mental health care, and dental care. The act is a 'bench-mark' bill setting the standard by which other proposals will be measured. Strong support for this bill is crucial to send a message for bold and systemic reform to the Clinton Administration as it develops its own health care proposal.[19]

The political opportunity presented by the state and national single-payer bills, as well as the political agents that sponsored them, encouraged grass-roots single-payer activists to continue to push for single-payer in order to reshape the dominant political discourse through their support of these single-payer bills. There is some evidence, beyond the increasing number of co-sponsors for the American Health Security Act, that this effort was having the intended effect.

> One Democratic Senate aide, who has strong misgivings about a single-payer approach, nevertheless said the influence of those who support it could not be discounted. "If we wind up with universal coverage, the single-

---

[18] Priest, Dana. 1993 "Central Health Care: 'Undoable' But No Longer on Political Fringe" The Washington Post May 7, Final Edition.

[19] Action: Interfaith Impact Newsletter June 1993.

payer people will deserve a lot of the credit for that," said the aide, who would speak only on condition of anonymity. "They'll have been the ones who kept up the pressure to cover everyone."[20]

While the SPM may not have been able to re-direct the development of the Clinton healthcare reform policy toward single payer, they had become the "left flank,"[21] with which the debate surrounding healthcare reform must contend and had "mustered a political constituency that the administration cannot safely ignore."[22]

While the opportunity presented by these single-payer bills encouraged single-payer activists to continue mobilization efforts in the face of a contrary dominant narrative of healthcare reform, they also began experiencing some signs of negative opportunity within the grassroots movement for healthcare reform. The MoSP minutes from June of 1993 indicate that members of UCHAN and MoSP had been interested in joining a "March on Washington" which was organized by the National Association of Community Health Centers. However, "Myrna reported that UHCAN has talked with the planners of the march, and there will not be a designated separate section for SPS groups."[23] During this time, single-payer supporters became increasingly marginalized, not only within the realm of the dominant political narrative of healthcare reform but also within the movement for healthcare reform.

However, single-payer activists continued to fight this marginalization. In the Summer of 1993, UHCAN, in conjunction with Public Citizen, organized a "Letter to President Clinton,"

in support of single-payer reform endorsed by nearly 1000 grassroots organizations from 47 states, Puerto Rico and D.C. Diane Lardie, UHCAN National Coordinator, moderated a Washington, D.C. press conference

---

[20] Toner, Robin. 1993. "Backers of Canada-Type Health Plan: Idealistic, Outmuscled, but Still Scrapping" Special to the New York Times May 4, Section A; Page 22; Column 4.

[21] Priest, Dana. 1993 "Central Health Care: 'Undoable' But No Longer on Political Fringe" The Washington Post May 7, Final Edition.

[22] Sternberg, Steve. 1993. "Health Care Reform TV ads push for Government-run Plan" The Atlanta Journal and Constitution June 10; Section A; Page 4.

[23] MoSP–E minutes June 1993.

releasing the letter at which a broad cross-section of grassroots leaders spoke.[24]

This letter indicated grassroots support for single-payer healthcare reform. Yet, this did not sway the Clinton's or the Health Care Task Force, which were still enmired in the dominant narrative of "political infeasibility" and argued that single-payer was not politically "doable." Activists recall single-payer being taken "off the table in ways that would make your head spin"[25] and being alienated by the Clinton administration,

> I covered a talk by Hillary in KC and there was a gentleman on the speakers platform, and some fellow was there representing single-payer, and he started to ask something about him and she turned to him and said 'single-payer is NOT on the table' very rude. That alienated me, and I was one of those people charmed by Hillary up to that point.[26]

While this alienation is significant, it is also important that this political alienation was not experienced in isolation. There was a generalized experience of alienation from the secretive process that resulted in the Clinton Health Security proposal.[27] Also key is the fact that the alienation experienced by single-payer activists did not result in a cessation of movement activity at this time. Single-payer activists continued to mobilize and push for single-payer in ever more creative ways.

"Then They Laugh at You": Clinton Health Security Proposed

When the Clinton administration released their proposal for "Health Security" on September 22nd of 1993, it became obvious that the "political infeasibility" narrative had been successful and that the counternarrative of political and grassroots support for single payer had not been able to influence the Clinton Health Care Task Force. The SPM continued to mobilize in new and inventive ways.

---

[24] United Health Care Action Network. "History: UHCAN's Story, written on the occasion of our 20th anniversary" Posted January 2012. https://uhcan.org/about/history/.

[25] Activist, Health Care NOW National Strategy Conference, Field notes, 2009.

[26] Interview: Roger Signor, November 2004.

[27] Skocpol, Theda. 1997. Boomerang: Health Care Reform and the Turn Against Government, W.W. Norton and Company, New York.

Directly following the release of the Clinton health security proposal, many organizations sent out materials indicating that the "debate is on" and that they would "continue to support the American Health Security Act, but at the same time be supportive of the useful parts of the Clinton, or any other proposal."[28] These organizations argued that they could use the pre-existing single-payer legislation—the American Health Security Act—to shape the debate surrounding the Clinton proposal for "Health Security." The narrative surrounding this push indicated that "Both the President and Hillary Clinton have stressed repeatedly that their plan should be considered a starting point for Congress, the President has shown himself to be a negotiator" and that it was the responsibility of single-payer supporters "to make sure that any changes that occur in the President's plans are ones that further guide us toward the goal of universal access to health care."[29] Also central to this push was contacting members of Congress who would be "lobbied extensively by the health industry, many with the intent of blocking real reform."[30] This discourse highlights that the definition of the opposition to the movement was securely in the realm of the industry agents that had developed a powerful hold on the provision of health care in the United States. Church Women United (CWU), a national organization that "unanimously voted to support a single-payer bill, The American Health Security Act (HR 1200/ S 491)" because it "most closely matched our principles" also stressed that "our position of support for the AHSA does not mean, however, that we will stand opposed to the Clinton proposal."[31] This example illustrates the continued support for national single-payer legislation and a strong focus on the American Health Security Act—the national single-payer bill. However, it also highlights that some single-payer supporters, especially those in multi-issue groups, were willing to consider other options as long as they complied with the principles that they had set forth. This position encouraged single-payer activists to continue to view the Clinton administration as potential allies, regardless of any experience of alienation.

---

[28] HEALTH CARE DEBATE: Time to Get Serious About It MO IMPACT Newsletter September 1993.
[29] "Let the Debate Begin" in a Church Women ACT Flier published by Church Women United (CWU).
[30] Ibid.
[31] Ibid.

Many organizations of this type became involved in the "Campaign for Health Security," at this time. Through this campaign "most national single-payer organizations are working ... to apply single-payer principles to health debate now taking place in Congress." They acted on the conclusion that "health reform is now in congressional committees, where the Clinton plan may be turned into something quite different." The campaign centered on "three essential tasks for advocates: to build mass demand for change, to attack the bad bills, particularly the 'bipartisan' Cooper bill, and to lobby single-payer co-sponsors and other supporters of reform to build a bloc that will hold fast to the principles of real reform."[32] This segment of the SPM continued to focus on pushing the discussion in Congress toward the principles that they argued would best be met through the implementation of a single-payer program.

This was a difficult task, due to the opposition that the Campaign for Health Security, as well as the SPM, faced. This was defined as a "war to establish people first health care." According to this narrative, the "enemy" within this war was the healthcare industry that was winning because they were "spending tens of millions of our health care dollars to flood the media and offices of our Congress with misinformation, lies, and six figure checks." Although this enemy was defined as extremely powerful due to their "big money PACS" and "slick Madison Avenue lobbyists with 100 million-dollar budgets," activists *kept on keepin on* with the belief that **"we do have the ultimate power. We have truth and moral people. We have YOU."**[33] In this narrative, the *enemy* in the *war* facing supporters of single-payer were the powerful corporate interests that, through their financial resources, have great influence on the media and political establishment. These elite forces were aligned against the SPM as well as the Clinton-led campaign for healthcare reform—they were an enemy that single-payer activists shared with the Clinton Administration. Activists were encouraged to fight this war using the "ultimate power" of grassroots mobilization.

[32] Cowell, Susan. 1994. "Round Two: What the Single Payer Movement Must Do in the Coming Months" Democratic Left March/April Democratic Socialists of America.

[33] Excerpts from a speech by Ustin Dar, former Chair of the President's Committee on Employment of People with Disabilities 1/17/94 at a Fairshake Legislative Rally in Charleston WV.

This narrative encouraged single-payer activists to mobilize in conjunction with the Clinton Health Security campaign and continue to see them as allies rather than work against them.

> Despite differences of tone and nuance within the single-payer camp, there is substantial unity over strategy, with very few groups seeking to defeat the Clinton plan outright. At the center now are five aspects of the Clinton plan that must not be compromised away—universal coverage by 1998, comprehensive benefits, an employer mandate to pay for health care, cost controls (including premium caps and fee schedules), and the state single-payer option. These are substantially the same elements promoted by the AFL-CIO and other liberal groups.[34]

Single-payer supporters were encouraged to develop strategies that continued to work alongside the Clinton Campaign rather than against it.

Although the single-payer option was ignored by the Clinton administration, single-payer supporters were encouraged to mobilize in support of passing universal health care through the Clinton campaign for Health Security. The Clinton administration did not initially invest in efforts to mobilize the public in support of Health Security, and there was a generalized experience of alienation from a secret process.[35] But, in the summer of 1994, as the national healthcare reform debate was drawing to a close, a focus on grassroots mobilization did arise. The "Health Security Express" bus tour was a major effort to mobilize the grassroots. The plan for this action was that through it,

> Thousands of citizens will do more than listen and watch. They will ride into history—on caravans of busses from every region of the country, arriving on Capitol Hill at the beginning of August. They will be nurses, doctors, working people and retirees, celebrities, and political leaders... The 'reform riders' will be carrying handwritten messages to elected representatives, demanding that Congress respond to President Clinton's leadership for universal coverage and guarantee that no American ever loses their health insurance.[36]

[34] Cowell, Susan. 1994. "Round Two: What the Single Payer Movement Must Do in the Coming Months" Democratic Left March/April Democratic Socialists of America.

[35] Skocpol, Theda. 1997. Boomerang: Health Care Reform and the Turn Against Government, W.W. Norton and Company, New York.

[36] Health Security Express Information Sheet, June 1994.

Organizations that supported single-payer were hesitant to become involved in the Health Security Express because it was still not exactly clear what plan the express would be supporting. CWU, for example, did not endorse

> the Health Security Express because the slogan is Pass It Now. We are unable to endorse something that is not clear. What is the "it" referring to (the Clinton Bill? The House Bill? The Bradley amendment?) and whether the issue of abortion will appear. We would have preferred that the slogan be modified to read: Universal Coverage: Pass It Now.[37]

Yet, organizations such as CWU did volunteer to support the express by providing meals to the riders. They recognized this as an opportunity to share the single-payer narrative with a wider grassroots audience.

> We believe that this second item[38] is KEY to our work as we can therefore control the visual on television. Most of the dinners and stops of the busses will be covered by the media. At this time, it is expected that someone from the White House, from staff to Cabinet members to either one of the Gores or Clintons, could be at these events. We will not know to the last minute. This is our opportunity to make CWU visible and advocate our key principles.[39]

Although the Health Security Express was not mobilized in support of single-payer, it became a location of grassroots opportunity in order to mobilize support for single-payer by sharing the single-payer counter-narrative with a wider population of people.

While single-payer supporters defined the opposition as those with corporate interests in the private insurance market and even mobilized in conjunction with last minute efforts to encourage mobilization in support of Clinton Health Security, they remained highly critical of the Clinton Administration's direction for reform.

---

[37] Letter from Church Women United Missouri President Mary Jane Schutzius July 30th, 1994.

[38] To provide visuals and posters at CWU hosted Health Care Express Events.

[39] Public letter from Sally Timmet, National President of CWU, July 15, 1994.

President Clinton is proposing something called 'managed competition.' Under managed competition, the multiple payer system will largely remain intact and the insurance companies will be protected. There will be one level of care for the 'haves' and another level for the 'have-nots.' This is not acceptable.

The alternative is a single-payer health care system modeled after the Canadian system. .... The battle for health care reform will be the people versus the insurance companies and big business. If the insurance companies win, the vast majority of poor and working people will be the losers. Therefore, it is in the best interest of African Americans to rally behind the single-payer bill in Congress—the McDermott-Conyers American Health Security Act.[40]

While single-payer activists were critical of many aspects of the Clinton plan—including the retention of private insurance companies within a tiered system—they continued to define the Clinton administration as an ally. Instead of defining this as a battle between the opposing options of "managed competition" and "single-payer," this narrative continued to define the "battle" for healthcare reform as being between the Movement for Healthcare Reform as a whole and the strong opposition presented by the well-financed insurance and pharmaceutical companies. This quote also illustrates a significant strategy of the SPM at this time—to encourage increased focus on the national single-payer bills in order to mobilize grassroots populations that had not yet been mobilized.

Many single-payer organizations focused on their support of the Wellstone–McDermott bills (The American Health Security Act) at the national level. These national bills in the House and Senate were viewed as the focus of a strategy through which the movement could convince the many congressional committees who were developing healthcare reform bills to reconsider single-payer. Central to this narrative is the argument that the American Health Security Act had more support than any of the bills being developed in Congress, both inside and outside of the legislature. In the March 1994 issue of "American Health Security News," Congressman McDermott argued that

---

[40] Ron Daniels—National Chairperson of the Campaign for a New Tomorrow (CNT)—led multi-racial independent political organization in the June 1994 ACTION Newsletter.

As congressional support for the Clinton health plan gets harder and harder to find, many are taking a second look at single-payer health care reform. Among those looking again—and liking what they see—are the editors of The Washington Monthly magazine. The March 1994 issue contains an eight-page examination of single-payer systems successfully controlling costs and delivering high quality health care in Germany and Canada.

The recently formed Single-Payer Across the Nation (SPAN) also discussed increasing support of single payer in the first issue of their newsletter in which they quote then General Motors Chairman Jack Smith as saying "I personally favor the Canadian system" and *Business Week* Magazine as saying "single payer is not 'socialized medicine.' Rather, it's by far the best way to control costs while preserving the freedom of choice and physician autonomy that made American medicine great" in their section "Quote of the Month." This narrative does not indicate that there was a downturn in activity following the introduction of the Clinton proposal but rather an upswing of activity in connection to the perceived support of the single-payer option embodied in the Wellstone/McDermott Bill.[41]

SPAN became an organizing force during this time of possible opportunity. SPAN began as a loosely organized coalition, headed by UHCAN. According to their origin story,

In early 1994, local and national activists affiliated with UHCAN formed SPAN to spearhead targeted grassroots legislative and political action on behalf of single-payer legislation in the U.S. Congress. In addition to organizing support for Rep. Jim McDermott's universal single-payer bill, the "American Health Security Act," SPAN helped organize nationwide support for Proposition 186, the single-payer ballot initiative in California.[42]

[41] Table 2.1 compares these two proposals. It is a condensed summary of just two of the bills during this era and is not exhaustive. A more comprehensive comparison can be found in the Congressional Research Office Report for Congress "Summary Comparison of Major Health Care Reform Bills." Written by Melvina Ford, Celinda Franco, Jennifer O'Sullivan, and Richard Price—Specialists in Social Legislation / Education and Public Welfare Division on January 6, 1994, on which this table is based.
[42] United Health Care Action Network. "History: UHCAN's Story, written on the occasion of our 20th anniversary" Posted January 2012. https://uhcan.org/about/history/.

According to this narrative, SPAN was formed specifically to support the single-payer bills introduced in the national legislature. This is markedly different from other national organizations, such as CWU, which were multi-issue organizations with a single-payer platform. Although these multi-issue organizations continued to support single payer, they also indicated that they were willing to accept other options that would fulfill the principles that they had set out to achieve. It is significant that several single-issue single-payer organizations (some with single-payer in the name) were formed during this period. Several state-based organizations also formed in connection with SPAN and continued to act on national-level issues. For example, the SPAN chapter in Washington (WA-SPAN), which was formed as a coalition of many groups, including the Gray Panthers, the Rainbow Coalition, League of Women Voters, WA Health Care for All, amped up their organizing in response to a media brownout.

In an attempt to break the media 'brown out' on the tremendous advantages of single payer, WA—SPAN has stated several mini-rallies and events prior to Health Care for People Week. When managed competition theorist Alain Enthoven addressed the American Pharmaceutical Association convention, SPANers were there picketing. When AARP hosted a "Health Care University" convention which promoted the Clinton health care plan, the audience was noisily single-payer. And when U.S. Sen. Patty Murray and Dr. Judith Feder hosted a meeting to hear about the impact to date of Washington's health care reform law, single-payer advocates organized a mini rally in front of the federal building ... Here, as elsewhere, the struggle goes on to rid the health care financing system of the private insurance industry. Regardless of the outcome in Congress this year, we are winning many converts among the populace.[43]

This action narrative indicates that this grassroots activity was encouraged by the negative cultural opportunity presented by an unresponsive media. My own analysis of the coverage of single-payer in news media, illustrated in Fig. 2.1, shows that while coverage of the Clinton supported

[43] Craig Salins in "Action for Universal Health Care "News from the Grassroots" March 1994.

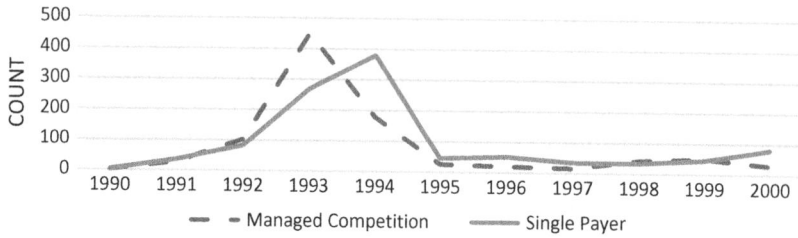

*Sample collected from all newspaper sources available on the database Nexis Uni.

Fig. 2.1 Single payer in newspapers during the Clinton era. (Source: Sample collected from all newspaper sources available on the database Nexis Uni)

option—managed competition—was initially greater than the coverage of single-payer, as the healthcare reform debate wound down on capitol hill, single-payer had greater representation in newspaper coverage.[44]

Grassroots activists in Washington found other ways to share their counter-narrative with a larger audience. While the main forms of material culture (i.e. television) were not accessible avenues through which to share their counter-narrative, they did work to find other ways of sharing their single-payer story. Activists in Washington were encouraged to act by the positive political opportunity presented by the support of political actors for single-payer bills and by the grassroots opportunity represented by the formation of grassroots organization such as SPAN. SPAN, and by proxy UHCAN, became leading forces in mobilizing the grassroots in support of single-payer. Later, it would become an organizing force in support of state-based single-payer initiatives.

Single-payer activists also hoped that the decisions being made in the national legislature would encourage the mainstream media to redirect its focus toward the grassroots organizing occurring in support of single-payer. In an article titled "Red Faces Busting Out All Over" single-payer activists linked the lack of mainstream media coverage of the Single Payer Movement with the dominance of the "political infeasibility" narrative.

---

[44] Chart 5.2 is based on the comparison of two searches limited to newspaper articles within the Lexis Uni database system using the search terms, "single payer" AND ("healthcare" OR "health care"), "Managed Competition" AND (Healthcare OR "Health care").

Look for the House subcommittees and committees to move legislations closer to the single-payer approach than the 'managed competition' approach, which will be an early indicator of where health reform is heading. Red faced reporters and editors who have bought the year-long White House spin that the single-payer plan is 'not politically viable'—and have, as a result, seriously under-reported it—will have some explaining to do at that point. Because the plan has been so under-reported, readers, viewers, and listeners are woefully uninformed about the single-payer proposal which is about to emerge as the clear front runner where it matters most: in Congress where the votes are cast.[45]

This excerpt clearly calls out the mainstream media establishment for ignoring the single-payer narrative in favor of managed competition, due to the supposed political "infeasibility" of the single-payer option. In lieu of mainstream coverage of support for single-payer, the SPM was pushed to develop media strategies that involved alternatives to the mainstream media while still utilizing the dominant form of material culture.

Single-payer activists responded to the ignorance of the mainstream media by concentrating on and developing a targeted media strategy. This targeted strategy involved hosting radio broadcasted healthcare town halls, posting full-page print ads in newspapers, and "A nation-wide call for op-eds to be sent to the *New York Times* for their special healthcare reform supplement to be published June 12th."[46] One ad, which was produced by the Public Media Center and Public Citizen, featured Ralph Nader and Jack Smith (then CEO of General Motors). It raised the question, "If these two can agree on a health care plan, why can't the Congress?" Both Nader and Smith were purported to be single-payer supporters and this ad countered the narrative that there was not a substantial amount of political or economic opportunity for single payer. These media strategies attempted to use the dominant aspects of material culture to tell the public a narrative that countered the dominant narrative of healthcare reform which labeled "managed competition" as the only feasible option.

[45] Action for Universal Health Care, UHCAN Newsletter, April 1994.
[46] Marilyn Clement—Director "Health Care—We've gotta have it" NYC in the May 1994 issue of ACTION for Universal Health Care Newsletter.

Single-payer supporters also developed creative ways to challenge the "Harry and Louise" ad campaign sponsored by the Health Insurance Association of America. In this ad campaign, the story of a couple—Harry and Louise—dealing with changes to the healthcare system is told. In the first ad, as Harry and Louise sit at their kitchen table "sometime in the future" trying to understand piles of paperwork, the narrator warns viewers that "things are changing, and not all for the better. The government may force us to pick from a few healthcare plans designed by government bureaucrats." Louise then frustratedly says "having choices we don't like is no choice at all." Harry and Louise then agree that "They choose. We lose." The narrative in this ad predicts a negative outcome of the Clinton reform proposal and encourages the audience to agree with this prediction.[47] The Harry and Louise narrative was successful at shaping the discourse concerning Clinton Health Security because it was very well funded and appeared in homes across the nation.[48]

An integral element of the single-payer media strategy was to create a counter-narrative to that of Harry and Louise. They did this through humor. An effort was made to create a set of ads which parodied the Harry and Louise ads. This was complimented by a fundraising effort supported by the National Health Care Campaign which was a project of the Democratic National Committee to raise funds in order to share this counter-narrative through the dominant form of material culture at that time—television. In an ad created through this endeavor, "Harry and Louise" are in bed—both covered in bandages, casts, and other medical equipment. Louise states that "They said universal healthcare was too complicated Louise. They said you'd never lose your job, so we'd always be covered. They said, what do we do when the government runs out of money. Well who's out of money now Harry." At this point, Louise pushes Harry out of bed and says, "There's got to be a better way." This narrative attempts to convince the audience that healthcare reform is needed and that there is a better way being proposed. The audience is then encouraged to contact Congress and urge them to support universal health care.

[47] You can view the Harry and Louise ads here, https://www.youtube.com/watch?v=CwOX2P4s-Iw.

[48] Skocpol, Theda. 1997. Boomerang: Health Care Reform and the Turn Against Government, W.W. Norton and Company, New York.

Two comedians, Jerry Stiller and Anne Meara, were central players in the production of another humorous counter-narrative presented in a commercial funded by Single-Payer Across the Nation (SPAN).[49] In this ad, the following exchange occurs,

JERRY STILLER: What's wrong, honey?
ANNE MEARA: I'm confused about Harry and Louise.
JERRY STILLER: You mean that worried couple on the insurance companies' commercials?
ANNE MEARA: They're so confused about health care.

The couple then explains that single-payer is simple to understand saying,

JERRY STILLER: Everyone is covered, you get full benefits, and you choose your own doctor.
ANNE MEARA: Harry and Louise, there is a better way.

Through this narrative, Stiller and Meara counter the narrative that reform is complicated and difficult to understand by telling the audience that the "better way" is actually quite simple—a single-payer healthcare system that covers everyone with full benefits while affirming patient autonomy to make choices about their healthcare provider. Although this campaign was not as well financed as the HIAA-financed Harry and Louise ads, single-payer activists used this ad campaign to promote their own counter-narrative—that what Harry and Louise really needed was a single-payer system.

These campaigns inspired more media attention on the SPM. One article in the May 3, 1994 issue of the *New York Times* discusses this ad campaign explaining that,

> The advertising campaign is small compared with the industry's: just $1 million, only a fourth of which has been raised, as against the more than $10 million spent by the insurance association. But the advocates of a

[49] Moyers, Bill. 1994. "The Great Health Care Debate" October 7, 1994 Transcript posted at https://billmoyers.com/content/great-health-care-debate/.

Canadian-style system, in which the government pays nearly all medical bills, have already demonstrated substantial support at the grassroots.[50]

This counter-narrative, which used humor to critique the narrative presented in the Harry and Louise ads, encouraged the mainstream media to re-direct their focus toward the activities of the SPM. The coverage of this ad campaign also encouraged more organizations to sponsor the campaign,

> Impressed by the success and the quality of the ads, the AFSCME international has decided to give a large grant to SPAN to further the ad campaign and keep up the heat for single-payer. It's wonderful to begin to get the solid backing needed to win this fight.[51]

This illustrates the success of the Harry and Louise counter-narrative in mobilizing not just grassroots single-payer support and increasing media coverage of the SPM, but also in encouraging the financial support of economic actors such as the American Federation of State, County, and Municipal Employees.

The alternative media strategies developed by the SPM used humor to challenge the dominant narratives of healthcare reform and the ignorance of mainstream media culture. Rather than being laughed at as working for something that was not politically feasible, they directed the laughter toward characters created by the insurance industry while critiquing the media establishment which had so easily been manipulated by the "politically infeasible" narrative and were thus narratively constructed as being shamed to the point of being "red faced." This media strategy was also important to the state initiatives that were developing around the country.

"Then They Fight You": Single Payer in the States

During this period (late 1993 to early 1995), focus also intensified on the possibility of implementing single-payer programs at the state level. An aspect of the Clinton proposal which would allow for federal support of

---

[50] Toner, Robin. 1993. "Backers of Canada-Type Health Plan: Idealistic, Outmuscled, but Still Scrapping" Special to the New York Times May 4, Section A; Page 22; Column 4.
[51] ACTION for Universal Health Care Newsletter June 1994.

these programs was of particular concern for single-payer actors. In an article titled "We're Everywhere, We're Everywhere," Representative McDermott argued that,

> Single-payer forces in Congress have revealed new support and opened a new front in the drive for single-payer health reform. HR 1200 cosponsors Reps. Bernie Sanders (VT) and Joe Kennedy (MA) are organizing an effort to complement the drive to enact HR 1200. They want to ensure that **every** plan moving through Congress includes a guarantee that states have the option to set up their own single-payer system. So far, **112 Members of Congress have enlisted in the effort**. Thirty-two of those Members are **not** HR 1200 co-sponsors. Even though they have not yet sponsored national single-payer legislation, they are making clear that they strongly believe their states should have the guaranteed option to create a state single-payer system.[52]

Support for this aspect of the Clinton proposal, which would allow single payer to be an option in the development of state-based programs, was defined as positive political opportunity for single-payer activism. This encouraged activists to continue to work at the national level, while also supporting state-level efforts. This aspect of national legislation was also of particular importance due to the increasing focus placed upon state single-payer initiatives at this time.

Many state-based organizations had been mobilized in support of state single-payer legislation or initiatives in the years leading into the debate surrounding Clinton Health Security. For example, the Missouri-based movement was also supporting the "Missouri Health Assurance Bill" and the Vermont-based movement was also supporting S-127, which was introduced by Vermont state senator Cheryl Rivers and supported by Bernie Sanders, who was then a Representative of Vermont in the U.S. House of Representatives. During the Clinton health security debate, state initiatives became not just a way to achieve single-payer at the state level but also a way for single-payer activists to affect the national debate on healthcare reform. Of particular importance during this time was Proposition 186—a grassroots ballot initiative in California.

---

[52] American Health Security News March 1994.

By June of 1994, the California-based movement had successfully gar-
nered the one million signatures needed in order to put Prop 186 on the
November 1994 ballot. The successful petition drive spearheaded by
Californians for Health Security involved more than 10,000 volunteers
and was supported by many California-based organizations such as the
California Nurses Association, the California Physicians' Alliance, the
California Professional Firefighters, the California Teachers Association,
the California Labor Federation (AFL-CIO), the California Council of
Churches, Catholic Charities, the Congress of California Seniors,
Neighbor to Neighbor, and Vote Health.

The California ballot initiative was implemented in the context of
national political, cultural, and economic opportunity that ignored and
delegitimized the single-payer position through the narrative of the "political infeasibility" of single-payer.

> Like voters everywhere, Californians have felt left out of the health care
> debate between insurance companies and other special interests and
> Congress. Until now, no one has listened to everyone else—health care con-
> sumers—who want comprehensive care whether they are health or sick,
> working or unemployed. **This campaign will inject the single-payer
> option into the national debate on health care reform and help win this
> kind of comprehensive coverage for all Californians—and then for all
> Americans.**[53]

Through the success of the petition portion of the campaign, single-payer
supporters showed that there was indeed extensive grassroots support for
single-payer healthcare in California. Coverage of this development also
"represented a major breakthrough for serious media coverage of single-
payer and the depth of popular support for it."[54]

As the passage of a healthcare reform bill at the national level became
less and less likely, the passage of Prop. 186 through a ballot initiative and
referendum became a major focus for the national SPM, as well as for
California-based single-payer activists. At their national meeting in May,
the Physicians for a National Health Program (PNHP) voted to support
the California initiative and great

---

[53] Action for Universal Health Care June 1994.
[54] Ibid.

optimism was accorded to the California single-payer petition victory with a firm commitment from PNHP to the drive to victory in November~ Plans include a 'Health Summer' volunteer campaign emulating the 'Freedom Summer' of the Civil Rights movement in 1964 ...

Clear-eyed about the awesome power of our opponents in government and elsewhere, PNHP came back home from Toronto more certain than ever that we can win, will win if the public's voice can be expressed in California and elsewhere![55]

While mobilization in support of health security was focused on the "health security express" heading toward the east coast and Washington D.C., single-payer supporters were gearing up for "healthcare summer" which would involve single-payer supporters across the nation committing to supporting Prop. 186 on the west coast in California.

Single-payer activists knew that while the insurance lobby had been focused on defeating health security, which by the fall of 1994 they had successfully accomplished,[56] the success of the Prop. 186 petition drive would force them to redirect some of that focus to fighting and defeating the ballot initiative. They warned that,

This very minute the insurance industry and numerous other lobbyists are planning to spend hundreds of millions of dollars to try to defeat passage of what can be the most important social legislation of the century. Winning this fight could capture the imagination of the country and set a precedent for the rest of the nation. The President's plan does give states the option to establish a single payer system. We will not try to match the distortions and lies of the opponents and we still can win, but not without your participation. If we don't win in California, we'll have to lie with what comes out of Congress and that would be a calamity for most of us.[57]

They began a nation-wide campaign to raise funds for an ad campaign in California. This involved house parties, educational programs, and the "Healthcare Summer."

[55] Quentin Young M.D. in "Action for Universal Health Care" Newsletter, June 1994.
[56] Skocpol, Theda. 1997. Boomerang: Health Care Reform and the Turn Against Government, W.W. Norton and Company, New York.
[57] Californians for Health Security Flier, Summer 1994.

The summer of 1994 involved mass grassroots mobilization by the SPM, not only in support of Prop. 186 in California but also as a final effort to redirect the dying debate in the national legislature. SPAN held a national lobby day in Washington D.C. in August during which over 200 activists visited over 130 congressional offices and personally spoke with 60 legislators. After summarizing the experiences of activists during this effort, activists concluded

> So, is the bottom line outcome of our effort....nothing?⁇ No more than Nelson Mandela's jail term was the final outcome of South Africa's struggle for justice. We're believers and WE'RE NOT GOING AWAY.[58]

Single-payer supporters were determined to continue pushing for single-payer, even in a context in which any type of substantial reform seemed less and less likely. Single-payer supporters still believed that their efforts would result in success of some sort. Representative Jerry Nadler (D-NY) is quoted as saying "There will be some states that adopt single-payer and over the next couple years, it will be so evident it is so superior that other states will follow suit. Insurance companies are afraid of the single-payer system because it serves the people and the people's needs."[59] After this day of action in D.C., focus was redirected toward the states.

The success of the petition campaign in California encouraged single-payer activists in other states to develop ballot initiatives of their own. The Massachusetts State Single Payer Referendum Campaign has some success when it gathered,

> enough signatures in seven senatorial districts and one representative district to place a single-payer question on the ballot in those districts for the November 1994 elections. This ballot initiative will help educate the public, build strong grassroots health care reform organizations, and lay the groundwork for a single-payer majority in the state legislature.[60]

As illustrated in the quote above, these initiatives became strategies for not just affecting the national debate on healthcare reform but also to build grassroots and political support for single-payer at the state level.

---

[58] Action for Universal Health Care Newsletter August/September 1994.
[59] Ibid.
[60] Ibid.

The initially successful ballot initiative in California was viewed not only as a strategy in which to change the debate or increase public awareness but as a legitimate opportunity for creating a state-based single-payer system. Don Cohen, Coalition Director for Californians for Health Security, urged nation-wide support saying, "This is a national fight. It cannot be won without the very active and aggressive support of every activist in the national Single Payer Movement. Nowhere else in the world is the single-payer system on the table to be scrutinized on its own merits."[61] Activists worked diligently to challenge the multi-million-dollar media campaign of the insurance industry.

The healthcare summer planned in support of Prop. 186 actually extended into the fall and the final days leading up to the November vote. Church Women United of California offered a "free trip to California" explaining that,

> During this "vacation", you will be asked to help build support for the Single Payer Initiative that is on the California ballot. In May, over one million signatures were collected to get the Single Payer Initiative on the ballot. Since then, the insurance companies have launched an all-out campaign ($60 million) in media advertisement to defeat this measure. Religious groups, the League of Women Voters, California AARP, and labor unions are working hard to show Congress and the nation that ordinary people support a single-payer system.
>
> Everyone in Washington will be watching what happens in California. Action in states has gained new importance as the possibility of national health care reform becomes less and less likely. Winning the CA Single Payer Ballot would have enormous consequences for the national debate. After all, the Canadian system began on a province by province basis back in the 70s.
>
> If you can afford the time and cost of a ticket, join the women of California and be a part of the action for reforming the health care system.[62]

People who took part in this free "vacation" worked in support of the initiative by telephone banking, leafleting, and canvassing in support of Proposition 186.

Activists in California used a broad range of tactics in their effort to garner public support for Prop. 186. Over 2000 house parties were held in California and around the country in order to raise money to

---

[61] Action for Universal Health Care Newsletter August/September 1994.
[62] Church Women United Flyer Summer 1994.

support the campaign for Proposition 186. Single-payer activists also held press conferences, became human billboards (telling Hillary Rodham Clinton that "We'll finish the job you started!"), and even chained themselves to the doors of insurance company headquarters. One notable action was committed by the California Nurses Association in which the nurses,

> wrapped the entrance of insurance company headquarters in Hollywood and San Francisco and with red tape on September 21st to signify their anger at the industry's use of 'nurse actresses' in ads attacking Proposition 186 blanketing the air waves during late August and early September.[63]

In the face of an extremely well-financed mobilization against the passage of Proposition 186, single-payer activists fought back with gusto.

In the weeks leading up to the November 8th elections, single-payer activists in California were still hopeful that their effort would be successful and that this would encourage future directions for national healthcare reform. In an article titled "California's Real-Life Blueprint for Single Payer," the author explained that

> as the November 8th election draws closer, the level of grassroots activity on behalf of the single-payer ballot initiative in California is rising. Massive public education from media ads down to neighborhood house parties is taking place all over the state. Leaders of the Yes on Proposition 186 campaign are optimistic that the major media campaign for which they are furiously raising funds this fall, together with the massive one-on-one voter education taking place under the auspices of thousands of grassroots groups supporting the initiative, **will make success on November 8th a REAL possibility.**[64]

Although the insurance industry was fighting their every effort, single-payer activists took this in stride and as a sign that such extensive countermeasures were only needed due to the real threat that they presented to the continuation of private insurance in California and due to the "real possibility" of succeeding.

---

[63] Action for Universal Health Care Newsletter October 1994 NO ISSUE/VOLUME NUMBERS.
[64] Ibid.

AND THEN YOU .... WIN?: THE "DEATH" OF HEALTHCARE REFORM

To "win" in the process of progressive social policy reform is an ambiguous issue. Due to the make-up of the political landscape in the United States, including the two-party system and campaign finance policy, achieving progressive reform is a difficult task for social movement actors who do not have traditional power within the political system and whose actions are often ignored or delegitimized. There is much debate within social movement literature over what constitutes success and failure in a social movement and how these issues should be measured.[65] Often the everyday "keep on keepin on" of social movements, which can at times result in the institutionalization of SMOs in "abeyance structures"[66] that serve to perpetuate the movement in negative times,[67] is not included as a measure of success. This act of "keep on keepin on" in the face of "failure" is largely dependent on the ways in which activists construct the story of their activities and the relationship between these activities and their perceived success or failure.[68] These action narratives guide future decision-making processes as the movement continues to mobilize. Although the Clinton era of healthcare reform is ultimately considered a failure by the public and academics alike, single-payer activists at that time initially constructed this period as successful in several ways. This action narrative facilitated future activity.

By mid-November of 1994 it became clear that healthcare reform at the national level had failed. Mid-term elections resulted in the first Republican controlled Congress in almost forty-five years and initiated a "Contract with America" that promised to cut social programs rather than improve them. The early success of the ballot initiative for Proposition 186 in California ultimately resulted in defeat, with 73 percent voting against the measure. While the SPM could have fizzled out at this point, in light of not only "failure" but also with knowledge of the changing trajectory of the national legislature, it did not. Instead single-payer activists discussed this period as a moment of success and as a reason to work

---

[65] Saeed, R. 2009. "Conceptualising Success and Failure for Social Movements" (2) Law, Social Justice & Global Development Journal Vol. 2.

[66] Tarrow. Sidney. 1994. Power in Movement. Cambridge: Cambridge University Press.

[67] Taylor, Verta. 1989. "Social Movement Continuity: The Women's Movement in Abeyance" American Sociological Review, Vol. 54, No. 5 (Oct. 1989), pp. 761–775.

[68] Polletta, Francesca. 2006. It Was Like a Fever: Story Telling in Protest and Politics University of Chicago Press.

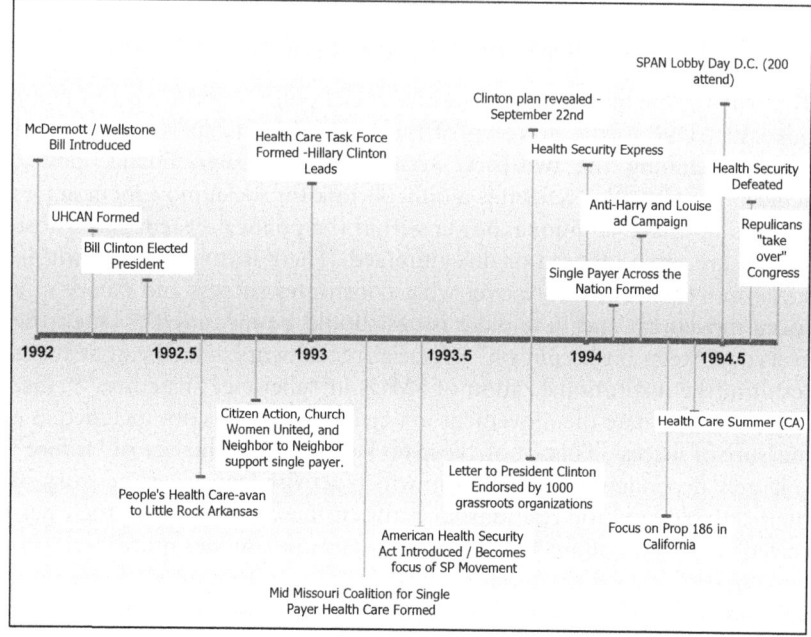

Fig. 2.2 The Movement for Single Payer Clinton era timeline

even harder in the future (see Fig. 2.2 for an accounting of all activities during this period).

Single-payer activists defined this period of healthcare reform as a success because they had built a movement.

> Our movement has never been stronger. Even though our strength in this latest round was not enough to put us over the top, our coalitions, here in Missouri and at the national level, grew to unprecedented size and influence. All across our state literally thousands of activists and volunteers engaged in a broad array of work to move the issue forward. Single-payer supporters provided the backbone of this growing movement and in most cases were its key leaders. There is no question that we come out of this phase of the campaign stronger than we went in.[69]

This aspect of the single-payer narrative reorients the concept of success to not just achieving one's goals but also to building the necessary

[69] "News from the Health Care Education Project" Missouri Citizen Action and Older Women's League.

components of a strong social movement. An important piece of this narrative is that the involvement within the movement grew and would continue to increase regardless of the outcomes of the Clinton reform attempt. At this time, organizations continued to be created. For example, Mid Missourians for Single Payer was formed in the aftermath of the failure of Clinton Health Security.

This period was also defined as a legitimatizing period for the movements' goals and strategy.

> The credibility and leadership role of the single-payer movement has been increased. Single-payer supporters have long been told by our allies in the health reform debate that single-payer may be the best health care policy, but that is made for poor health care politics. The argument has been that small scale, incremental reforms are less threatening to the insurance industry and other special interests. They should, therefore, provoke less opposition and be easier to pass. Single-payer advocates have always believed that the special interests would do everything they can to kill even modest reforms; and that the best strategy is to offer the kind of real reform proposal that can mobilize genuine outpouring of public support to counteract our well-financed opponents. The furious insurance attack on President Clinton's less than complete proposal, and the public's uneasiness about its complexity (born of an attempt to find some role for the insurance industry) have proven that the single-payer strategy makes sense.[70]

While healthcare reform may have failed at the national level, this failure was constructed by single-payer activists as evidence that their strategy for achieving real healthcare reform was legitimate. This countered the argument that working for single-payer was not worthwhile because it was not politically feasible.

This period of healthcare reform also encouraged and facilitated the development of state-based single-payer movements around the country. While these movements also ultimately failed to implement single-payer systems, there were also examples of traditional success such as single-payer legislation successfully passing through the Vermont House of Representatives and the relative success of the single-payer ballot initiatives in California, Massachusetts, and Colorado. These state-based movements also served to grow the movement by educating and encouraging the public to support single-payer.

[70] Ibid.

While single-payer activists recognized the power of their "enemies," they also believed that this period of healthcare reform had served to weaken this power in some ways.

> While our movement has grown in strength and learned a valuable strategic lesson our opponent's coalition is showing signs of wear and tear. The unified front that the insurance industry, the AMA, and the hospital industry once showed has cracked under the strain of the Congressional debate. Providers are becoming daily more aware that the massive insurance bureaucracy is as much their problem as it is consumers. More and more Doctors and other health care professionals are coming to the realization that single payer is the best route to their long-held goal of universal access.[71]

Single-payer activists assessed the situation and concluded that the changes that were made during this period (i.e. the rise of managed care) would result in a reduction in the autonomy of healthcare providers and would thus result in more support from this arena in future efforts for healthcare reform. Looking to the future, they concluded that although they had lost this battle, their enemies were very concerned about the "war" (See Fig. 2.3 for a visual summary of this period).

While single-payer activists worked to counter the narrative that single-payer was not politically feasible throughout the healthcare reform debate, they did not work to counter those who were the perpetrators of this narrative. As the healthcare debate was coming to a close, this began to change. Single-payer supporters began to be more confrontational with their critique of this narrative.

> The Political Unfeasibility argument is anti-democratic because it elevates corporatism above democracy. It assumes that the country can be governed from inside the Beltway and that the aspirations of the majority of Americans can be safely ignored.... Acceptance of the Political Unfeasibility argument, and support for managed competition, are therefore not signs of progress in health policy, or evidence of political realism, but rather symptoms of intellectual failure, moral insensitivity, and political cowardice.[72]

The quote above indicates that the relationship between single-payer activists and those who rejected single-payer due to political feasibility was

---

[71] Ibid.

[72] Robert G. Stubbings—The Texas Observer / Quoted in Action for Universal Health Care Newsletter, July 1994.

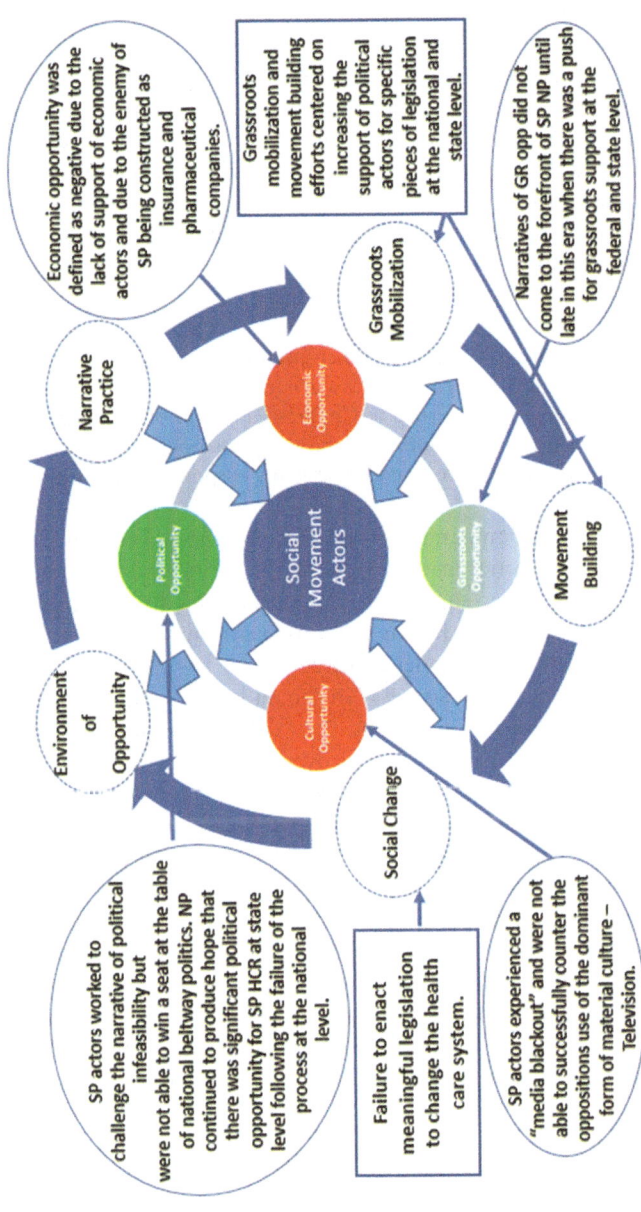

Fig. 2.3 Clinton era narrative practice

changing. It counters the argument that "realism" is more feasible than the idealism represented by the single-payer option and calls out those who support this argument for their "intellectual failure, moral insensitivity, and political cowardice." This is a major change from the start of the debate when single-payer activists continued to be supportive of those who perpetuated the argument of political infeasibility who they ultimately viewed as allies in the fight for healthcare reform.

The continued success of single-payer supporters in the context of a power-shifting political arena was also taken as a sign of success for the SPM.

> Rep. Mc Dermott is hopeful that he can gain at least as many cosponsors as in the 103rd Congress. The HR. 1200 cosponsors fared much better in the November elections than Democrats as a group, since only nine of the original 91 sponsors have not returned to Congress, and four of these left due to retirement. McDermott is counting on the avid grassroots support for single payer to keep up the pressure to ensure as many cosponsors as possible.[73]

While many of the Democratic proponents of the political infeasibility argument lost their congressional seats in the 1994 mid-term elections, most of the single-payer supporters retained theirs. In the single-payer narrative, this signified that there is still significant support for single payer, both inside and outside of the legislature.

Each of these aspects of "success" in the midst of "failure" encouraged further action immediately following the "death" of national healthcare reform. Single-payer activists were ready to continue the "long haul"[74] that would eventually lead to greater success. The combination of their narratives of opportunity and their action narratives detailing their activities during this period encouraged continued action oriented toward gaining political support for single-payer legislation. Activists were successfully able to, through the practice of producing narratives of hope, construct and act upon their narratives of opportunity. The SPM did experience a period of denouement but it did not occur until several months after the "death" of healthcare reform at the national level—during the era in which the "Contract with America" narrative dominated the political, economic, and cultural opportunity that single-payer supporters faced.

---

[73] Public Citizen D.C. Office. In Action for Universal Health Care Newsletter, December 1994/January 1995.
[74] Church Women United Letter.

Table 2.1 Comparison of Clinton era healthcare reform bills

Clinton era healthcare reform legislation	Clinton health security (Administration Plan) H.R. 3600 / S. 1757	American health security (McDermott / Wellstone) H.R. 1200 / S. 491
General approach	Managed Competition through Health Alliances/Cooperatives	National Health Insurance / State Administered Single Payer
Federal administrative role	National Health Board Establishes Standards for regional and corporate alliances and regulate state programs.	American Health Security Standards Board Establishes budget, policies, procedures, and guidelines for system at national and state level
State administrative role	States establish state specific plan including one or more regional alliances for approval by National board.	States establish plan for universal health security program for approval by national board. States make payments to providers.
Employer role	Required to pay premiums—fixed percentage of "weighted average premium."	Finance the system through payroll taxes. Top corporate tax rate increased.
Employee (Patient) role	Pay part of premium not covered by employer.	Finance system through taxes.
Financing	In addition to premiums, supported by change in tax code. Federal subsidies cover shortfalls.	Establishes American Health Security Trust Fund through taxes and already established funds (i.e. Medicare Trust)—makes payments to state budgets.
Benefits	Approved plans must cover comprehensive benefits—such as hospital services, preventative care, and prescription drugs.	Comprehensive services such as hospital care, primary care, preventative care, long term care, prescription drugs, and mental health care.
Cost sharing	Tiered cost sharing based on copayments deductibles. Out-of-pockets limits of 1500 for individuals or 3000 for families. No balance billing.	No deductibles, coinsurance, or copayments. No balance billing.
Payments	Provider agreements with health plans—state-wide schedule for fee for service plans based on negotiated fee schedule.	Global budget would be used for each state to pay hospitals and nursing facilities via global fees. Other services paid by mechanism developed by state (fee for service, capitation, global budget, etc.).
Role of private health insurance	Sold through regional or corporate alliance if certified as compliant with Federal standards.	Prohibited by the state if payment by private insurance would duplicate payment made by state program.

This is a condensed summary of just two of the bills during this era and is not exhaustive. A more comprehensive comparison can be found in the Congressional Research Office Report for Congress "Summary Comparison of Major Health Care Reform Bills." Written by Melvina Ford, Celinda Franco, Jennifer O'Sullivan, and Richard Price—Specialists in Social Legislation / Education and Public Welfare Division on January 6, 1994, on which this table is based

CHAPTER 3

"Newtered": The Contract with America Era

I arrive at the pleasant middle-class home of Mary Jane on a chilly morning in January of 2005. I'm thrilled to be speaking with Mary Jane, who has been involved in the Single Payer Movement since it's conception in the late 1980s. Mary Jane was at the first meeting of Missourians for Single Payer in the early 90s and recalled the "growing pains" that the organization had experienced following the failure of the Clinton administration's attempt to reform federal healthcare policy. In addition to sharing with me what she remembers about that period throughout our conversation, Mary Jane shares with me her meticulously kept files—a veritable historical archive with materials produced by participants within the movement during the previous fifteen years. Mary Jane shows me the transcript of a keynote address that took place at the United Health Care Action Network (UHCAN) annual conference in September of 1995. In this address, Nick Unger discussed the challenges that the movement was facing within the post Health Security context in which the rise of the Contract with America narrative had resulted in a push to retract previously enacted progressive social policies. Unger also discussed the narrative battle in which the movement was now enmired saying, "Ideas matter. Ideas make the difference of whether you will be ground into the dirt or stand up and fight. ... And ideas matter how we will do it. Whether we will stand and resist or accept being ground into the dirt."[1] This fight with the Contract with America narrative was new, but the principles or ideas on which the fight was based were not. Mary Jane explained, that while there were many hurdles to overcome, she, and many other single-payer supporters, decided to stand and resist.[2]

---

[1] Nick Unger Address to UHCAN Conference September 1995.
[2] Field notes from interview with Mary Jane—January 2005.

© The Author(s) 2020
L. S. F. Hern, *Single Payer Healthcare Reform*,
https://doi.org/10.1007/978-3-030-42764-1_3

Although they "lost the battle at the national level,"[3] directly following the "death" of the Clinton era of healthcare reform grassroots single-payer groups still remained positive about the possibility of achieving single-payer healthcare because "opportunities are multiplying."[4] Many began to focus on supporting Proposition 186 in California as a shining example of the grassroots support for single-payer, while others began to build movements for single-payer within their own states. Not all leaders within the Single Payer Movement (SPM) were positive about the opportunity for "real reform" at the national level. Many believed "that real health-care reform—that is reform that both controls costs and expands coverage—will not occur, during the remainder of the Clinton term."[5] Yet, most did continue to encourage state-level efforts for reform. However, the 1994 election season would change the environment that single-payer supporters faced as it would result in the dominance of a political-economic narrative that would alter the ideological and material environment in which the SPM mobilized (see Fig. 3.1 for a visual summary of this era).

During this era, issues related to economic opportunity came to the forefront of single-payer narrative practice. Several factors are important components of the economic sphere to which a social movement must adapt. The amount of financial resources that an organization is able to acquire is tied to its organizational structure.[6] In addition to economic resources it is important to consider the ways in which economic actors can facilitate or constrain action. Elite economic actors—such as businesses, unions, and professional organizations—not only facilitate the work of grassroots organizations by providing some of the financial resources needed for action but they can also constrain action by financially sponsoring the competition or using their financial resources to utilize dominant aspects of material culture to counter movement goals.[7] All

[3] Church Women United Letter, Nov. 21, 1994.

[4] Health Care Education Project Newsletter/Missouri Citizen Action and Older Women's League November 1994.

[5] Marcia Angell M.D., notable single-payer supporter, former editor in chief of the *New England Journal of Medicine*, and faculty member of Harvard Medical School, "New Life for health reform in 96?" *USA Today*, September 29, 1994. 13A.

[6] McCarthy, John D. and Mayer Zald. 2002. "The Resource Mobilization Research Program: Progress, Challenge, and Transformation," pp. 149–174 in J. Berger and M. Zelditch, editors, *New Directions in Contemporary Sociological Theory*. Lanham, MD: Rowman and Littlefield.

[7] Luders, Joseph. 2006. "The Economics of Movement Success: Business Responses to Civil Rights Mobilization." *The American Journal of Sociology* Vol. 111, No. 4.

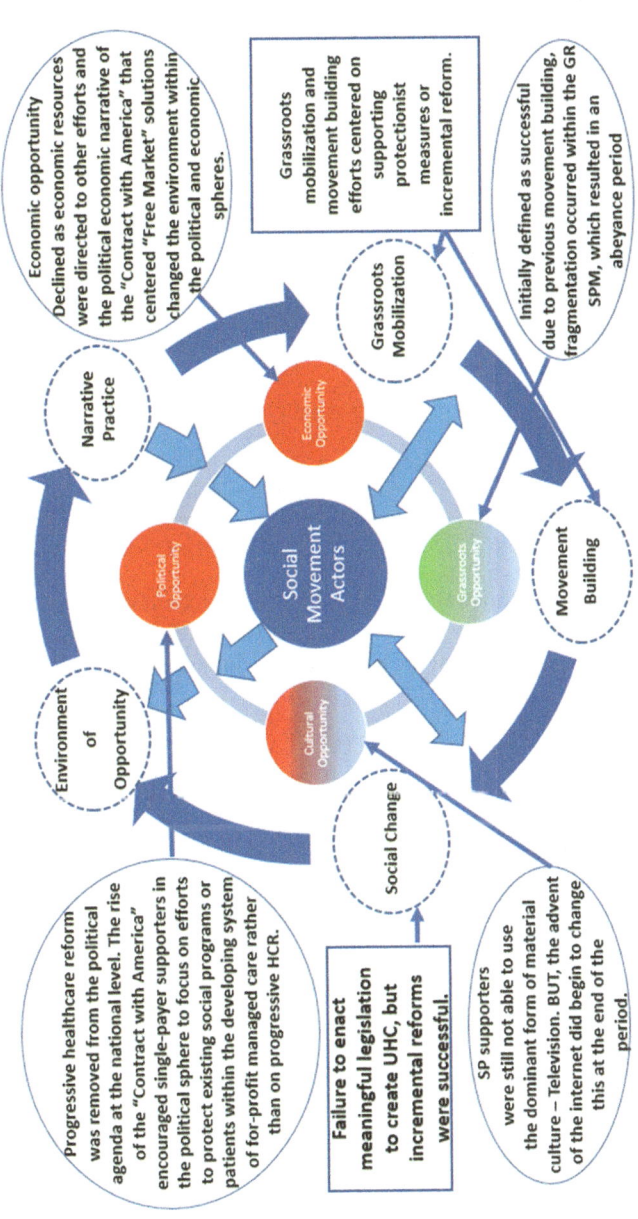

Fig. 3.1   The Contract with America era narrative practice

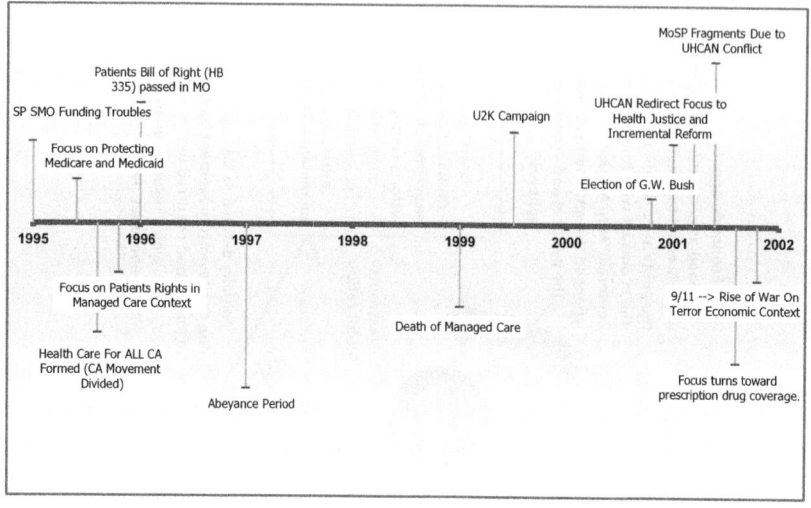

Fig. 3.2   Contract with America era timeline

social actors are also constrained or enabled by macro-level economic factors, such as the stability of the economic system and dominant economic narratives or ideologies (see Fig. 3.2 for a timeline summary of this era).

"DEAD IN THE WATER?"

Following the failure of the attempt to reform the healthcare system at the national level, proposition 186,[8] California's ballot initiative for a state-based single-payer system, as well as other state-based initiatives, became a primary focus for the SPM. However, Prop 186 was defeated during the 1994 election season by a margin of 77–23. If this initiative had been enacted, it would have validated the SPM by showing the nation that grassroots mobilization for progressive reform could be successful. Instead, its defeat further solidified the power of insurance lobby in deciding health policy. Although the California-based SPM initially continued their work with a positive mindset, disagreements within this group of activists eventually led to the movement becoming divided. *Health Care for All California* was formed due to critiques that were made about the ways in

---

[8] For a more detailed discussion of this, see Chap. 2.

which *Californians for Health Security* had run the *Yes on Prop 186* campaign. Both groups proceeded by focusing on single-payer legislation rather than on another single-payer ballot initiative, but were divided in support of different bills, neither of which was successful. The California-based movement remained divided for many years. Many single-payer groups around the nation had supported the California movement with their time and resources. The consequences of its failure were felt across the country.

> Leaders in New Mexico feel that the heavy loss in the California single-payer initiative campaign (77–23%) has had a negative impact on the New Mexico organizing effort. If the revised New Mexicare is reintroduced, Health Care for All plans to do more organizing and to reach out to key interest groups such as seniors and Native Americans.[9]

While some state single-payer groups continued to develop their own state-based legislation, and some, such as the movement in Colorado, thrived,[10] by the winter of 1995 the national movement was in disarray. Many organizations, including UHCAN, were experiencing funding difficulties as the foundation funding that they had previously depended on dried up.

In his address to the gathering of some 130 activists at the UHCAN national conference in September of 1995, Nick Unger, UHCAN board member, questioned the effect of the reduction in funding on movement activities saying, "all the movements we built, we built without a dime. And now we don't have enough money to continue the fight. I am somewhat confused by that. Perhaps someone will explain it to me later." This question of funding, while important, was a small aspect of Unger's address which primarily focused on the economic narrative that was becoming dominant within the political sphere.

"NEWT-ERED": A CONTRACT WITH AMERICA

Perhaps more problematic than decreased funding, was the political-economic narrative that became dominant following the 1994 election season. The election of Republican candidates to the U.S. House of

---

[9] Action for Universal Health Care Newsletter, February 1995.
[10] Ibid.

Representatives and U.S. Senate resulted in the first Republican-controlled Congress in 42 years.[11] The conservative effort to defeat the Clinton agenda for healthcare reform had also resulted in a "turn against government" and in increasing the right-wing influence within the Republican Party.[12] The new majority found its voice with the "Contract With America" narrative. This narrative was rooted in the hegemonic economic narrative of free market capitalism and in a strict moral code.

The Contract With America (CWA) which was signed by a majority of GoP congressional office holders, became a rallying point for the GoP during the 1994 election cycle. Some argue that the success of the GoP in this election cycle resulted in the nationalization of the key issues presented in the CWA.[13] The newly elected republican-controlled House of Representatives centralized authority around the new Speaker—Newt Gingrich (R-GA), who developed a ten-point program to implement the CWA.[14] A central premise of the CWA was that "the government is out of touch and out of control. It is in need of deep and deliberate change."[15] Accomplishing this task would involve reducing government spending and relying on free-market solutions for the problems facing the country. When explaining the CWA, Gingrich used many narrative elements— referring the "American family" as a core value that the CWA would support. This narrative strategy allowed the GoP to argue that they supported "values" while at the same time defunding programs for the poor and cutting taxes for the wealthy. This political-economic narrative had extensive ramifications for organizations working to challenge the status quo.

Focus in Washington D.C., for Democrats and Republicans, became directed toward the financial matters of "balancing the budget" and decreasing the deficit. Even key supporters of single-payer in the political sphere, such as Senator Ted Kennedy (D-MA), shifted their support to

---

[11] Republicans last held the majority in the House of Representatives during the 83rd session elected in 1952. The 1994 election resulted in a Republican majority in both the House and the Senate.

[12] Skocpol, Theda. 1997. *Boomerang: Health Care Reform and the Turn Against Government*, W.W. Norton and Company, New York.

[13] Clucas, Richard A. 2009. "The Contract with America and Conditional Party Government in State Legislatures." *Political Research Quarterly* Vol. 62, No. 2: 317–328.

[14] Riley, Russell L. 1995. "Party Government and the Contract with America." *Political Science and Politics* Vol. 28, No. 4: 703–707.

[15] Gingrich, Newt. 1995. "The Contract With America: A Report on the New Congress." Televised Address Washington, DC. April 7, 1995.

more incremental goals that would have a higher likelihood of success within the new context or to protecting pre-existing social programs. Rather than focusing on creating new programs that would provide universal access to health care, attention was redirected toward "reforming" social programs, such as Medicare and Medicaid, in order to "cut waste" and curb spending. A central goal of the CWA was to "improve Medicare" by including more free-market mechanisms in the universal public program. This forced single-payer activists to refocus their energy. Rather than operating within an environment in which progressive healthcare reform was on the table, they began operating in an environment in which cuts to social programs became the focus of the legislative body. They began to reframe their efforts as defending what was already there, Medicare and Medicaid, rather than fighting to create what did not yet exist—single-payer. A key aspect of defending these programs was critiquing and deconstructing the narrative of the Contract with America.

Activists critiqued the claim made by republicans that "it is their particular message that Americans want. More specifically, Republicans claim that it is their 10-point 'Contract With America' which over 350 Republicans have signed."[16] Instead they argued that the public was concerned that this contract would result in cuts to valued social programs, including Medicare and Medicaid. Building a defensive strategy became an important way for single-payer advocates to spread the message of single-payer. Diane Lardie, UHCAN organizer and board member, warned single-payer supporters about the transition to a defensive position saying,

> As Medicaid and Medicare cuts and waivers are considered, and as ERISA comes up for review, these are the questions to ask. When welfare reform, campaign finance reform and other social change legislation is introduced the links to the healthcare reform must be made. These next months will be critical for education of the public and policymakers alike. Committed health activists have some real work ahead.[17]

Single-payer activists became focused on defending Medicare and Medicaid within the context of the Contract with America.

One tactic used by single-payer activists was to push single-payer as a "counterweight" in discussions dealing with proposed cuts to Medicare

[16] CWU Church Women INFORM Dec. 2, 1994. "The Republican Contract With America: Do Voters Really Know What They Voted For?"
[17] Diane Lardie in Action for Universal Health Care Newsletter Dec 1994/Jan 1995.

and Medicaid. Single-payer became the savior of Medicare and activists
proudly declared "single-payer to the rescue!"[18] According to this single-
payer counter-narrative,

> Medicare must be PRESERVED! MEDICARE is the key to dignity, needed
> support, the security of having the proper medical assistance available when
> necessary. ... THE ULTIMATE ANSWER: In these United States, no lon-
> ger can we expect a band-aid to cure what ails the health care system. The
> System now needs major surgery. Our entire health care system is in critical
> condition, and in need of fundamental change, not tinkering, fundamental
> change. People want a health care system that is available and affordable to
> every American Citizen without bankrupting the country. ... A Single Payer
> Health care system is the ANSWER.[19]

The defense of Medicare and Medicaid in the face of the CWA initially
became an opportunity for single-payer activists to push for their primary
goal of single-payer.

Single-payer advocates recognized that the elements of the "free market" and the fear of government interference that were such integral
aspects of the CWA would also need to be dealt with,

> The G-word, it has to be taken seriously. There are some good reasons to be
> fearful of government solutions. If health reformers are serious about the
> government administrative function in a single-payer solution, then there
> must be a much better explanation of the proper functions of government.
> Otherwise, gentle folks hear "government" and think license bureau lines
> and IRS hassles. GOVERNMENT'S REASON TO EXIST IS THE
> REALIZATION OF THE COMMON GOOD.[20]

They began to concentrate on developing messaging strategies that would
counter the narrative that government in and of itself was bad and that a
free-market strategy was always the best solution. The positive aspects of
government involvement became an important focus for their CWA
counter-narrative.

---

[18] Action for Universal Health Care Newsletter December 1994/January 1995.
[19] Meeting Handout 1995.
[20] Action for Universal Health Care Newsletter Dec. 1994/Jan 1995.

These efforts culminated in the "Contract Out on America" counter-narrative. This narrative deconstructed the tenets of the CWA and made those who supported the CWA the antagonists in the story rather that the protagonists who were fighting for American values and freedom. In his keynote address to the 1995 UHCAN annual conference, Nick Unger reframed the CWA as a "box" that could kill movements for progressive change. According to Unger, this battle went beyond the material to the realm of ideology,

> I measure their victory by their control of institutions, a little. I measure their victory by control of the ideas that govern American political discourse. They won the battle of ideas ... and they won it so big and so heavy that almost everything and our ideas sound fanciful. The full measure of their victory is that both political parties use their language. And our language is outside of discourse. They have won the battle for the ideas of the country. They think ideas matter, perhaps much more than we do. This is radical change. This is not just one party wins, another party wins, the pendulum swings. This is a radical change to restructure the organization of American society. These things ... The previous economic contract, political contract and social contract that existed for sixty years is being broken and is being replaced by a new one.[21]

According to this argument, single-payer activists had a much more difficult battle to wage following the CWA than before. Although the SPM had always faced the free-market narrative that was dominant in the United States, they now faced a "fundamental shift" in the social contract that had previously been rooted in ideas developed during the "New Deal" era. The CWA narrative defined health care as a commodity best left to the rule of the free-market rather than a public good that should be guaranteed by the state.

The counter-narrative developed by the SPM critiqued this dominant economic narrative. They worked to develop the case that health care is not only a right but also that as a public good it should be guaranteed by the state. Along with forming a defensive strategy to protect Medicare and Medicaid, single-payer activists developed an ideological strategy through which they defined health care as a human right, not a commodity. At the UHCAN's 1996 national conference, Bob Griss of the National Disability

[21] Nick Unger Keynote Address Transcript UHCAN National Conference September 1995.

Group expressed concerns about moving away from this framing of the issue in order to capitulate to the demands of the CWA agenda. He discussed,

> the Healthcare as a Human Right Model. He said that we are presently moving from this model and substituting compromises. However, he felt that this is an essential criteria for our struggle. He posed the problem as: how to develop public policy with healthcare as a right (1) for everyone (2) equal quality because, he said, that's what a right means. It's not a right if it limits choice or costs more money for some. He said that the civil rights model is an untapped tool for health care rights.[22]

Discussing health care as a right and as an issue of social justice continued to be a way for single-payer activists to counter the dominant economic narrative of this time which concluded that health care was a commodity best bought and sold in a free market.

THE RISE OF MANAGED CARE

Just as single-payer activists were becoming adept at countering the dominant economic narrative of the CWA, their efforts were also challenged by a significant material shift in the provision of health care in the United States. Although managed care had existed in some form in the United States since the 1930s,[23] following the failure of Clinton Health Security and in the context of the CWA narrative, the vertical integration and corporatization of health insurance continued with a frenzy that was unprecedented. Unlike earlier forms of managed care, this restructuring of healthcare financing arose as the health insurance industry's response to their failure to provide adequate health care for everyone.

According to the single-payer narrative, the rise of corporatized managed care had serious consequences for the SPM. An article titled "Health Care Justice: A New Focus" explains that,

> Advocates for universal health care are increasingly expanding their agenda to focus on the challenges of managed care and the threats to entitlement

---

[22] Notes, Myrna, UHCAN Conference 1996.
[23] Hill, Lewis E., and Robert F. McComb. 1996. "A post-mortem on the Clinton health-care proposal: Lessons from history and hopes for the future." *International Journal of Social Economics* Vol. 23, No. 8: 21.

programs, especially Medicaid. New coalitions focused on managed care and Medicaid are springing up across the nation. This issue of Action highlights issues involved, including efforts to: oppose Medicaid cutbacks, expose abuses and establish protections for consumers in MCOs and capture funds generated by the transformation to managed care to provide health care for more insured people rather than increase MCO profits.[24]

Challenging the most abusive aspects of the new system of managed care became intimately tied with the defense of Medicare and Medicaid. A consequence of this shift was that efforts to promote single-payer were pushed to the side while efforts to confront managed care were brought to the forefront as the new focus within single-payer organizations.

Legislative battles became focused on bills that would protect health-care "consumers" from the abuses of corporatized managed care. Single-payer activists were affected by the transition to managed care on a very personal level. In her letter to the Joint Bipartisan Legislative Committee on Managed Care, Mary Jane wrote,

> I am very dissatisfied with Group Health Plan and its policies. We have no recourse: It's either stay with them, or take a chance on another inefficient insurer. I believe the health care system needs better and closer regulation and that everyone has a right to the care they need.[25]

In Missouri, although they still endorsed the "Missouri Health Assurance" bill, single-payer activists began to promote HB 335, which included a "Patients' Bill of Rights." This would eventually pass and become a hallmark bill for the regulation of managed care. Many other organizations around the country began working for a "Patients' Bill of Rights" in relation to managed care rather than for single-payer as a way to protect the "human right" to health care.

Even single issue single-payer organizations began to directly focus on managed care issues. UHCAN took this a step further by obtaining grant funding to *perform a service* in relation to managed care. In 1996 they secured a Managed Care Workshop Grant from the Ohio Developmental Disabilities Planning Council. These workshops were designed to help people with disabilities learn how to get their health needs met under

[24] Action for Universal Health Care Newsletter Feb./Mar. 1996.
[25] Mary Jane, letter to the Joint Bipartisan Legislative Committee on Managed Care, August 1, 1996.

managed care. Although this service orientation is commendable, it represents a significant shift away from promoting social change through a complete restructuring of the provision of health care and toward a service orientation that works within the current system.

Single-payer activists were critical of this redirection of focus, some going so far as to conclude that "single-payer" was dead. However, others saw the managed care mobilization efforts as examples of a movement that was still actively working toward valuable goals,

> I am perplexed at the June 3 editorial "the Merits of The Single-Payer Plan." It states that the "expansion of managed-care programs has silenced the once-lively debate over a single-payer health insurance system" and portrays the fortunes of single-payer legislation as dependent upon lack of success in reforming managed care. This is an interesting bit of historical revisionism (and soon after the passage of HB335!) because single-payer advocates have been front and center in the struggle to make managed-care insurers accountable for their impact on health care decision making. These are not contradictory goals.[26]

These single-payer activists continued to view their efforts to increase government regulation of managed care as complimentary to the promotion of a single-payer system.

Critiquing and controlling managed care was also intimately tied to the critique of the CWA and its free-market orientation.

> The same people who never wanted us to have these camels in the first place are saying, 'Look at that, they just sit there and spit,' and they are trying to kill Medicare and Medicaid. They say they want to save the camels, but don't believe it. They are trying to poison them. And one way they do that is to twist the idea of managed health care in a way that brings the free enterprise profit motive into the process. ... **There is nothing wrong with managed care. But under free enterprise**, which is what they're doing in health care now, they are taking in as much money as possible, giving as little service as possible, and paying enormous dividends to the shareholders who do whatever they want with it.[27]

[26] Joy Martin, Letter to the editor, June 14, 1997—St. Louis Post Dispatch.
[27] Address by Rep. Jim McDermott (D-WA) to the "Health Consumers' Summit on the Future of Medicare and Universal Coverage." Washington DC (April 26, 1997).

The challenges to free enterprise managed care were tied to challenges of the CWA, both of which were incompatible with the goal of single payer. The "camels" in this narrative are the government-funded programs of Medicare and Medicaid, which were being threatened by those who wanted to "cure" these programs by using free-market mechanisms such as for-profit managed care.

The actual outcomes of the corporatized managed care system—including rising costs and decreasing autonomy of healthcare professionals—resulted in adaptation through changing narratives of opportunity. During the late 1990s, single-payer groups continued to focus on fighting the CWA and the newly evolved corporatized managed care system. They also concentrated on convincing those with the highest *conformity* costs in the managed care system, healthcare professionals and unions, to support their cause. This effort to mobilize economic stakeholders in support of health justice would continue into the new millennium. While some incremental changes to healthcare policy happened during the Clinton period, such as the implementation of the State Children's Health Insurance Program (SCHIP) and the Health Insurance Portability and Accountability Act (HIPAA), there was not any additional movement toward a universal healthcare program. Although managed care had become the institutional framework in which health care was delivered, by the end of this decade, many people, activists and scholars alike were declaring that "managed care is dead." Nick Unger explained this transition saying,

> The HMO reorganization of health care after the collapse of the Clinton plan in 1994 temporarily stopped the crisis. The financial crisis was postponed. Costs were shifted from employers to employees, and from employers to the public as a whole. The new HMO system was chaotic from inception, but the public was willing to be tolerant, and use the legislative/political arena to fix specific outrages and abuses. What about now? The crisis is back with a vengeance.[28]

This renewed crisis in the healthcare system left room for a revived discussion about the possibilities for healthcare reform. A new campaign would capture the attention, and the resources, of the movement for healthcare reform.

---

[28] Nick Unger May 1999 U2K Summary.

U2K or There Is NO WAY

The U2K campaign developed in response to the "death" of managed care and in the midst of the potential for shifts in the realm of political opportunity represented by the 2000 Presidential election season. Although supported by organizations that had previously been focused on single-payer, U2K represented a significant shift away from support of single-payer. Materials dealing with the U2K campaign do not center single-payer as a possible solution to the current healthcare crisis. Instead, the more general terms "universal health care" and "healthcare justice" are used.

According to the writers of the U2K Campaign, it represented a significant shift from the healthcare reform attempts of the past five years.

> U2K comes from a recognition that the struggle for health care justice proceeds best when the entire country is talking about what to do with the entire health care system. Universal health care in any form is a fundamental, systemic change. The best conditions for a discussion of systemic change exist when people are talking about the whole system, not just about any one part.[29]

This narrative insists that while recent reform efforts had been focused on minor changes to the managed care system, U2K would once again push for the fundamental systemic changes that would result in universal health care.

The U2K campaign used the term "universal health care" in order to become a more inclusive movement that formed alliances with many groups because,

> the relatively small group of health care justice activists will not serve the cause of healthcare justice by spending the next year arguing among ourselves over which form of universal health care is the best, then dividing potential allies over which plan to endorse. Rather, now is the time to create a popular political demand for fundamental health care reform and indicate the directions of that reform. Working for U2K is the best thing we all can now do for health care justice.

[29] Nick Unger "Universal Health Care 2000—U2K: The Political Steps to Solve America's Health Care Crisis," May 1999.

The creators of the U2K campaign believed that focusing on the more ambiguous goal of "universal health care" would serve to create a united front of all supporters of "health justice." This transition arose from a critique of earlier periods of the SPM in which,

> One of the biggest mistakes in past health care fights was a 'with us or against us' style of working with other groups. Instead of growing and unifying, we often split and divided. Instead of creating enduring relationships among groups, we often found ourselves with enmity and recriminations. U2K has to be different.
>
> The challenge every U2K supporter faces is how to get the widest grouping into the struggle for universal comprehensive affordable care. We think joining the U2K Campaign is a good thing to do. A group that is not ready to join, but is willing to educate its members is a friend, not a foe. A group that has a slightly different wording about universal health care is an ally, not a rival.[30]

This focus on building alliances was deemed more important than refocusing on the earlier goal of a specifically single-payer system because it would help the campaign to reach its primary goal which was to "change the national political landscape around fundamental health care reform during the 2000 election season."[31]

While U2K was successful in that it did create a broader and more diverse coalition of "over 400 national, state, and local coalitions,"[32] it was not successful at drastically altering the main focus of the presidential candidates.

> It must be acknowledged that U2K did not achieve one of its key goals, which was to make universal health care a hot election issue. The anticipated potential for real health care advances did not materialize this past year.
>
> Now, as the nation prepares for the next President Bush, the health care justice movement must take what we learned this past year, redouble our commitment, and build the structure we need to keep going and get ready for the 2002 election.[33]

[30] Universal Health Care 2000 Campaign Policy Document, Nov. 1999.
[31] U2K informational booklet 1999.
[32] Letter from U2K campaign, Fall 2000.
[33] ACTION for Universal Health Care Newsletter Dec. 2000/Jan. 2001.

While U2K supporters and new members of the "Health Justice" movement continued to gear up for the next election season and replenish depleted resources, groups that had remained ardently single payer were going through transitions of their own.

SINGLE PAYER, IT'S WHO WE ARE

The U2K campaign promoted by the national, formerly single-payer, organization UHCAN represented a significant breaking point for some state-based single-payer organizations. This had profound effects on Missourians for Single Payer (MoSP) in particular. As one of the longest continually operating state single-payer organizations in the country, MoSP is a good case for understanding the impact that national-level movement changes had on state-level processes. A more in-depth look at this particular case will illuminate the effects of this transitional period.

Although MoSP members also focused on issues of managed care during the mid-1990s, especially in their support of HB 335, which included a patient's bill of rights, their identity as an organization remained resolutely tied to single payer. Unlike many other state-based organizations, MoSP actually experienced some growth during the early years of the CWA time period with the creation of two regional chapters—Mid Missourians for Single Payer Health Care and MoSP-East—in addition to the state-wide organization. MoSP seemed to be on its way to becoming a stronger state-wide organization, especially after receiving a grant for 30,000 dollars from the Incarnate Word Foundation. However, the changes occurring in UHCAN—illustrated by the U2K campaign—also impacted progress within this state-based organization.

MoSP-East, which successfully acquired the Incarnate Word Grant, had remained tightly devoted to the goal of single-payer and was critical of the new direction that UHCAN was taking. This became an important focus of discussion,

> Myrna said the conference focused on the U2K campaign for elections, on universal health care, not Single Payer, with the campaign going through the elections in Nov. 2000. The campaign will not talk about Single Payer nor about insurance companies, but concentrate on points in the U2K Statement. The campaign will be housed in the UHCAN! Office in Cleveland. They hope to hire staff people to enlist the 20,000 organizations.[34]

[34] MoSP East Steering Comm. Meeting Minutes Summer 2000.

This movement away from the single-payer position was rejected by MoSP-East, which critiqued the transition as evidence that,

> UHCAN doesn't have the guts to take on the insurance and political establishment. There is no way we can get real comprehensive universal, non-tiered healthcare coverage without eliminating the overhead and bureaucracy of for-profit making entity. UHCAN will settle for sound good, "reform" half measures. That will just marginalize the effectiveness of citizen advocacy groups. We should stick with PNHP.[35]

But, the transition away from single-payer was embraced by the chapter based in Columbia MO—Mid Missourians for Single Payer. Members of MoSP-East became suspicious that members of the Mid-MO chapter wanted to use the newly won grant money to

> convert MoSP from a state single-payer healthcare membership-based organization to his grandiose MO "universal healthcare as a right" UHCAN affiliate where he would coordinate a state coalition of church, labor and community groups.[36]

This combination of influences—the economic opportunity that the grant represented coupled with a disagreement over goals and affiliations—resulted in a break between the Mid Missouri group and MoSP-East. The Mid Missourians for Single Payer did not renew their membership with MoSP State in 2000 and by 2001 MoSP-East was being restructured as the only MoSP organization.

The reformed MoSP, based in St. Louis, used its grant money to hire Pat Harvey as an Outreach Coordinator in an effort to rebuild MoSP as a state-wide organization. Although some members of MoSP were weary of reforming an alliance with the mid Missouri group, the general consensus was that this would be a good first step in recreating a state-wide organization. In Pat Harvey's notes on his work as Outreach Coordinator, healing the rift between these two groups is of primary concern. This was not an easy task as the organizations still disagreed on some key issues. In the following excerpt, Julia, then the newly elected Chair of MoSP, recounts one of her first exchanges on this road to recovery,

---

[35] MoSP Email, Rick, 2000.
[36] MoSP email, Rick, August 7, 2001.

So evidently, she is still enthralled with UCHAN ... I was irked that she made her pitch for UCHAN. I also found some UCHAN leaflets that she must have been passing out. She wanted to know if we could all work together. I really felt like saying that it was you who dropped out and went for UCHAN. But I kept my big mouth shut ... In my MoSP history, it's the largest event I have ever seen. Perhaps years ago, there may have been others? I didn't see anyone from Columbia, so I certainly won't feel obligated to attend theirs. It's just a UCHAN rally anyway.[37]

This action narrative makes it clear that the tension between single-payer activists in Missouri was intimately tied to the shifts that had occurred in UHCAN the year before. While efforts were made to heal the rift between these two organizations, they were not entirely successful.

As the sole chapter of MoSP (Pat Harvey's attempts to create new chapters around the state were not successful), MoSP members in St. Louis became even more tied to their identity as a single-payer organization. They also began to confront the problematic consequences of having an organizational structure still rooted in a coalition framework. Increasingly, coalition members—mostly multi-issue organizations—were refocusing on more incremental directions for healthcare reform.

INCREMENTAL STEPS TO HEALTH JUSTICE

After the 2000 election season ended with the election of G.W. Bush to the Presidency of the United States, some single-payer organizations continued to shift away from single-payer by increasingly being focused on supporting incremental reforms. The then chair of UHCAN, Ken Frisof, built an argument in support of incremental reforms saying,

> Haunted by Clinton's debacle in 93–94, mainstream politicians have been reluctant to consider proposals for comprehensive health care reform. In its place, they talk about 'piecemeal' or 'incremental' reform as if the two are interchangeable. But they are not. An incremental reform definitively and permanently provides health coverage to a part of the population. A piecemeal reform allows for both increments and decrements of coverage.[38]

[37] Julia, MoSP Email, Fall 2001.
[38] ACTION for Universal Health Care Newsletter Apr/May 2001.

Frisof goes on to argue that because a universal healthcare bill was not feasible given the economic and political context "It is important to build towards it through solid increments rather than through unreliable piecemeal measures."[39]

The difference between incremental and progressive reform became a divisive point of debate within the movement. Organizations that remained resolutely in support of single-payer experienced increasing marginalization as multi-issue organizations that had previously supported them redirected their resources toward incremental reform measures. For example, MoSP experienced a downturn in activity due to the coalition structure of its board and the non-participation of its coalition members. This resulted in single-payer organizations focusing on individual, rather than coalition, members. Although state-based single-payer organizations did support some of the incremental measures promoted by the larger movement, such as efforts to promote equitable prescription drug legislation, they were no longer tied to a strong national single-payer movement or organization. This downturn in support and activity would become even more apparent following the events of September 11, 2001.

The War on Terror: A Redefined Economic Narrative?

Following the tragedy of 9/11 and the advent of the War on Terror, there was another shift in the economic narrative that dominated the country and the actions of healthcare justice activists. The dominance of the CWA narrative of the mid-1990s had resulted in the supremacy of free enterprise in the healthcare system and piecemeal attempts to reform it. The rise of the "War on Terror" economic narrative, which directed federal spending toward the war effort, further reduced the perceived chances of passing progressive healthcare reform.

According to this narrative, the possibilities for progressive healthcare reform, even in small increments, were next to nil and it had gone "from possible to very unlikely that any political races in 2002 will be won or lost on the basis of positions on health system issues."[40] This narrative correctly assumed that the focus of the legislature would be on the new war

---

[39] Ibid.

[40] Sept. 17th, 2001 Ken Frisof—UHCAN Initial Thoughts on health care justice strategies and timing in the wake of the terrorist attacks.

and that funding would be directed toward the war effort. Others agreed with this assessment but still tried to develop ways to use this period to talk about healthcare reform,

> The Terrorist attack of September 11 acutely changed America's political preprimary priorities, making national security and economic recovery our primary concerns. But these new realities, including the threat of bio-terrorism also highlight the failings of America's health system. The deteriorating economy threatens the security of health coverage of millions.[41]

The economic downturn and military crisis of this time period were reframed by some as an opportunity to continue to work for some type of healthcare reform. Directly following the events of 9/11, critiques of the President and the War on Terror were not tolerated and many progressive individuals and groups began organizing in more anonymous ways.[42] While the intersection of protest against the war and activism for single-payer would once again become a primary focus of the single-payer narrative as part of the "Health Care Not Warfare" campaign during the second term of G.W. Bush, initially the effort to define this as a location to mobilize for single-payer was not successful.

Many single-payer groups, such as MoSP, experienced a greater downturn in activity and participation from coalition members and individual members alike. Organizations that had redirected their focus to "health justice" through incremental reforms also began to refocus their energies on confronting the effects of war. Both the economic narrative of the CWA and the new economic narrative of the "War on Terror" had serious consequences for the goals and organizational form of single-payer organizations.

Although the SPM actively worked toward grassroots mobilization in practice by constructing narratives that countered the political-economic narrative of the CWA, they were not able to increase or sustain their mobilization efforts through these counter-narratives. While they were able to mobilize in efforts to protect social programs that already existed (i.e. Medicare), and to limit the negative effects of for-profit managed care, these efforts resulted in a shift away from single-payer for many

---

[41] Email Dec 11, 2001, from Rachel DeGolia of UHCAN.

[42] Rohlinger, Deana A., and Jordan Brown. 2009. "Democracy, Action, and the Internet After 9/11." *American Behavioral Scientist* Vol. 53, No. 1: 133–150.

organizations. The redirection of focus of national single-payer groups such as UHCAN resulted in divisions within state-level organizations such as MoSP. During this time period, single-payer activists were unable to construct the hope-producing narratives of opportunity that were needed for the push to mobilize in support of single-payer to be effective. Although attempts were made to construct these narratives of opportunity, these attempts were not effective because the actual **material** aspects (including the rise of managed care and the material aspects of the War on Terror) of the environment of opportunity were so prohibitive in relation to progressive reform.

Eventually, the negative effects of these material aspects (i.e. managed care) that increased the conformity costs for economic stakeholders became a useful narrative location for encouraging more support of single-payer. Increasing healthcare costs coupled with the decreasing autonomy of health professionals, unions, and patients within the managed care system would play a role within both the economic and grassroots opportunity narratives produced within the SPM. Julia Lamborn, President of MoSP (2001–2012), explained that she, as a small business owner, found that she "was struggling to provide health insurance" for her six employees. She "finally decided that there had to be a better option. So, I educated myself and found single-payer. Now, five years later, I'm the President!"[43] Julia went from being an economic stakeholder struggling with the conformity costs of the managed care system to being not just a supporter of single payer but a leader in the SPM.

The first years of the new millennium were spent regrouping in an economic and political context that was increasingly prohibitive of progressive reform. However, changes in grassroots and cultural opportunity would within a few years result in a rejuvenation of the SPM. Single-payer organizations were able to act on grassroots and economic opportunity by adapting to a new form of material culture—the internet.

---

[43] Interview, Julia Lamborn, January 2005.

CHAPTER 4

"American Sickos": The Rise of Digital Mobilization During the G.W. Bush Administration

It is a gloomy night. It is cold, dark, and wet. As I, and the leaders of Missourians for Single Payer (MoSP), walk into the University City Library in St. Louis Missouri the rain has decreased to a light drizzle. It's funny how a light drizzle can be more depressing than a full out shower. The weather is not the only gloomy aspect of the evening and the dark clouds are not the only depressing force hanging over our heads. On this mid-November evening, the results of the recent presidential election are also looming overhead. A majority of American voters had decided to give another four years in the oval office to a man whose stance on social issues was notoriously anti-social. What would the re-election of a man known for his goals of privatizing social services mean for a group working diligently towards a more socially oriented system of health care—a system in which everyone, regardless of employment or state of health, would receive the best care possible? On this night, the first bi-monthly meeting of MoSP since the election, these were the questions that were going through my head, as I am sure they were on the minds of the leaders of MoSP.

When I say leaders of MoSP, I am referring to Julia Lamborn—President of the organization and Mimi Signor—Legislative chair of the organization. These two women are currently the driving force behind MoSP and they spend much of their time and energy fighting for this cause. Most of the time, they are pretty positive about their goals and the realization of them, but on this gloomy night, optimism is harder to come by. Comments are made regarding doubts that anyone will even show up on this dismal evening. As we enter the meeting hall and begin setting up these doubts are lingering.

Then, as we are waiting for people to come and the meeting to start, a surprising thing happens … people do begin entering the room! More and more familiar faces arrive, those stalwarts that have been involved in the organiza-

© The Author(s) 2020
L. S. F. Hern, *Single Payer Healthcare Reform*,
https://doi.org/10.1007/978-3-030-42764-1_4

tion for some time, but many of whom hadn't seemed to be as active anymore. New faces also enter. There is a woman from AARP who guarantees that her people are not afraid of talking to the legislators in Jefferson City and a couple of women representing the Green Party who are very ready to "take action." More and more people are coming, turning this gloomy night into a night of possibilities. Why was this night after a very depressing turn of events in the political environment, host to the MoSP meeting with the largest attendance for several months? Why did this change in events occur?[1]

Directly following the events of September 11, 2001 and the start of the "War on Terror," the Single Payer Movement (SPM) was still enmired in a period of "abeyance"[2] in which the leaders of organizations worked to maintain some infrastructure and mobilization potential in a context that was not tolerant of social protest or critiques of the war-time president. Some progressive voices were silenced during this period as the nation waited for the end of the war. Other progressive voices were directed toward critiquing the war effort, rather than addressing internal domestic issues. Yet, just a few short years later following the re-election of George W. Bush, there was a resurgence of the SPM. Understanding why this occurred at this particular time requires looking beyond political opportunity, to other forms of opportunity that arose from changes to both the material and subjective conditions within the environment of opportunity. The frustration of the political left with the actions of a conservative president along with the rise of new forms of mobilization via internet-based technologies were of central importance to the single-payer narrative practice during the G.W. Bush era. The use of new digital media forms within social movements demonstrated that "with every new advance in technology comes the promise of a broadening of democracy."[3] The democratization of the media, through the development of the internet and of digital video technology, became an issue of primary importance during this time period as it expanded the options available for organizing and for sharing marginalized narratives with a wider audience. This democratizing shift within the sphere of cultural opportunity became a catalyzing force that

[1] Field notes: Missourians for Single Payer Meeting, St. Louis Missouri, November 2004.
[2] For an extensive discussion of abeyance as a concept, see Taylor, Verta. 1997. "Social Movement Continuity: The Women's Movement in Abeyance," in Doug McAdam and David Snow (eds), *Social Movements: Readings on Their Emergence, Mobilisation, and Dynamics.* Los Angeles, CA: Roxbury.
[3] Jones, Robert. 2011. "Does Machinima Really Democratize?" *Journal of Visual Culture* 10(59): 59–65.

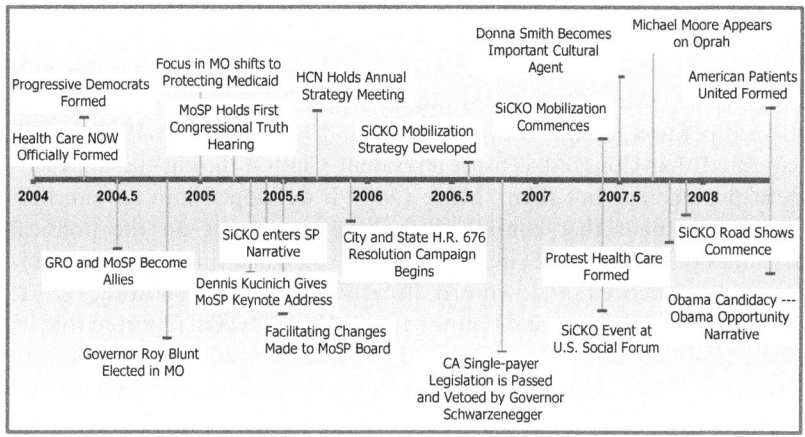

Fig. 4.1 SiCKO era timeline

would help to pull the SPM out of abeyance into a period of renewed action and vitality (See Fig. 4.1 for a visual summary of this time period).

Internet-Based Organizing and Resurgence

The advent of the internet and virtual forms of networking represented a significant shift in the environment of opportunity within which single-payer supporters worked after the events of 9/11 and the start of the War on Terror. While scholars have addressed the ways in which Social Movement Organizations (SMOs) take advantage of this form of opportunity, a more complicated discussion of the process that traditional SMOs went through to adapt to this new technology is warranted. Many activists who had been involved in the SPM since the Clinton era, and who were born a generation or two before the digital generation, initially experienced this shift in material culture as a constraining factor rather than an enabling one. SMOs with a membership that did not adeptly use this new form of material culture were faced with competing for participants with organizations that could recruit through the use of these new technologies. It took several years for the veteran single-payer organizations to be able to use the internet in order to effectively advance their cause.

MoveON to the Digital Age

An exemplar of internet organizing during the early years of the new millennium was MoveOn.org. Although MoveOn initially started as an emailed petition, designed by Wes Boyd and Joan Blades in 1998, which requested that Congress censure President Clinton during the impeachment proceedings but then "Move On,"[4] it developed into an internet-based movement that continued to have an impact on the political dynamics of the United States for many years. While single-payer organizations experienced a downturn in activity directly following 9/11, MoveOn "grew in leaps and bounds after 9/11. MoveOn reported that its membership increased from 500,000 in September 2001 to 3 million in December 2005, noting that these figures represent members in the United States alone."[5] MoveOn became a digital location "where millions mobilize for a better society—one where everyone can thrive."[6]

It is likely that the success of this organization increased the number of people who saw the possibility of successful grassroots action via the use of the internet and thus actively sought progressive social change in the early years of the new millennium by utilizing this new resource. Indeed,

> the Internet can be an important democratic resource in the wake of political shocks because some segments of the citizenry are likely to disapprove of the policies and practices of state actors but find it difficult to voice their dissent. Specifically, the Internet is an important democratic resource because it provides a free space for citizens to articulate their dissent in a less public way and cultivate oppositional identities, which, in turn, can provide a foundation for activism in the real world.[7]

While the climate following 9/11 and the nationalistic sentiment that arose discouraged social protest or criticism of any kind, the "political shock" that the commencement of the War on Terror caused encouraged activism. The internet created a space within which new activist identities could develop. MoveOn became a place where individuals could engage in

---

[4] Moveon.org "A Short History of MoveOn," https://front.moveon.org/a-short-history.
[5] Rohlinger, Deana A., and Jordan Brown. 2009. "Democracy, Action, and the Internet After 9/11." *American Behavioral Scientist* 53, no. 1: 133–150.
[6] Moveon.org "A Short History of MoveOn," https://front.moveon.org/a-short-history.
[7] Rohlinger, Deana A., and Jordan Brown. 2009. "Democracy, Action, and the Internet After 9/11." *American Behavioral Scientist* 53, no. 1: 133–150, p. 132.

protest without experiencing many of the costs associated with protest. This encouraged a larger population of people to develop activist identities through their involvement in MoveOn, which is related to the grassroots opportunity experienced by single-payer activists following the 2004 election season.

An Example Case: Missourians for Single Payer

Although the 2004 elections did not result in a positive change to political opportunity at the national level, single-payer organizations did experience what they defined as significantly more grassroots opportunity. Missourians for Single Payer (MoSP) in particular experienced greater attendance at meetings (see Fig. 4.2) and more support from larger nation-wide organizations. MoSP is an important case to consider because it is one of the few organizations that survived the abeyance period that followed the death of healthcare reform during the Clinton era with the goal of single-payer intact. MoSP persisted primarily by remaining tied to the core goal of implementing a single-payer system and by concentrating their mobilization efforts on state policy changes that did not require mass mobilization efforts. The perceived shift in grassroots opportunity during the second G.W. Bush term was related to the shift in cultural opportunity that the advent of the internet represented to organizations like MoSP.

Prior to the 2004 election season, MoSP had experienced low levels of grassroots opportunity with poor attendance at meetings (15 in September

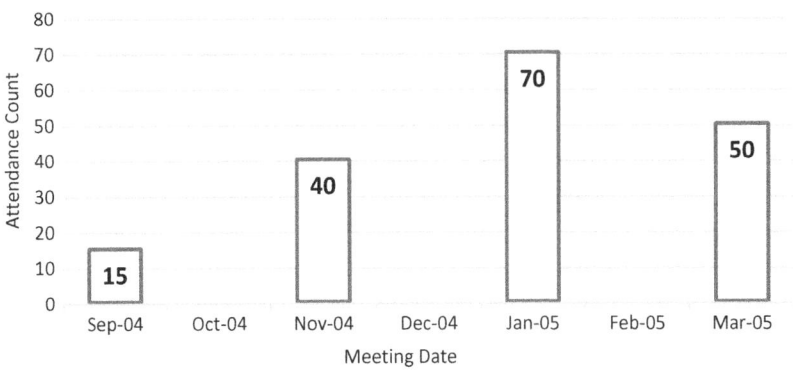

Fig. 4.2 MoSP meeting attendance during the 2004 election cycle

2004) and the inability to do much organizing due to an inactive board. Leaders of MoSP expected more of the same at the bi-monthly meeting that directly followed this election cycle and were surprised that the opposite occurred, with forty individuals attending the November 2004 meeting. In addition to greater attendance, those who attended were energized and "ready to act." The attendance of seventy individuals at the following meeting in January of 2005 was a valuable indicator to single-payer activists that there was sustained grassroots opportunity to mobilize for single-payer.

MoSP also experienced greater grassroots opportunity due to the formation of three new organizations—Grassroots Organizing (GRO), Healthcare NOW (HCN), and the Progressive Democrats of America (PDA). While these three organizations differ in many ways (including goals, strategy, and political affiliation), they became important allies in the SPM. Their use of internet technology differed depending on their targeted audience and their knowledge regarding the use of this technology. These are both factors that are related to the "digital divide"[8] that SMO's experience when using new forms of communication technology.

Grassroots Organizing was formed in October of 2000 by "three women in a Pizza Hut."[9] It developed as an organization based around the mission to "create a grassroots voice to win economic justice and human rights for all Missourians."[10] GRO supported the development of a healthcare system that would fulfill their goal of health justice for the economically disadvantaged. GRO initially worked toward this goal by actively supporting the SPM. An alliance between GRO and MoSP was formed through Mary—who was a MoSP board member and one of the co-founders of GRO. While it initially seemed as though GRO would become more involved in the SPM, even paying their 50 dollars in MoSP membership dues to "show our sincerity,"[11] eventually GRO became, according to MoSP members, just another multi-issue organization that supported single-payer in theory, but not in practice.

Several issues contributed to this disconnect between GRO and the Missouri-based SPM. First, the context in which these state-based

---

[8] Modarres, Ali, 2011. "Beyond the Digital Divide." *National Civic Review* 100, no. 3: 4–7.

[9] Robin Acree, GRO activist, Public Lecture, October 2005.

[10] Ibid.

[11] Mary Hussman MoSP Board Meeting Feb. 2005.

movements were working shifted due to changes in state government that resulted in the transformation of the way in which health care was financed and delivered in the state. When Matt Blunt defeated Claire McCaskill in the 2004 Missouri Gubernatorial election, the state of the Missouri Medicaid program became a primary focus. At a MoSP board meeting in January of 2005, Mary urged the MoSP board to actively work to stop possible cuts in Medicaid,

> I would like to talk about Medicaid. I don't think that we can do reform incrementally, but we do need to protect the programs that we already have. Holden may not have been the best governor, but he went to bat for Medicaid, the new administration will not. Medicaid as it is … it is not a very generous program. When they canceled the program in Tennessee, many doctors fought it. This may not happen in Missouri. Blunt made a statement while campaigning that he would not cut Medicaid, but he has not said anything about that for quite some time. Medicaid enrollment in MO has almost reached the million mark, and that might trigger a countermovement against Medicaid. MoSP has cosigned a letter to Blunt asking him to stick to his commitment. The state senate has called for hearings Monday, Jan 24th, dealing with health care. GRO is going to testify on behalf of Medicaid and general relief. It would be good if MoSP would also testify.

The threat of cuts in healthcare provision for this vulnerable population was a central topic of concern for both MoSP and GRO, whereas GRO largely limited their efforts to preventing these cuts; MoSP saw this as an opportunity to insert single-payer into the debate. These differing orientations involved mobilizing different constituencies. MoSP focused on using citizen lobbying to encourage the state legislature to stop the cuts to Medicaid, while also encouraging the legislators to support the state single-payer bill. They held citizen lobbying days in Jefferson City Missouri, during which they would talk to as many legislators as possible about defending Medicaid and achieving single-payer. GRO focused on mobilizing the population that would be most greatly affected by these cuts—the economically disadvantaged.

Mobilizing economically disadvantaged populations comes with certain constraints. Populations that are economically disadvantaged have less access to the resources and social capital that are important to the process of mobilization.[12] There is also a "digital divide" between the haves—who have access to computers and thus the internet—and the have nots—who do not have access to digital resources.[13] Disadvantaged individuals are less likely to have access to personal computers, and disadvantaged communities are less likely to have access to the infrastructure needed for high speed internet access.[14] This digital divide, especially in the early 2000s, made using the internet to mobilize disadvantaged populations unpractical. The advent of the internet did not represent an increase in cultural opportunity for GRO, which was focused on mobilizing disadvantaged populations in Missouri. So, they continued to focus on mobilizing through face-to-face grassroots efforts such as going door to door to register voters, collecting petition signatures in person, and holding funeral processions in order to memorialize the "demise of Medicaid in Missouri."[15] These types of activities were considered to be more productive by organizational leaders.[16]

The advance of the internet also resulted in a digital divide between those who have the human capital to use the new technologies and those who do not have these skills.[17] MoSP tried to adapt to the new internet aspect of material culture in order to act on the cultural opportunity that it represented. However, MoSP experienced this opportunity differently from other organizations that were mobilizing at this time because most of the active members of MoSP were individuals in their 50s, 60s, and 70s who had not yet become adept at using new internet-based technologies. They were, in the words of one activist, "technologically handicapped."[18] A digital divide developed between organizations that had members who were able to use this new technology and those that did not. In order to act on perceived grassroots opportunity, the MoSP board became concerned with creating a new webpage to replace the old one, which was created in 2001 and had not been updated. They knew, from the example

[12] Piven, Frances Fox, and Richard Cloward. 1979. *Poor People's Movements: Why They Succeed: How They Fail.* New York: Vintage Books.

[13] Epstein, Dmitry, Erik C. Nisbet, and Tarleton Gillespie. 2011. "Who's Responsible for the Digital Divide? Public Perceptions and Policy Implications." *Information Society* 27, no. 2: 92–104.

[14] Modarres, Ali. 2011. "Beyond the Digital Divide." *National Civic Review* 100, no. 3: 4–7

[15] Mary, MoSP board meeting April 2005.

[16] Robin, GRO Organizer, Informal Interview, October 2011.

[17] Uğuz, Hülya Eşki. 2011. "Digital Divide in Turkey and Bridging the Digital Divide." *Journal of US–China Public Administration* 8, no. 6: 629–639.

[18] Bev, Informal Interview, November 2007.

set by organizations like MoveOn, that this was now an integral way in which to act on the grassroots opportunity of this time period. While they had quickly become adept at using email as a way to share information and have discussions, other types of digital networking, such as developing a website that was interactive as well as informational, were beyond their skill level.

Although members of MoSP had always wanted a more age diverse membership, and often bemoaned the lack of interest of the young who "expected to be healthy forever,"[19] they began to seek out the participation and input of younger generations more earnestly in order to develop the organization in a way that would allow them to positively confront the new digital age. Although I was not the most technologically savvy person, as a millennial I was one of the youngest participants in MoSP. I was often asked to use my digital "expertise" in some way. The addition to the board of a student at Webster University, Mark, who was technologically adept, hosted an internet radio show, and wanted to "use that media to help get out the word for MoSP,"[20] was taken as a good sign that MoSP was on the right track. However, MoSP was not able to mobilize a significant young adult population, and Mark eventually resigned from the board due to other obligations. Although the leaders of MoSP continued to use email to spread information and a new web page was created, they were not able to use the internet to significantly increase their membership at that time. Their alliance with another new organization would begin to change this dynamic.

The Birth of Healthcare NOW

Healthcare NOW (HCN) was formed when Marilyn Clement was asked by Representative John Conyers (D-MI) to mobilize grassroots groups in support of H.R. 676—the single-payer healthcare bill that he had just introduced in the House of Representatives in February of 2003. Conyers had previously co-sponsored The American Health Security Act with Representative Jim McDermott (D-WA). Senator Paul Wellstone (D-MN), who had sponsored the companion bill in the senate had passed in 2002, which had left a hole in the heart of the SPM. According to this origin story, Clement "took this call to heart" and

[19] Julia Lamborn, Interview, January 2005.
[20] Mark, MoSP Board Meeting 2005.

didn't care that George W. Bush was president, or that there was not a lot of money to build a new organization. She didn't care that many said she couldn't make this new group viable and important. She didn't care that many scoffed at the very notion of healthcare reform.[21]

Clement began this new organization by contacting pre-existing organizations that supported single-payer (such as MoSP) and also by reaching out to a wider audience through new democratized internet-based technologies. By the summer of 2004, HCN had a website in addition to their New York based office. HCN began to fill the hole in national-level organizing that had existed since United Health Care Action Network (UHCAN) had shifted focus away from single-payer.

Healthcare NOW quickly became adept at using internet-based technology to not only share information but also to build the movement networks that would be needed to mobilize a mass movement in order to achieve their goal of passing H.R. 676. On their website, HCN staff shared "single-payer news," updated their members about progress with H.R. 676, and shared important educational information—including power point slides and videos—with their members. The website also encouraged those visiting the site to become actively involved by signing their online petition or by attending one of the actions around the country, which were listed on the events calendar. HCN had enough start-up funding to hire a web designer to create this initial website, which also included a digital donation mechanism through which HCN could continue to raise funds.

This adept use of the internet also allowed Healthcare NOW to more easily reach out to and form alliances with pre-established single-payer organizations, which allowed HCN to start the process of re-establishing a national movement for single-payer. While there were still active single-payer organizations in many states, there had not been national organizational leadership in the SPM since UHCAN had transitioned to focusing on more incremental measures during the late 1990s. Before the formation of HCN, state-based single-payer movements sometimes knew of each other, but a call from activists in other states was cause for excitement

---

[21] Gerard, Leo. International President of the United Steelworkers. 2009. "Tribute to Marilyn Clement," https://www.healthcare-now.org/blog/leo-gerards-tribute-to-marilyn-clement/.

due to its rarity.[22] MoSP leaders learned about HCN early on, and two representatives—Julia Lamborn and Mimi Signor—attended the first HCN national strategy meeting held in the fall of 2005. MoSP was also the first state organization to hold a "Congressional Truth Hearing" about healthcare (in the spring of 2006). These hearings were the first major nationwide mobilization effort developed by HCN. MoSP, although still concerned about the changes occurring in the provision of health care in Missouri, began to focus on supporting H.R. 676. At the 2006 HCN national strategy meeting, Mimi explained to the gathered activists that "with the current political environment in Missouri, the (Missouri Health Assurance) bill has no chance of being passed and is really just a way to keep the dialogue open for the time being while we focus on H.R. 676."[23] While MoSP still retained their identity as a distinct state-based organization, state-based reform efforts took a backseat to organizing around H.R. 676, which included a campaign to encourage state and local governments to pass resolutions in support of H.R. 676.[24]

Alliances between state-based single-payer organizations and HCN would later prove to be beneficial for SMO's caught on the wrong side of the digital divide. The founders of HCN encouraged the support of unions and professional organizations. Some of these organizations became the primary financial backers of this fledgling organization. These financial resources allowed the founders to hire trained individuals who would create and operate this empowering technology. From the start, HCN was on the empowered side of the digital divide. The relatively younger population that became involved in this new organization (including representatives of the American Medical Student Association—AMSA) pushed HCN to use new social media and digital video technologies as they developed their mobilizing potential.

Young adults who were participating in the movement also encouraged the use of social networking sites. In my field notes for the 2006 annual meeting of Healthcare NOW I wrote,

---

[22] MoSP board meeting minutes Fall 2005.

[23] Mimi Signor, then VP of MoSP, HCN National Strategy meeting, Nov. 2006.

[24] While the California movement did successfully remobilize and pass their single-payer legislation through their state legislature in 2006 and 2008, this was vetoed by then Governor Schwarzenegger both times. This encouraged many California single-payer activists to become involved with HCN and national reform efforts.

I said that I thought a very good way to target a younger constituency would be through the internet. That on internet networking sites, such as Myspace, the possibility for reaching people is exponential (I have 100 friends, those friends have 100 friends, etc.). They agreed that this would be a good idea, but I had a feeling that they didn't really know what I was talking about.[25]

The media strategy group with which I was working at that meeting did make developing their use of MySpace and the newer social networking platform, Facebook, a priority. HCN would eventually use these networking tools to connect with many communities. At the January 2006 board meeting for MoSP, I was directed to create a MoSP Myspace page after giving the board a lesson on the workings of the site. Although I did create this page and was able to network MoSP with my "friends" on MySpace, the board members of MoSP never created individual MySpace pages or became involved with the development and activities of this page. The page became inactive when focus of the social networking world transitioned to Facebook.[26]

An awareness of this digital divide within the movement eventually led HCN to implement programs through which they could help their state and local allies adeptly use internet technology. Through a formal "affiliation program," organizational members could use the resources of HCN—including its technologically adept professional staff—to develop their internet-based organizing efforts and connect with a wider audience through the HCN website. This formal affiliation also included a long list of "tech services" including—database and email management; online donation management; and website design and maintenance. This affiliation program became a useful avenue through which organizations could overcome the digital divide.[27]

The technological adeptness of HCN also facilitated the alliances that HCN formed with other nascent national organizations such as the Progressive Democrats of America (PDA). PDA was founded at the 2004 Democratic National Convention, by attendees who were committed to creating a strong progressive caucus within the Democratic Party.

[25] Lindy Hern, Field notes, HCN National Strategy Meeting, 2006.
[26] MoSP eventually created a Facebook page in the fall of 2010.
[27] By the end of 2011, HCN had 43 official affiliates in 33 states.

A thousand activists—many from the presidential campaigns of Howard Dean and Dennis Kucinich—gathered in Roxbury to hear talks by Dean, Kucinich, Reps. John Conyers and Barbara Lee, Tom Hayden, Granny D, Medea Benjamin, and many others.[28]

Tim Carpenter, a founding member and original executive director of PDA, created this organization because "Democrats were not doing enough to oppose the war in Iraq or to advance a "Medicare for All' reform of a broken health-care system."[29] PDA eventually became involved in the SPM and an important ally to HCN. Mimi, who was then the legislative chair of MoSP, attended the first national meeting of PDA and brought back the news that she had spoken with Howard Dean. She explained that it "seems he's going to keep an open mind on this"[30] and that MoSP needed to direct this new organization toward talking about single-payer instead of universal health care. She got the impression from this meeting that they would be "open" to this and this impression became reality when PDA made single-payer part of their platform.

Although local chapters of PDA focused on grassroots organizing at the local level, the national PDA organization used the internet for its mobilizing efforts in many ways.[31] Much like HCN, PDA built a website through which they could share information, acquire donations, build a network, and call a wider audience to action. PDA urged the newly formed progressive caucus to support H.R. 676. PDA would fill an important hole in the SPM as a political organization that would support single-payer regardless of the desires of the mainstream Democratic politicians. PDA threw its energy behind single-payer through the "Healthcare NOT Warfare" campaign, which directly tied the lack of funding for social programs to the enormous amount of military spending that was occurring due to the Iraq War. It was "organized to slash excessive military expenditures and shift the funding to meet human needs."[32] Unlike HCN and MoSP, which could not support specific candidates due to their tax status,

[28] Progressive Democrats of America "About" http://pdamerica.org/about-pda.

[29] John Nichols for The Nation, May 2014, Found via https://www.healthcare-now.org/blog/tim-carpenters-politics-of-radical-inclusion-in-the-streets-and-in-the-polling-booths/.

[30] Mimi, MoSP Board Meeting, Feb 2005.

[31] Progressive Democrats of America "Homepage" http://pdamerica.org/.

[32] Progressive Democrats of America "Healthcare not Warfare Campaign," https://pdamerica.org/healthcare-not-warfare/.

PDA became an overtly political arm of the SPM that was tied to the Democratic Party.

The greater interest of these new organizations, as well as that of individuals, in mobilizing for single-payer, encouraged the leaders of MoSP to make the changes necessary in order to act on this period of increased opportunity for grassroots mobilization. Julia Lamborn, then President of MoSP, used a clause in the MoSP bylaws to change the make-up of the MoSP board. By dropping several coalition-based board members who had shown no interest in participating for some time, MoSP was able to create "a great new board and great movement forward"[33] and consistently hold board meetings that fulfilled the requirements of a quorum. This more centralized board was able to quickly organize those interested in participating in the 2005 MoSP healthcare weekend, which included new actions such as street theater, and to convince Representative Dennis Kucinich (D-OH) to give the keynote address at MoSP's Health Care Sunday held at the Ethical Society of St. Louis. This event became immortalized in an action narrative as the most successful event in MoSP history.

The development of this weekend was facilitated by MoSP's new alliances with HCN and PDA. MoSP's interaction with the national PDA organization resulted in the connections that were needed to contact and encourage Kucinich to travel to Missouri in order to be the keynote speaker. These alliances also encouraged the development of new tactics that played a role in this particular healthcare weekend. Members of the local PDA were active organizers of and participants in the Single Payer Street Theater that took place as part of the weekend of events. MoSP leaders were also proud to hold the first state "Congressional Truth Hearing" as part of the weekend. Truth hearings were one of the first nation-wide action campaigns sponsored by HCN after this tactic was developed at the 2005 HCN national strategy meeting. At these hearings, participants would give testimony about their experiences in the healthcare system to a public audience that included invited politicians.

The keynote address made by Kucinich at the event drew the largest crowd that MoSP had ever experienced, with over 600 attendees. Kucinich was introduced by Julia as "one of the few politicians who actually talks the talk AND walks the walk. I really believe he is a man of the people."[34] Kucinich then gave a speech about the need for single-payer and how

---

[33] Field notes: Julia Lamborn, MoSP board meeting, Feb. 2005.
[34] Field notes: Julia Lamborn, MoSP Health Care Sunday, April 2005.

everyone in the room should support MoSP in their efforts to achieve it, concluding that "NOW is the time for real healthcare reform."[35]

Although a digital divide developed between those who adapted to internet-based technology and those who did not, MoSP was able to remain active while its members developed the skills necessary to take advantage of this digital revolution by allying itself with HCN and other social movement actors that adroitly utilized the internet. This facilitated their mobilization efforts even within a context of negative state-based political opportunity. Veteran organizations, like MoSP, were also able to "pay back" emerging organizations such as HCN for their help with adapting to new technologies by sharing their expertise, existing networks, and time-tested resources with them. While other state-based organizations, such as GRO, focused on protecting social programs rather than promoting single-payer, MoSP was able remain committed to single-payer by redirecting its focus to supporting new national legislation. Another aspect of the digital revolution, the democratization of film making, would also become an important focus of the single-payer narrative as it also allowed the SPM to share their narrative with a wider audience.

SiCKO AND SINGLE PAYER

Michael Moore gave us a great gift, we can capitalize on SICKO.[36]

The democratization of film making was another significant shift in cultural opportunity. This became important to the SPM during the second term of President G.W. Bush. This democratization involved both the development of ever more accessible and user-friendly digital video-recording technology and the development of ways in which to digitally distribute these videos via the internet. These advances served to free "the medium from the tyranny of up-front financing"[37] and have resulted in more people having access to video recording devices[38] as well as the

[35] Field notes: Representative Dennis Kucinich (D—OH) keynote address at MoSP Health Care Sunday, April 2005.

[36] Field notes: Mimi at MoSP board meeting, February 2008.

[37] Hancock, Hugh. 2011. "Machinima: Limited, Ghettoized, and Spectacularly Promising." *Journal of Visual Culture* 10:31 PG 2.

[38] Buckingham, David, Maria Pini, and Rebekah Willett. 2007. "'Take back the tube!': The discursive construction of amateur film and video making." *Journal of Media Practice* 8, no. 2: 183–201.

means to share their films with a wider audience.[39] While this opportunity was not empowering for everyone as there was also a significant skills gap between organizations in relation to using this new video technology, it allowed for the production of films by others outside of these organizations that represented significant opportunities for grassroots mobilization.

The most significant early example of this opportunity took the form of a film about the dysfunction present within the United States healthcare system. A discussion of a new film about the healthcare system entered the single-payer narrative in the spring of 2005, a few years before the film, *SiCKO*, was released in the summer of 2007. Although single-payer activists had organized around films in the past, *SiCKO* had longer lasting effects on the SPM than previous examples. *SiCKO* became a focus of the single-payer narrative of cultural opportunity years before it actually premiered. This narrative became important to the process of mobilization for years following its release as it produced hope even within the context of negative political opportunity.

Although Michael Moore, the director of *SiCKO*, eventually became the director of the highest grossing documentary film of all time,[40] he had much more humble beginnings. Moore's film career began when he mortgaged his house in order to make the documentary "Roger and Me" about the effects of the General Motors factory closing on the residents of Flint Michigan. Although he eventually sold the distribution rights for this first film for 3 million dollars, he began with very little financial backing. While *SiCKO* did have more significant financial backing, its director came from very humble beginnings and benefited from the democratization of film making which was developing when Moore was becoming a filmmaker at the tail end of the 1980s.[41] Moore also used internet-based resources to develop the film *SiCKO*. In order to find the healthcare stories to tell in the film, Moore posted a call for patients to send in their stories via email. When the number of submissions reached 25,000, Moore and the *SiCKO* team narrowed the selection down to just a few patients whose stories would be preserved in the film. The *SiCKO* team also used

[39] Lowood, Henry. 2011. "A 'Different Technical Approach'? Introduction to the Special Issue on Machinima," *Journal of Visual Culture* 10: 3.

[40] Fahrenheit 9/11.

[41] Michaelmoore.com "About."

internet-based resources, such as YouTube, to create a buzz for the film which is a good example of the use of new media for marketing strategies.[42]

This strategy was successful at creating a public conversation about the film even before it was available to view. Before *SiCKO* was even finished filming, single-payer activists began to discuss the organizing that might take place around this film. At the 2006 HCN national strategy meeting, it was decided that there would be a nationwide organizing effort surrounding the release of this film. Single-payer activists around the country began to plan to "capitalize" on the opportunity presented by this film by discussing various tactics that could be used.

Organizing around this film took place in several forms. A few national events were organized as "premieres." Many single-payer activists attended a rally and showing of the film at the 2007 U.S. Social Forum in Atlanta, Georgia. State and local *SiCKO* events were also organized. Some organizations set up "permanent" single-payer tables outside theaters where the film was being shown. Activists took turns handing out information about H.R. 676 and manned these tables around the clock. Other organizations held local premiere rallies when *SiCKO* opened in their area. MoSP, for example, held a rally that was attended by over 100 "nurses and health care advocates."[43] When the DVD of *SiCKO* was released, Michael Moore and the California Nurses Association (CNA) teamed up to provide copies of the DVD for all of the activists who attended the 2007 national strategy meeting of HCN with the direction to "literally hold hundreds of showings in people's communities."[44] Organizing around *SiCKO* picked up again when it was nominated for an academy award. Activists held award parties because this was "a good time for partying and for strategizing together."[45]

Organizations such as the California Nurses Association (CNA), which would later form National Nurses United (NNU),[46] and Physicians for a National Health Program (PNHP), played an important role in the grassroots mobilization effort around the *SiCKO*. They engaged in the "Scrubs

---

[42] Potter, Wendell. 2010. "The Campaign Against Sicko." *Deadly Spin: An Insurance Company Insider Speaks Out on How Corporate PR Is Killing Health Care and Deceiving Americans.* Bloomsbury Press, pp. 29–43.

[43] Field notes 2007.

[44] HCN Conference Call, August 2007.

[45] HCN Conference Call February 2008.

[46] NNU is currently the largest nurses' union in the United States.

for SiCKO" campaign and supported grassroots mobilization efforts. The mobilization around *SiCKO* became a

> big campaign for a lot of people, not the least of which was the nurses. The California Nurses Association really launched into a campaign in many states. First in Sacramento with Michael where he came and premiered in Sacramento and did a hearing there. And also, in Washington D.C. where there was also a hearing held on capitol hill to talk about Sicko and to really launch those issues strongly. The film really spoke to the issues that the nurses had been talking about for a very very long time.[47]

CNA facilitated the mobilization around *SiCKO* by funding grassroots efforts, by planning actions, and by putting boots on the ground for *SiCKO* events around the country.

SiCKO also resulted in a new tactic for this wave of the movement—"The Sicko Cure Road Show," which was planned and sponsored by CNA and also involved the participation of several national and state-level organizations, including HCN. The goals of this road show were to

1. reach the public with information about H.R. 676 via events and related media and internet publicity;
2. energize local coalitions that have already done some work on the issue;
3. serve as a catalyst for the formation of new local coalitions where none existed; and
4. apply pressure on targeted Congress people to co-sponsor H.R. 676.[48]

The first road show left in the "Sicko Bus" directly following the 2007 annual strategy meeting of HCN. This road show made stops in twenty-one cities in the south-east. One road show participant, Donna Smith, who was one of the "stars of SiCKO," said this about the experience,

> The five people on the bus are as diverse as their histories and cultures might suggest but we all believe in a healthcare system with the simple message: "Everybody in, nobody out." And so far, we've only had one person tape a

---

[47] Michael Moore and Donna Smith Interview on "The Nurses Station," https://www.healthcare-now.org/blog/video-michael-moore-donna-smith-still-sicko/.
[48] Road Show Evaluation Report 2008.

little handmade note on the side of the bus that read: "Socialism." The note was quite colorful, and we kept it aboard for the ride to remind us of all misinformation and myths we have to overcome as we take the message deeper into the south and across the nation.[49]

The participants in the road show were able to keep the rest of the SPM informed about their actions by using the blog function on the HCN website. Through this medium, activists all around the country were able to support the road showers through their attention and comments. The first road show made stops in Indiana, Kentucky, Tennessee, Alabama, Mississippi, Louisiana, Florida, Georgia, South Carolina, North Carolina, Virginia, West Virginia, and Pennsylvania. The success of this initial road show and the continued salience of the narrative presented in *SiCKO* encouraged other activists to plan regional road shows of their own in the northwest, southwest, north east, and midwestern United States. At each stop, activists would hold *SiCKO* showings, rallies, educational programs, and other activities that were desired by the local contact groups. This became an important tactic to raise awareness and support for single-payer at this time.

The organizing around *SiCKO* reinvigorated the SPM. By the fall of 2007 Marilyn Clement, who was then the National Coordinator for HCN, was already calling their efforts a success saying that HCN's list of participants "is just growing by leaps and bounds because of SiCKO."[50] Several new organizations were formed and became affiliated with HCN during this time. These organizations were able to form quickly and start sharing their "message" with a large audience by using the internet. The origin stories of many of these organizations directly referenced a *SiCKO* viewing as the catalyst for creating the organization. A thirteen-year-old boy from New York State explained that,

> I saw SICKO and it moved me. And I realized that I wanted to do something to help change things. Joel gave me this great idea. Launch a website. As many stories that I can get—put them on website so anyone can see it. Bring people onto the floor of Congress. My other idea is to have students call in to local Congressmen to have this arranged and have these people taken care of.[51]

[49] Donna Smith, Nov. 10, 2007. "On the Road Again"—https://www.healthcare-now.org/blog/on-the-road-again-the-sicko-cure-road-show/.
[50] HCN Conference Call September 2007.
[51] HCN Conference Call February 2008.

Although his website is no longer active, it is significant that even a child who was affected by *SICKO* could use the internet in order to become involved in the movement. This was taken as a very good sign by Marilyn Clement who said, "we've got a youth developed movement, that's what we need, great!"[52]

Other individuals were inspired to create organizations that would go beyond organizing on the internet and would also organize boots on the ground actions. Katie, who founded Protest Health Care (an organization that was based in Texas) with the help of her family, explained that

> This year started off so differently and has come to a close in the most humbling way I could have ever imagined. The film, SiCKO, touched my heart— and my mind will be changed *forever*. I was angry as to why our healthcare system was run by profiteering insurance and pharmaceutical companies. The audacity of our government to allow this to *keep* happening to our citizens. The film allowed me to consider other people's situations—not just my own—and to ask questions. **I am now a healthcare activist.**

This organization quickly "partnered with Healthcare NOW" and began organizing efforts in support of H.R. 676.

These are just a few examples of organizations and mobilizing efforts that were created following the release of *SiCKO*. These examples are clear indicators that *SiCKO* became a catalyst for mobilization within the SPM, but there is also evidence that the film became a catalyst for the discussion of healthcare reform for a larger population outside of the SPM.[53] A Kaiser Family Foundation poll, which used a representative sample of 1500 adults, asked about *SiCKO*, among other healthcare reform questions. While only 4 percent of respondents had seen the film, 46 percent indicated that they had at least read or heard something about it only one month after the release. A significant percentage of those who viewed the film indicated that they had not only discussed it with others but also

---

[52] HCN Conference Call February 2008.

[53] Holtz, Andrew (September 25, 2007). [National Survey Shows Michael Moore's Sicko Did Indeed Provoke Discussions about US Health Care System "National Survey Shows Michael Moore's Sicko Did Indeed Provoke Discussions about US Health Care System"] Check |url= value (help). *Oncology Times.* Lippincott Williams & Wilkins, Inc. 29 (18): 28–29.

that it had shaped their opinion on healthcare reform.[54] The organizing around this film was not only facilitated by advances in internet technology, but it was supported by *cultural agents* that arose from the film. These individuals became important heroes within the single-payer narrative of cultural opportunity.

A primary agent of cultural opportunity is the director of *SiCKO*, Michael Moore. Although neither the film, nor the DVD extras, discussed single-payer or any specific bills as a solution to the crisis explicated in the film, according to the single-payer narrative at the time, "*Sicko*'s director Michael Moore supports the Congressional bill for Medicare for All, H.R. 676."[55] Moore did actively support the "Scrubs for SiCKO" campaign[56] and eventually included links to the websites of single-payer organizations, such as HCN, on his website. Joe, aid to Representative Conyers at the time, said this about the role of Michael Moore in the movement— "the country is at a tipping point—a forum to discuss healthcare and have a quality discussion about that. The movement has started through Michael Moore, I think it started before that, but that was a (catalyst)."[57] According to this action narrative, Michael Moore was a spark for the movement building and grassroots mobilization that followed. Moore also engaged in other forms of internet-based activism during the SiCKO period by collecting even more healthcare horror stories which he both requested and shared via his "Sicko the Movie" YouTube channel. In his video request for these stories, Moore specifically references the opportunity presented by YouTube for sharing these stories.[58] Moore, who consistently emphasizes the importance of grassroots mobilization, had this to say about the film,

[54] Levitt, Larry, Craig Palosky, and Kate Schoen. "Michael Moore's Sicko—Broad Reach and Impact Even Without the Popcorn?" Kaiser Family Foundation. Published: Aug. 23, 2007, https://www.kff.org/other/poll-finding/michael-moores-sicko-broad-reach-and-impact/.

[55] MoSP Sicko Rally August 2007.

[56] Nurses, Doctors Announce "Scrubs For SiCKO" Campaign in Conjunction With Debut of Michael Moore's Film to Spark Genuine Healthcare Debate, June 21, 2007, https://www.medicalnewstoday.com/releases/74779.php.

[57] Joe Segal, Aid to Congressman Conyers, HCN Conference Call, July 2007.

[58] Michael Moore, "SiCKO Movie: Michael Moore Wants to Hear From You." Posted on June 6, 2007, https://www.youtube.com/watch?v=VEFoq_5RbC4.

It is just a movie. It requires a lot of political action by millions of people to get involved. But the good news is that, you don't have to convince anybody anymore that we have a very unfair and kind of rotten health care system, especially health insurance system. That, I think a majority of Americans get.[59]

SiCKO may have been "just a movie" but Michael Moore became a key cultural agent for the movement and would be an outspoken proponent of single-payer in the years to come.

A few of the stars of SiCKO, whose healthcare stories were told in the film, also became involved in the movement at this time. While they did not have the same level of "star power" as Michael Moore, they became active participants in the movement itself. One star of SiCKO, Donna Smith, became a leader in several organizations that supported single-payer. Of her involvement in the film and the "transformation"[60] that happened through her role in the film Smith said,

Dignity heals. That was and is my lesson. I was blessed to be featured in SiCKO, and I was determined to make the experience count. I was acutely aware that 25,000 people sent their stories to Michael for possible inclusion in the film and yet somehow ours would represent millions of other stories. It was humbling and hopeful. Though we did not earn any money from that as no one is paid to be in a documentary film, the chance I have had to impact the healthcare justice movement has been rewarding and reinforcing of the notion that the vast majority of working class Americans really do care about one another. I also was blown away by the care I received in Cuba. It made me so angry to think of the years I had spent fighting for access to care in the U.S. while other nations provide healthcare to all as a matter of right. That was eye-opening.[61]

Donna explains in this action narrative that her involvement in *SiCKO* was the catalyst for her participation as an activist because she was empowered through her participation in the film. This process of empowerment that Smith experienced through sharing her personal healthcare narrative in *SiCKO* resulted in the extensive positive contributions that Donna made to the efforts of the SPM. Donna acted for some time as a cultural agent

---

[59] Michael Moore & Donna Smith: Still Sicko, GritTV with Laura Flanders. March 19, 2011.
[60] Ibid.
[61] Donna Smith, Interview, July 2017.

in her role as a "star of Sicko." She traveled around the country giving talks and answering questions before and after showings of the film. She became an important ally for the leaders of MoSP and was the keynote speaker for their 2008 Annual Health Care weekend, which also involved a radio interview and a showing of *SiCKO*. At this meeting, Donna told the gathered activists "Dignity really does heal people. You are valuable just because you are a human being. You all are so powerful."[62] Donna also used her star power to mobilize constituencies that had not previously been mobilized. She created a new organization "American Patients United" in order to empower and mobilize individuals who had patient experiences like her own. Donna also became an important liaison between the California Nurses Association (CNA) /National Nurses United (NNU) and HCN. As a member of the HCN board, a paid organizer for CNA, and later as the executive director of Progressive Democrats of America (PDA), she continued to work diligently for single-payer.

SiCKO also inspired some less likely characters to take on an active role in the fight to end private for-profit health insurance through the creation of a single-payer system. Wendell Potter, who was then the Vice President for Corporate Communications at CIGNA, a giant in the health insurance industry, wrote that America's Health Insurance Plans (AHIP) had sent a "reconnaissance agent" to the world premiere of *SiCKO* at the 2007 Cannes Film Festival. They anxiously awaited a report about this secretive project. Upon finding out that CIGNA was a "target" in the film, Potter was relieved to know that AHIP was working with the insurance industry to discredit Moore and his film. According to Potter, the plan to counterattack Moore started a few years before the film's release and then went into full effect once the content of the film was made public. AHIP formed "Health Care for America" which would work to reify a fear of government run health care in the United States.[63] In preparation for his role in this counterattack, Potter was able to score tickets to the Sacramento premiere of the film which was hosted by PNHP and CNA. Of his experience at this premiere Potter says,

[62] Donna Smith, Field notes, MoSP Healthcare Weekend, Ethical Society of St. Louis, April 2008.

[63] Potter, Wendell. 2010. "The Campaign Against Sicko." *Deadly Spin: An Insurance Company Insider Speaks Out on How Corporate PR Is Killing Health Care and Deceiving Americans*. Bloomsbury Press, pp. 29–43.

But the movie had an effect on me that I didn't expect. Because of all the experience I'd had handling "horror stories" like the ones depicted, I knew that they were a common occurrence—that many Americans found themselves in similar situations every day. I also found the film very moving and very effective in its condemnation of the practices of private health insurance companies. There were many times when I had to fight to hold back tears. Moore had gotten it right. If I hadn't been with a colleague, I probably would have joined all the others in the audience in giving the movie a standing ovation, just as the people at Cannes did when it was first screened.[64]

Potter soon retired from CIGNA and then became an active contributor to the SPM and a "whistleblower" from within the insurance industry. Potter became both a supporter and vocal critic of future healthcare policy proposals—such as the Affordable Care Act—and wrote several books dealing with the issue. In addition to becoming an influential cultural agent via his somewhat celebrity status, Potter also became the President of "Business for Medicare for All," which works to make the business case for single-payer healthcare reform.[65] Potter has also participated in grassroots single-payer events at which he has advised grassroots activists by using his expertise in marketing and public relations—an expertise that was once utilized in support of the for-profit insurance industry. At the 2012 One Payer States annual strategy meeting, he advised the gathered activists on strategy saying, "No offense, but you all have been at this for quite a long time, so maybe you might think that there are some things that you might try differently."[66] Potter continues to be a cultural and economic agent of opportunity within the single-payer narrative practice.

Yet another cultural agent who played a small role in the single-payer narrative surrounding *SiCKO* was Oprah Winfrey. According to this narrative of cultural opportunity, following her viewing of *SiCKO* and her interview with Michael Moore in the summer of 2007 she said, "you've opened my eyes and my heart and I'm gonna have a forum about it this

[64] Potter, Wendell. 2010. "The Campaign Against Sicko." *Deadly Spin: An Insurance Company Insider Speaks Out on How Corporate PR Is Killing Health Care and Deceiving Americans*. Bloomsbury Press, p. 41.

[65] Business for Medicare for All "Wendell Potter," https://www.businessformedicare-forall.org/wendell-potter.html.

[66] Potter, Wendell. *Field Notes, One Payer States/Healthcare NOW National Strategy Meeting*, Philadelphia PA, June 2012.

fall,"[67] because "when she saw the film, it completely changed the way she looked at health care."[68] According to this opportunity narrative, as "the most powerful woman in the world"[69] any level of support for single-payer from Oprah had the potential to push the goals of the movement into the realm of political feasibility.

This idea, about the "Oprah effect," is not a new one. As an icon with an extensive amount of "cultural authority,"[70] Oprah could have impacted the political, economic, and cultural opportunity that the movement would face during the upcoming election season in ways that other cultural agents, with less cultural authority or economic power, such as Michael Moore, could not. This cultural authority has allowed Oprah to turn "books into best sellers, products into must have holiday gifts, and social issues into political movements."[71] Scholars have argued that Oprah has single-handedly put books on the best seller list,[72] started a reading revolution,[73] affected voting behavior,[74] and convinced even conservative voters to support more government involvement in family issues.[75] Having the cultural authority, not to mention the "deep pockets,"[76] of Oprah

[67] Julia Lamborn, MoSP Board Meeting July 2007. For a summary of this episode see Oprah.com "Michael Moore's Sicko," http://www.oprah.com/world/michael-moores-sicko_1/1 and "Health Care Crisis," https://www.oprah.com/health/sick-in-america-it-can-happen-to-you_2/all.

[68] Wilson, Dan. "Oprah Winfrey Talks to Michael Moore About Sicko and Health Care Insurance Industry." Posted on September 27, 2007, http://www.pnhp.org/news/2007/october/oprah_winfrey_talks_.php.

[69] Julia Lamborn, MoSP Board Meeting July 2007.

[70] Peck, Janice. 2002. "The Oprah Effect: Texts, Readers, and the Dialectic of Signification." *Communication Review* 5, no. 2: 143.

[71] Glynn, Carroll J., Michael Huge, Jason B. Reineke, Bruce W. Hardy, and James Shanahan. 2007. "When Oprah Intervenes: Political Correlates of Daytime Talk Show Viewing." *Journal of Broadcasting & Electronic Media* 51, no. 2: 228–244.

[72] Butler, Richard J., Benjamin W. Cowan, and Sebastian Nilsson. 2005. "From Obscurity to Bestseller: Examining the Impact of Oprah's Book Club Selections." *Publishing Research Quarterly* 20, no. 4: 23–34.

[73] Peck, Janice. 2002. "The Oprah Effect: Texts, Readers, and the Dialectic of Signification." *Communication Review* 5, no. 2: 143.

[74] Baum, Matthew A., and Angela S. Jamison. 2006. "The Oprah Effect: How Soft News Helps Inattentive Citizens Vote Consistently." *Journal of Politics* 68, no. 4: 946–959.

[75] Glynn, Carroll J., Michael Huge, Jason B. Reineke, Bruce W. Hardy, and James Shanahan. 2007. "When Oprah Intervenes: Political Correlates of Daytime Talk Show Viewing." *Journal of Broadcasting & Electronic Media* 51, no. 2: 228–244.

[76] Field notes: Becky, 2008 HCN national strategy meeting.

behind the SPM would have likely resulted in some positive changes for the movement.

However, as the debate surrounding healthcare reform was heating up in anticipation of the upcoming 2008 Presidential election, single-payer activists began to doubt that Oprah's earlier statements would result in any real opportunity for the SPM. Activists were eager to capitalize on the possibility of Oprah's support, but the candidacy of Barack Obama would change their outlook. Donna explained that "Oprah is complicated because of how loyal she is to Obama" and that, "the political reality is— once she came out for Obama, she wasn't going to do anything to rock the Obama boat. Maybe she'll do something in the future, but what?"[77] The opportunity that Oprah's support could have created was no longer defined as a possibility, and this was directly tied to the candidacy of Barack Obama within this single-payer opportunity narrative. This was just a fore-shadowing of the tension that would develop between the SPM and the new administration in the years to come.

THE NARRATIVE PRACTICE OF CULTURAL OPPORTUNITY

The events of this time period, from 2000 to 2008, illustrate the ways in which shifts in material culture can affect social movement organizations (SMOs) in positive ways as new forms of cultural opportunity develop. The G.W. Bush Administration and the dominance of the Republican Party in Congress, along with the emphasis on a wartime budget and economy, made it unlikely that progressive healthcare reform would be possible. Although some incremental changes to healthcare policy did occur, such as the addition of prescription drug coverage to Medicare through the "Medicare Prescription Drug, Improvement, and Modernization Act of 2003" that created Medicare Part D, these reforms were critiqued by single-payer activists as changes that further empowered the enemy of single-payer—private for-profit health insurance and pharmaceutical companies. Although the SPM experienced low levels of opportunity in the political sphere, activists were able to mobilize in support of new single-payer legislation (H.R. 676) by acting on positively defined opportunities in the cultural and grassroots spheres. It is significant that single-payer activists continued to mobilize the grassroots in

---

[77] Field notes: Donna Smith, 2008 HCN National Strategy Meeting.

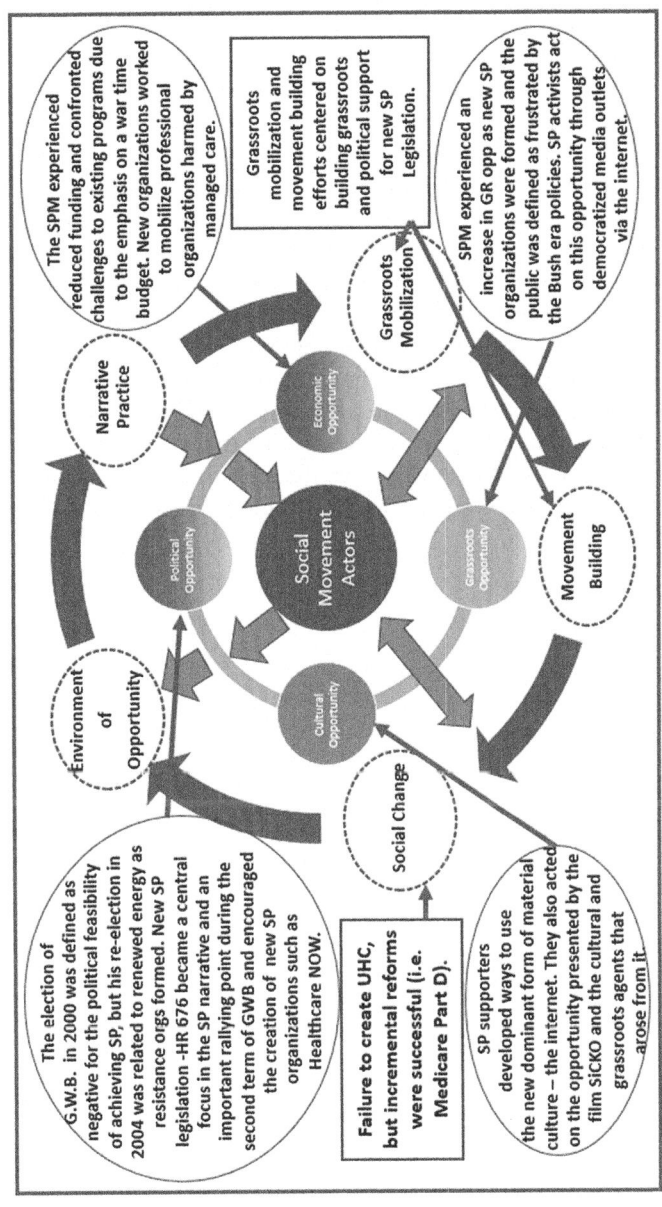

Fig. 4.3 *SiCKO*/G.W. Bush era narrative practice

order to increase support in the political sphere for specific pieces of legislation, even within such a negative political context (see Fig. 4.3 for a visual summary of this era).

Single-payer activists acted upon the frustration and energy in the public sphere, or grassroots opportunity, by utilizing newly developed internet-based resources and by forming new grassroots organizations that were adept in the use of these resources. However, rather than concluding that the resources made available through the democratization of media technology are always enabling, I have examined the ways in which the reality is much more complicated. These shifts in material culture were initially negative for SMO's that didn't have the skills to utilize new forms of technology. I have also given several examples of the ways in which alliances with other organizations and the interest of cultural agents can serve to sustain these organizations as they learn new skills in order to develop their use of new technologies. In the case of the SPM, this process of democratization resulted in new allies in the form of cultural agents. All of these changes would continue to affect single-payer supporters as they entered the Obama era.

CHAPTER 5

Resisting "Politics as Usual": The Obama Era of Healthcare Reform

"Happy birthday dear Medicare. You're red white and blue. Uniquely American and we all want you too." As Donna Smith leads the hundreds of gathered activists in song while standing on a stage situated on the upper senate park lawn on this hot sunny day in July 2009, I am delighted to find that I am singing just as loud as the activists standing near to me. I have spent the morning meeting with politicians and activists to discuss the mobilization for single-payer that is on-going, and also the ignorance of this mobilizing effort by mainstream Democratic officials who are debating the issue of healthcare reform on capitol hill. I am already exhausted at this point in the day, but the enthusiasm of the gathered activists energizes me. We hear from a young girl named Frankie who tells us that she was recently arrested at a Blue Cross Blue Shield facility when the CEO refused to meet with her to discuss the denial of patient care by his company. She asserts that "The only way that we can get healthcare for everyone. Is to get healthcare for everyone" and I marvel at the fortitude and the depth of character present in this 12 year old girl which allowed her to not only stand up to a powerful corporation, but also to stand before a crowd of more than 1000 activists to tell her story. Although the debate in the capitol is focused on more incremental measures of healthcare reform, speakers at the rally are still positive, with one exclaiming that "I expect that 10 years from now, we will not only be celebrating the 54th birthday of Medicare, but the 10th anniversary of Single Payer Healthcare!"[1] Even President Obama's own personal physician, Dr. David Schneider, speaks at the rally and explains that, "I respectfully differ with him on his approach to healthcare

---

[1] Fieldnotes: Jos Williams AFL CIO President Metro Washington Council, Medicare Birthday Rally, July 2009.

© The Author(s) 2020
L. S. F. Hern, *Single Payer Healthcare Reform*,
https://doi.org/10.1007/978-3-030-42764-1_5

reform. I speak to you today as an advocate for the single-payer approach to healthcare reform—expanded and improved Medicare for All, but I am hoping that President Obama and congress will hear me also." While this is a rally for single-payer supporters, the day of action that surrounds it is intended to re-shape the congressional debate about healthcare reform and bring single-payer "to the table." I can feel the power and urgency of the gathered activists as they chant together,[2] "Healthcare is a human right—don't stop now, don't give up the fight."[3]

In the final years of the G.W. Bush administration, single-payer activists began to heavily critique the argument that their goals could not be achieved due to a lack of "political will." The single-payer narrative included a discussion of earlier movements that pushed for their goals regardless of whether or not there was significant political support for them. The argument that "we can make it politically feasible" and the mantra that "there is no NO!"[4] were regularly used by single-payer activist leaders. They began using new strategies and new forms of material culture to act on what they perceived to be grassroots opportunity.

During the Obama era of healthcare reform, narratives of grassroots opportunity came to the forefront of the single-payer narrative in unprecedented ways. Single-payer activists had experienced greater grassroots opportunity during the years of the G.W. Bush administration, especially during his second term, and their ability to act upon this opportunity was facilitated by the development of new internet-based methods of organizing. *Grassroots opportunity exists when there is active interest and participation of members, non-members, and new members in a social movement, when grassroots mobilization is seen as a legitimate outlet for political action, and when there are resources available to take advantage of this opportunity.*

In this chapter, I will examine the ways in which narratives of grassroots opportunity—or the opportunity to mobilize the public in support of single-payer—became dominant within the single-payer narrative. These narratives were related to a movement building strategy oriented toward increasing public support for the concept of single-payer, and the development of increasingly radical tactics that were designed not only to support the goal of single-payer healthcare but also to critique the "politics as

---

[2] Fieldnotes: Mikuak Rai of the Coalition of the Uninsured and Underinsured for Single Payer led this chant, Medicare Birthday Rally, July 2009.

[3] Fieldnotes: Lindy Hern, Medicare Birthday Rally, Washington D.C., July 2009.

[4] Julia Lamborn, President of Missourians for Single Payer, MoSP annual meeting, Dec. 2006.

usual" process occurring in the capitol. In this opportunity narrative, the Obama administration was eventually constructed as the opposition and sometimes labeled as the enemy of "real" healthcare reform. This narrative practice resulted in single-payer activists concluding that the public must be mobilized to change the political sphere through challenges to establishment politics in order to actually achieve the changes needed to create a single-payer healthcare system.

"We Are the Change That We Seek"[5]: The Obama Candidacy

Healthcare reform once again became a central focus of political discourse during the 2008 election season. The economic recession and healthcare crisis were of primary concern for most Americans and were prevalent within the political discourse surrounding the election season. Each of the presidential candidates, regardless of political affiliation, developed political rhetoric, if not specific plans, for dealing with these issues. The campaign of then Senator Barack Obama (D-IL) was rooted in a narrative of change. This campaign was built upon the preposition that an Obama presidency would not result in "politics as usual." Characteristics of the campaign, such as the focus placed upon grassroots mobilization and a political frame centralizing hope and change, led the public to believe that this would be the case. Single-payer activists were also inspired by this narrative of change.

Central to the single-payer narrative was a conclusion that Obama was a supporter of single-payer. A key point in this narrative occurred at an AFL-CIO convention in the summer of 2003 when Obama stated that,

> I happen to be a proponent of a single-payer universal healthcare program. I see no reason why the United States of America, the wealthiest country in the history of the world, spending 14 percent of its Gross National Product on health care, cannot provide basic health insurance to everybody. And that's what Jim is talking about when he says everybody in, nobody out. A single-payer health care plan, a universal health care plan. And that's what I'd like to see. But as all of you know, we may not get there immediately.

[5] Barack Obama, Speech, February 5, 2008.

Because first we have to take back the White House, we have to take back the Senate, and we have to take back the House.[6]

This, coupled with a declaration from Obama that,

> He requires a **mandate** from the voters, as he stated to a reporter. That word "mandate" relates to the suggestion that he made in the meeting. He said citizens can get a specific healthcare policy by sending a thousand to two thousand letters from every U.S. Congressional District that communicate the need for whatever healthcare policy we want. He promised that the U.S. Representatives will listen. Barack Obama clearly recognizes that the immense power of the health insurance companies must be overcome with the overwhelming force of thousands of educated constituents communicating to their U.S. Representatives.[7]

made single-payer supporters hopeful that the opportunity to pass single-payer legislation would increase if Obama became the democratic presidential candidate.[8]

Many single-payer supporters threw their support, as individuals, behind candidate Obama due to this narrative, as well as due to lingering distrust of the other democratic candidates who had not supported single-payer during earlier debates on healthcare reform. The alienation experienced by single-payer supporters during the Clinton era of healthcare reform filtered into perceptions of what then Senator Hillary Clinton (D-NY) would do as president. According to this narrative, the other Democratic candidates were "pushing half measures that don't matter"[9] and focusing on individual mandates for insurance. Obama was narratively defined as opposed to individual mandates "except for children."[10] The specter of "individual mandates," which were, according to the single-payer narrative, an extensively flawed aspect of the earlier reforms that had happened in Massachusetts, became an important dimension of the single-payer mobilization efforts during the 2008 election season and throughout the Obama era of healthcare reform. Single-payer activists had learned

---

[6] Barack Obama, Speech to Illinois AFL-CIO "Civil, Human, and Women's Rights" Conference, June 30, 2003.

[7] Bob, Healthcare NOW member and organizer of the "Million letters" Campaign Healthcare NOW Conference Call Oct. 2008.

[8] This prompted the start of a "Million Letters Campaign"—to send 2000 letters from each congressional district.

[9] Representative John Conyers (D-MI) Healthcare NOW Conference Call September 2007.

[10] Jim, CNA organizer, HCN Conference Call February 2007.

from the Massachusetts experience how easily movement toward single-payer could be derailed by a solution based on compulsory participation in the private insurance market and concluded that they must "stop individual mandates which force people to give more money to greedy insurance companies."[11]

Single-payer actors were encouraged to support congressional elections instead of specific presidential candidates because "what will get this bill through is the election of a progressive Congress, that must be reminded that we pay their bills."[12] Yet many single-payer supporters remained hopeful that an Obama presidency would result in real change of the healthcare system through the implementation of a single-payer program. This narrative of opportunity was powerful, even though Obama did not support the single-payer option in his campaign, except to say that it would be the best option if the United States could "start from scratch."[13] This *hope producing narrative of political opportunity* was related to the changes in grassroots opportunity that single-payer supporters experienced at this time, in part due to the Obama campaign process.

The Obama campaign focused on mobilizing the grassroots. This mobilization was facilitated by the use of the internet and social media networking sites. Perhaps the most interesting and influential aspect of the internet-based aspects of the Obama campaign is that by using these resources it was able to not only accumulate an exceptional amount of campaign funds through small donations,[14] but that it was able to translate virtual organizing to on-the-ground grassroots organizing in unprecedented ways.[15] This served to further legitimate conventional grassroots activity within the context of traditional American politics. At this time, single-payer activists were also committed, for the most part, to conventional and non-disruptive forms of grassroots organizing (see Fig. 5.1 for a visual representation of this time period).

This campaign played an important role in narratives of grassroots opportunity by legitimizing grassroots efforts in the context of mainstream

[11] Donna Smith, MoSP Funeral March Event, St. Louis MO, April 2008.

[12] Donna Smith at MoSP SICKO showing—April 2008.

[13] Barack Obama, Town Hall, Rio Rancho New Mexico, May 2009.

[14] Luo, Michael. 2008. "Small Online Contributions Add Up to Huge Fund-Raising Edge for Obama." *The New York Times*, February 20, 2008.

[15] Cogburn, Derrick and Fatima K. Espinoza-Vasquez. 2011. "From Networked Nominee to Networked nation: Examining the Impact of Web 2.0 and Social Media on Political Participation and Civic Engagement in the 2008 Obama Campaign." *Journal of Political Marketing* 10:1–2, 189–213.

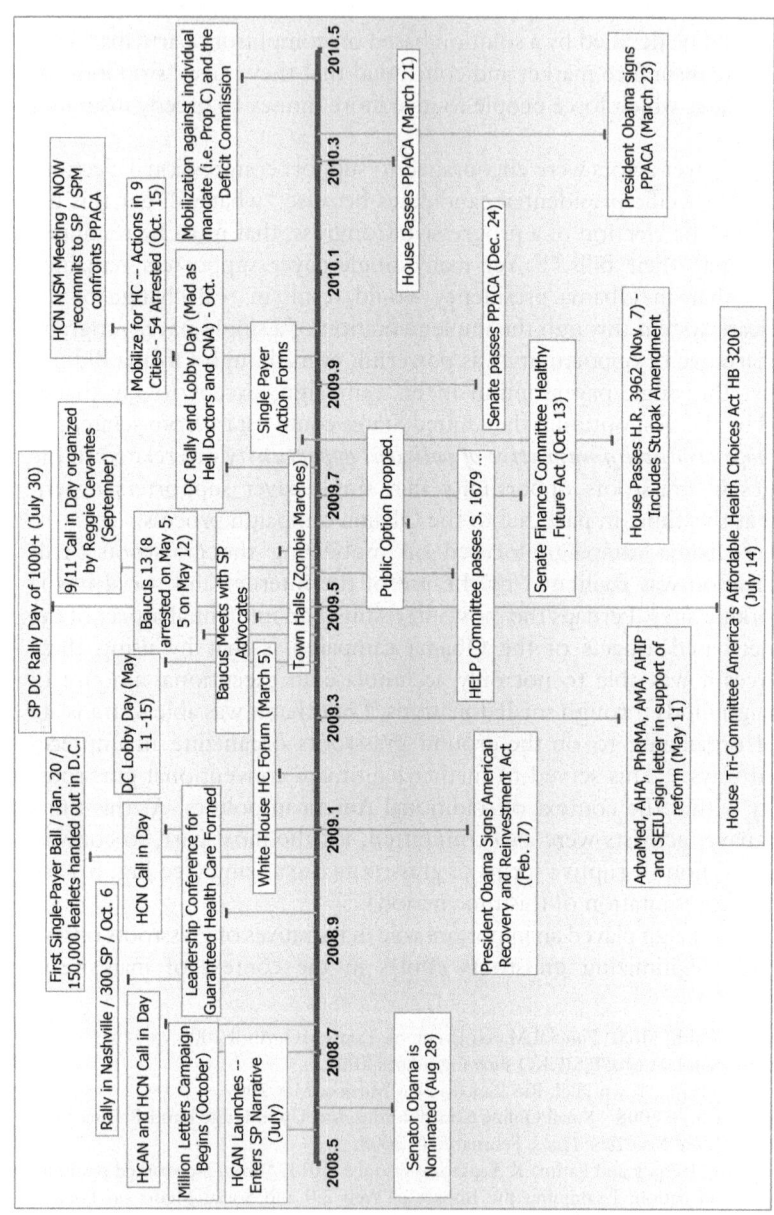

Fig. 5.1 The Obama era timeline

politics. For single-payer activists, the Obama campaign became a lesson that they should learn from and a lingering opportunity on which they should act. Although single-payer activists cautioned that "pinning our hopes on him directly would not be the right way to go,"[16] they also believed that the Obama campaign had "really taught us that you still can organize to make change."[17] A few important lessons learned were that the campaign was "decentralized, but focused,"[18] that adopting slogans used in the campaign, such as "Yes We Can," could also be effective,[19] and "how to reach out to all people regardless of their political opinions."[20]

Single-payer supporters also defined the mobilization of a larger progressive constituency during the Obama campaign period as an indicator of grassroots opportunity. The Obama campaign was able to mobilize large numbers of people, especially young voters, in support of his candidacy.[21] Because these participants were mobilized in the context of the narrative of "change" developed during the Obama campaign, they, according to single-payer activists, could also be supportive of more progressive changes such as single-payer. However, the formation of a new grassroots organization specifically directed toward less progressive options for healthcare reform would serve to undermine this narrative of grassroots opportunity while also becoming an important factor in a developing an *identity building narrative of opportunity* which concluded that the Single Payer Movement (SPM) was the "real grassroots."

"We Are the Real Grassroots!"[22]: Countering the Push for the Public Option

The grassroots opportunity that was narratively defined as increasingly positive during the final years of the G.W. Bush administration resulted in the formation of new grassroots organizations and in greater participation

---

[16] Fieldnotes: Donna Smith, HCN National Strategy meeting Nov. 2008.

[17] Ibid.

[18] Fieldnotes: Ethel, HCN National Strategy Meeting Nov. 2008.

[19] Fieldnotes: Sandy, HCN National Strategy Meeting Nov. 2008.

[20] Interview: Aileen, Vice President of United for National Healthcare in Bellingham Washington, Internet based open ended interview.

[21] Keeter, Scott, Julianna Horowitz, and Alec Tyson. 2008. "Young Voters in the 2008 Election." Pew Research Center for the People and the Press Nov. 12, 2008.

[22] Dr. Steve B, Single Payer to HCAN: We Will Not NOT Be Listened To! Posted on July 19, 2008 www.pnhp.org.

in the SPM. This was initially a benefit to the SPM, but the effects of this opportunity were complicated by the combination of this grassroots opportunity and the political opportunity for healthcare reform that the campaign of Barack Obama represented because they also encouraged the formation of new social movement organizations (SMOs) that focused on reforming the healthcare system in ways that were not in line with the SPM. Health Care for America NOW (HCAN) became a primary focus of the single-payer narrative of grassroots opportunity in the months leading up to the election. The grassroots competition that arose between Healthcare NOW and HCAN resulted in HCAN being constructed as a member of the opposition to the SPM.

Health Care for America Now (HCAN) entered the narrative practice of those involved in the SPM during the summer of 2008 and quickly became a focus of the single-payer narrative of grassroots opportunity. According to the HCAN origin story, it was formed in order to

> create a nationwide movement for comprehensive health care reform. We knew the only way to succeed was to build a base of grassroots activists and to ignite a national movement to demand action, lay out an agenda for change and answer the powerful forces arrayed against quality, affordable health care for all.[23]

Single-payer activists were initially cautious about this new organization that had a name which was "confusingly similar to an existing coalition called 'Healthcare-Now'" and which "threatened to divide the progressive movement for health care reform."[24] During the July 2008 Healthcare NOW conference call, activists were warned that,

> HCAN will launch this week, and it seems that they do not support single-payer because their ten-point plan states that people should have the choice between public and private insurance. They campaign for a publicly funded Medicare system that will compete with the private insurance. New York Times stated they are pushing a $40 million ad campaign. Healthcare-NOW

[23] Health Care for America NOW "History" http://healthcareforamericanow.org/about/history.

[24] Mogulescu, Miles. 2008. "Why not Single Payer? Part 6: New 'Health Care for America NOW' May Reflect Divisions in the Movement for Universal Health Care." *Huffington Post* Posted Online July 9.

is putting together a position paper that is going to be approved by the steering committee on what role we should play in exposing this group.

Although the 40 million dollar budget and coalition membership of several major labor unions, including the AFL-CIO and SEIU, were both constructed as a benefit for healthcare reform by some involved in this movement, single-payer activists were critical of the policy recommendations of HCAN and the source of its funding. In a position paper circulated by Physicians for a National Health Program (PNHP), one of the core intellectual leaders of the movement, David Himmelstein, stated that

> HCAN's proposal tries to avoid a head-on collision with private insurers, but the result is a plan that cannot achieve universal coverage or make care affordable. For physicians, offering a placebo in place of effective treatment is a serious ethical violation. Hence, while we salute the good intentions of the members of the HCAN coalition, we must warn against their proposal.[25]

Although HCAN was oriented toward the goal of "universal" healthcare and toward building a movement in support of this goal, their use of the term "universal" and the principles that went along with the use of that term were not compatible with the goal of the SPM to implement a universal single-payer healthcare system that eliminated the need for private insurance companies for the coverage of basic care. It became essential to single-payer activists that they make these differences clear.

> Partly because the name of the new group is so similar to our own, it is important that we point out what distinguishes the HCAN position from ours. Even more essential, the distinction is important because the policy issue is the crucial foundation of successful healthcare reform. We have to get it right this time around.[26]

It was imperative that they "get it right" because, "it would take 10–15 years to really see the effects of such a plan at the national level, so the movement for real reform would be put back that many years. So, it is important that they make Single Payer an option now."[27] The SPM's rela-

---

[25] David Himmelstein MD "A Policy Response to Health Care for America NOW" July 9, 2008, http://pnhp.org/blog/2008/07/09/a-policy-response-to-health-care-for-america-now/.

[26] Healthcare NOW Position Paper "Regarding HCAN" Nov. 7, 2008.

[27] Donna Smith. MoSP Healthcare Weekend. St. Louis MO. April 2008.

tionship with HCAN became progressively more contentious as Healthcare NOW was forced to compete with this new organization for economic, grassroots, and political support.

While the budget of HCAN was impressive, the source of this funding became another location for single-payer criticism of this organization. According to the single-payer narrative, much of this funding came from a contradictory source.

> I want to talk to you about the alternative movement to single-payer. There is an organization called HCAN that supports a universal insurance plan. The driving forces and funding source is AHIP—Americas Health Insurance Plans—an insurance lobby organization that is trying to push for an all insurance universal plan for America.[28]

Single-payer activists frequently called out HCAN for being critical of private health insurance while at the same time including private insurance as an integral aspect of its proposed legislation. This was tied to the funding behind the organization as well as its political ties. The marginalization of single-payer activists within the larger movement for healthcare reform had in the past been tied to the funding sources of multi-issue organizations. This made single-payer activists concerned about the source of the funding for other progressive groups working for healthcare reform, but who did not specifically support single-payer. So, the narrative that HCAN had accepted funding from an oppositional force—AHIP—made single-payer activists even less likely to seek out a positive relationship with HCAN. However, this was a false narrative. HCAN itself was critical of organizations that took funding from AHIP and heavily critiqued the Chamber of Commerce for accepting AHIP funds saying

> This reflects poorly on everyone involved. The Chamber of Commerce—ostensibly a principled interest group with its own constituency and goals—is revealed to be nothing more than a front group for hire. And the insurance companies and AHIP not only lied about their support for reform (as we've known all along) but lacked the courage of their convictions to put their money into their opposition publicly.[29]

---

[28] Activist, Missourians for Single Payer Annual Meeting, Nov. 2008.

[29] HCAN Blog. "Breaking AHIP and Insurance Companies Funding Chamber of Commerce Attack Ads" Posted on Jan. 1, 2010, http://blog.healthcareforamericanow.org/2010/01/12/breaking-ahip-and-insurance-companies-funding-chamber-of-commerce-attack-ads/.

While single-payer activists critiqued HCAN for being funded by corporate special interests, those on the right who were opposed to "Obamacare" critiqued HCAN for accepting funds from "leftist" organizations and unions.[30] Single-payer activists eventually learned that HCAN was actually being funded by a "consortium of unions and liberal groups,"[31] some of which had also supported single-payer in the past (i.e. SEIU—Service Employees International Union), but the funding for the organization was still a questionable issue in this narrative of opportunity. It is possible that single-payer activists initially conflated HCAN with the Families USA coalition—which was partially funded by special interests or The Campaign for an American Solution (CAS) which was a project of AHIP that claimed to be a grassroots mobilization effort developed to "build support for workable health care reform based on core principles supported by the American people: coverage, affordability, quality, value, choice and portability."[32] Some of HCAN's first activities actually involved protesting The Campaign for an American Solution's "listening tour" that was held in the summer of 2008.[33] While it was not clear what reform CAS supported, it was clear that as an arm of the insurance industry this campaign would be opposed to any reform that limited the autonomy of industry actors in any way. In this way, it was an enemy that Healthcare NOW and HCAN shared. While the saying—the enemy of my enemy is my friend, could have applied in this situation, concerns about the way in which HCAN was funded and how this affected the goals of HCAN continued to limit any possibility of an alliance between the two organizations. HCAN was actually funded through 500,000 dollar commitments from each organization on the executive committee and substantial grants from The Atlantic Philanthropies and The California Endowment (TCE) which was a "conversion foundation" established when Blue Cross Blue Shield

---

[30] Michelle Malkin, Conservative Blog/Columnist, "Funding the Obamacare Astroturf Campaign" Posted on June 24, 2009. http://michellemalkin.com/2009/06/24/who%E2%80%99s-funding-the-obamacare-astroturf-campaign/.

[31] Eggen, Dan. 2010. "How interest groups behind health-care legislation are financed is often unclear," Washington Post Website. Posted on January 7, 2010. http://www.washingtonpost.com/wp-dyn/content/article/2010/01/06/AR2010010605160.html.

[32] American Health Solution Webpage "About" http://www.americanhealthsolution.org/ (No longer active).

[33] Kirsch, Richard. 2012. *Fighting for Our Health: The Epic Battle to Make Health Care a Right in the United States.* NY: Rockefeller Institute Press.

of California transitioned to for-profit status in 1996.[34] Neither of these entities supported a single-payer option. Richard Kirsch, one of the founders of HCAN, explained the situation this way,

> While a growing number of groups decided to support HCAN's approach, many single-payer advocates remained highly skeptical. Rumors circulated on the web that we were an insurance industry front group. I was even asked by a prominent single-payer advocate if Atlantic Philanthropies was financed with insurance company money (it's not). Other single-payer advocates engaged in convoluted dissections of the Herndon research[35] to show that it was biased and based on faulty assumptions. While I respected the single-payer champions' concerns about the many potential shortcoming of reforms that kept much of the nation's health financing system in place, we were no longer debating theory. We were actually trying to get a president and Congress to pass a law that provided affordable health coverage to everyone in the United States.[36]

Even though HCAN was indeed entirely funded by progressive and liberal groups or individuals (i.e. Billionaire George Soros),[37] this still created a competitive relationship between the two mobilization efforts because it resulted in less economic opportunity, in the form of large organizational donations, for single-payer organizations. However, HCAN continued to be tied to special interest funding in the single-payer narrative of grassroots opportunity centered on this new organization. This served to further decrease the likelihood that these organizations could ever work together. These issues also resulted in activists increasing use of the motto "the revolution will not be funded."[38]

---

[34] Starr, Paul. 2010. *Remedy and Reaction: The Peculiar American Struggle Over Health Care Reform*. Yale University Press.

[35] This was a poll used by Kirsch and others to sway single-payer supporters to support the public option and the principles of HCAN (Kirsch 2012). Single-payer supporters were very critical of this research done by Celinda Lake which concluded that the American public favored "guaranteed affordable choice" over single-payer. http://www.pnhp.org/news/2008/december/why_does_celinda_lak.php.

[36] Kirsch, Richard. 2012. *Fighting for Our Health: The Epic Battle to Make Health Care a Right in the United States*. NY: Rockefeller Institute Press.

[37] Starr, Paul. 2010. *Remedy and Reaction: The Peculiar American Struggle Over Health Care Reform*. Yale University Press.

[38] Fieldnotes: Mimi, V.P. of Missourians for Single Payer, Spring 2009.

Jacobs and Skocpol[39] found that progressive groups had planned ahead for this round of healthcare reform and, much like the Obama administration, did not want to make the same mistakes that were made during the Clinton era of healthcare reform.

> What is more, this time around in the long-running quest for universal health insurance in America, most liberal health care reformers decided in advance that they would not insist on the single-payer approach, but would, instead, champion a compromise idea called the 'public option', a proposal to create a publicly run health insurance plan to compete side by side with private insurance.[40]

Jacobs and Skocpol go on to argue that most would-be supporters of single-payer joined forces with the "chief orchestrator of pressure"—HCAN—which began to ardently press for the public option.[41] Single-payer activists who did not join HCAN were critical of HCAN's support of the "public option" over single-payer. According to this narrative of grassroots opportunity, those who funded and supported HCAN purposefully co-opted the grassroots opportunity of this time period by convincing would-be single-payer supporters to support an inferior financing mechanism—the public option—that left for profit insurance in place.[42] It became important for single-payer activists to "chip away the HCAN support—people are not aware that there is a contradiction between HCAN principles and H.R. 676—we need to explain and clarify"[43] to HCAN supporters who were "buying Healthcare NOW T-shirts."[44]

After Barack Obama was elected president and officially rejected single-payer in favor of the public option, HCAN became tied to specifically

---

[39] Jacobs, Lawrence, and Theda Skocpol. 2010. *Health Care Reform and American Politics: What Everyone Needs to Know.* Oxford University Press.

[40] Jacobs, Lawrence, and Theda Skocpol. 2010. *Health Care Reform and American Politics: What Everyone Needs to Know.* Oxford University Press, p. 78.

[41] It is significant that single-payer is present, even on a very small scale, in this state level analysis of health care reform. Although Jacob's and Skocpol's analysis does account for the significant role that HCAN played, it does not account for the extensive organizing of the SPM during this time.

[42] In his memoir, Richard Kirsch explains that the HCAN founders developed a specific procedure using "power maps" to convince single payer supporters, such as Public Citizen Action, to support the Public Option and join HCAN (Kirsch 2012).

[43] Kay, Healthcare NOW conference call, Nov. 2008.

[44] Rebecca, Healthcare NOW conference call, Nov. 2008.

supporting the Obama administration's agenda for healthcare reform. The degree to which the policy recommendations of HCAN affected the policy initially recommended by the Obama administration, and vice versa, is unclear. However, it is clear that the focus on the public option and the activities of HCAN became increasingly tied together within the single-payer narrative of grassroots opportunity. Single-payer activists became more critical of President Obama's apparent rejection of the single-payer option and the continued emphasis on insurance company financing. When President Obama was challenged to the point of rejecting single-payer by conservative opponents, these exchanges were constructed as a sign that single-payer had become the "unattractive alternative" instead of "irrelevant because it is not politically feasible."[45] The positioning of the SPM as the straw man during the 2008 election cycle became, "how we know we're on the map my friends—when John McCain accused Barack Obama of being for single-payer. That's how we know we're in the mix."[46] However, single-payer's new role as the straw man for the newly elected Obama administration's healthcare reform agenda did not result in significantly increased political opportunity.[47] HCAN came to be viewed by single-payer activists as an extension of the Obama agenda for healthcare reform.

> Obama is also helped by a grassroots campaign known as Healthcare for Americans Now (HCAN), made up of progressive groups and unions across the country backing Obama on his health care plan.[48]

This tie between HCAN and the Obama administration signified to single-payer activists that single-payer would not be on the table in the upcoming debate about healthcare reform. It became a central aspect of their narrative practice as they made sense of political, as well as grassroots, opportunity.

According to this narrative, the focus on the "public option" served to decrease the likelihood that their perspective would be heard in the debate,

---

[45] Quentin Young M.D., Head Organizer for PNHP, Interview, March 2007.

[46] Fieldnotes: Activist, Healthcare NOW National Strategy Meeting October 2008.

[47] When H.R. 676 was Reintroduced on Jan. 26th, it only had 33 original co-sponsors, a significantly lower number that the 90 final cosponsors that it had in the previous legislative season. Single-payer activists struggled to bring that number back up.

[48] Ricardo Kaulessar for Hudson Reporter, Filed under Single-Payer News, www.healthcare-now.org.

as well as lessen the amount of grassroots support the SPM would be able to mobilize. Single-payer activists began asking if Healthcare NOW had a plan to "combat HCAN in any way."[49] Single-payer activists attended HCAN events in order to "move the discussion to the left,"[50] and Healthcare NOW also organized actions on the same day as HCAN actions. Kirsch discusses the involvement of single-payer activists in HCAN events as evidence that they were able to "turn around single-payer activists with our actions, not our words,"[51] rather than as evidence that there was still a vibrant, critical, and dedicated SPM that was committed to having a voice in the debate. While single-payer activists viewed HCAN as a major competitor in the grassroots movement for healthcare reform, they were also confident that the opportunity to push single-payer into the discussion was there, largely due to "real" grassroots support for single-payer.

According to the single-payer narrative, the Obama administration's and HCAN's focus on a public option was based on problematic research[52] and flew in the face of increasing popular support for single-payer. Several polls that were completed in the years leading up to the 2008 election season were used as evidence of public support for single-payer healthcare.

> Meanwhile, an Associated Press poll in December, 2007 asked voters "Do you consider yourself a supporter of a single-payer health care system that is a national plan financed by taxpayers in which all Americans would get their insurance from a single government plan, or not?" 54% said "Yes" and 44% said "No". A CBS News poll last September asked "Which do you think would be better for the country: having one health insurance program covering all Americans that would be administered by the government and paid for by the taxpayers, or keeping the current system where many people get their insurance from private employers and some have no insurance?" 55% chose "One Program for All" and only 29% chose "The Current system".[53]

---

[49] Jill, Healthcare NOW conference call, September 2008.

[50] Joan, Healthcare NOW conference call, September 2008.

[51] Kirsch, Richard. 2012. *Fighting for Our Health: The Epic Battle to Make Health Care a Right in the United States.* NY: Rockefeller Institute Press, p. 82.

[52] All Unions Committee for Single Payer Health Care "Why Does Celinda Lake Oppose Single Payer?" Posted on December 1, 2008. http://www.pnhp.org/news/2008/december/why_does_celinda_lak.php.

[53] Miles Mogulescu, "What Do MoveOn Members Think About Health Care? Who Knows?" *Huffington Post,* August 15, 2008.

These figures, coupled with the extensive response[54] of single-payer activists to the HCAN statement of principles and to other grassroots groups that signed on in support of these principles (i.e. MoveOn), indicated to the SPM that they should have the support of a large percentage of the public. This encouraged single-payer activists to focus on mobilizing public support in order to force single-payer into the beltway policy debate, rather than on staging protests against the Obama administration's agenda for healthcare reform. Unlike the conservative protests that occurred at early town hall meanings, the presence of single-payer activists was intended to push the debate in a particular direction, not to challenge it or prohibit it from continuing. At this early stage, single-payer activists were still focused on working within conventional forms of political action.

As HCAN grew in numbers and political influence, single-payer activists became progressively more critical of anyone who supported this organization, including their own political leader at the time, Representative John Conyers (D-MI). In October of 2008, Conyers endorsed HCAN and released the following statement,

> I am proud to join HCAN's broad progressive campaign to raise awareness about the need for true universal health care reform. The HCAN coalition and I are united by our belief that the current non-system of health care run by profit hungry insurance companies is unsustainable and inhumane. It will take a monumental effort to defeat the entrenched special interests that benefit from the status quo. I remain firmly committed to the passage of my single-payer universal health care bill, H.R. 676, and believe that private insurance will never provide the kind of guaranteed affordable health care America needs. However, I agree with HCAN that a true policy debate in the Congress can only begin when there is broad consensus that the sham reform trumpeted by the industry is off the table.[55]

This endorsement resulted in an uproar in the SPM that had the potential to create a drastic shift in the identity of the organization. Single-payer activists were immediately critical of this statement and suggested that Healthcare NOW ask Conyers to retract it. This was cause for much debate within the single-payer community as some activists were convinced that HCAN was the "enemy" and they needed to hold Conyers'

[54] Single Payer activists attended HCAN house parties, HCAN Rallies, and flooded HCAN's website with comments about single-payer.
[55] Representative John Conyers (D-MI) statement in support of HCAN. October 2008.

"feet to the fire."[56] There was even some discussion of no longer calling H.R. 676 the "Conyers Bill" or developing a new bill altogether. Others argued that Conyers was "playing a waiting game" until Obama was elected, at which point he would start pushing for single-payer in earnest. They encouraged activists to focus on building the movement and not arguing about this divisive issue. This event illustrates the contradictory—and yet collective identity building—aspect of narrative, which can result in disagreements about which narrative understanding, and thus which actions, will become dominant within a SMO.[57]

Conyers was quick to address this conflict by attending the annual strategy meeting of Healthcare NOW in November of 2008 where he directly addressed the 100 activists that were present. In his keynote talk, Conyers explained that, although H.R. 676 had over 90 cosponsors at that time, single-payer supporters were up against incredible odds in the current debate about healthcare reform. He also explained that President Elect Obama was not going to support single-payer and that many single-payer supporters still believed that it was not politically feasible. Thus, they would remain in the "closet" while supporting the Obama administration's agenda for healthcare reform. However, he assured the gathered activists that he was still one of them saying,

> I consider you my extended family, because we believe in the same thing, we're related by ideology. Because we share the same world view, not on everything, but on this subject we are one and that's why we're gonna win.[58]

This reassurance mollified single-payer activists, but the tension between this grassroots group and the political figures that had supported single-payer in the past would be a reoccurring issue as the debate surrounding healthcare reform came to the forefront of public and political discourse.

Politicians who did not sway from the goal of single-payer became important protagonists in the single-payer narrative at this time. The election of Eric Massa (D-NY) to the House of Representatives played a prominent role in their narrative practice at this time. According to the action narrative of his election, Massa, a cancer survivor and former Navy

---

[56] Fieldnotes: Activist, Healthcare NOW conference call October 2008.

[57] Polletta, Francesca. 2006. *It Was Like a Fever: Story Telling in Protest and Politics.* University of Chicago Press.

[58] Fieldnotes: Representative John Conyers, Key Note Address, Healthcare NOW Annual Strategy Meeting, 2008.

sailor who was "alive due to single-payer health care,"[59] was elected in a conservative district in New York through a campaign based on a single-payer platform, making him the most "improbable member of Congress."[60] Although Massa encouraged activists not to make the Obama sponsored plan that would be developed the "enemy of perfection,"[61] he became a stalwart supporter of single-payer during the healthcare reform debate that ensued. While other political agents important to the SPM were perceived as wavering in their support, Massa became known as the politician who would absolutely not accept anything less than single-payer. This was an important boon for the SPM. However, the most salient aspect of the narrative surrounding Massa's election was not that it resulted in another political agent that supported single-payer, but that it illustrated what single-payer activists narratively defined as grassroots support for single-payer. Even after Massa resigned due to allegations of sexual harassment in March of 2010, the narrative of his election was still useful as an illustration of positive grassroots opportunity for the SPM because he had been elected by a conservative public using a single-payer platform.

According to this identity building opportunity narrative, the SPM was the "real grassroots movement," regardless of how much funding or political support HCAN had.

> We are doing that [holding meetings] around the country. We don't have the funding that HCAN has but I have in front of me the list[62] of tactics and activities that are going on. We've got a lot of energy behind us. The movement **for H.R. 676** is strong and HCAN knows that.[63]

The grassroots activities that were happening around the country, as well as the creation of new grassroots single-payer organizations, such as the "Private Insurance Must Go Coalition" and the "Leadership Conference for Guaranteed Health Care," were cited as evidence that the grassroots support that would be necessary to push for single-payer, via support of H.R. 676, during the upcoming debate on healthcare reform was there. Although this narrative indicated that there was less grassroots

---

[59] Fieldnotes: Representative Eric Massa, Key Note Address, MoSP Annual Health Care Weekend April 2009.

[60] Ibid.

[61] Fieldnotes: Representative Eric Massa, MoSP Dinner Party, April 2009.

[62] See Fig. 5.1 for a timeline sampling of activities.

[63] Katie, Healthcare NOW conference call, Oct. 2008.

opportunity for single-payer due to the activities of HCAN and it disconnected the focused single-payer organizations from HCAN, it also served to support the empowering identity building action narrative that Healthcare Now, and its affiliate organizations, was the center of the "real grassroots" movement for healthcare reform. This identity building action narrative encouraged single-payer activists to continue to act in ways that would convince a wider audience that they should support the "real grassroots" which was rooted in a grassroots, rather than political, understanding of the case for healthcare reform. As the debate surrounding healthcare reform came to the forefront of most political discourse in Washington D.C., it became even more important that those groups that did support single-payer join forces, organize, and form a collective strategy.

FIGHTING FOR A SEAT AT THE TABLE: COALESCENCE WITHIN THE SINGLE PAYER MOVEMENT

One of the most significant differences between the Obama period of healthcare reform and the Clinton period of healthcare reform is the extent to which mobilizing structures existed *before* the start of each period. Mobilizing structures are "those collective vehicles, informal as well as formal, through which people mobilize and engage in collective action."[64] While several pre-existing multi-issue organizations supported single-payer during the Clinton era (i.e. Church Women United, The Gray Panthers, Neighbor to Neighbor, etc.) and these acted as important mobilizing structures during this period, the organizations that were focused on the sole issue of single payer (i.e. United Health Care Action Network, Missourians for Single Payer, etc.) did not really develop until that period of healthcare reform debate was already underway. Their development was rooted in the political opportunity that the new Clinton administration represented. Although the grassroots movement in support of single-payer at the national level did go through a period of abeyance following the failure of that period, its infrastructure and mobilizing potential continued to develop after the "death" of healthcare reform—largely through state-based movements. "While the beltway and people 'who knew better' did little after 1994, it has been single-payer advocates who continued more than anybody to do the hard work of actually

---

[64] McAdam, Doug. 1999. *Political Process and the Development of Black Insurgency. 1930–1970*. Second Edition. Chicago: University of Chicago Press, p. 3.

building a grassroots infrastructure and support."[65] Several organizations had continued to mobilize at the state level, and several new national organizations (i.e. Healthcare NOW and Progressive Democrats of America-PDA) were formed during the G.W. Bush period.[66] By the time the Obama era healthcare reform debate started, the SPM had developed an extensive network of mobilizing structures that used traditional, as well as newly formed internet-based structures, to push for single-payer.

The political, professional, and grassroots organizations that supported single-payer prior to the Obama era of healthcare reform refined their alliance structure during this period in order to more efficiently push for single-payer through a collective strategy focused on beltway politics. Two organizations had formed during the administration of G.W. Bush and eventually became allies in the SPM—Healthcare NOW and Progressive Democrats of America (PDA). Two professional organizations also played a major role during this period of healthcare reform—Physicians for a National Program—PNHP (which had formed in 1987 in order to specifically push for single-payer) and the California Nurses Association (CNA),[67] which had also played a major role in supporting the California-based single-payer ballot initiative during the Clinton era. In the period between the Clinton era and the Obama era, these organizations had grown substantially. The membership of PNHP had grown to 16,000 by the start of this period, and CNA was forming a national organizing force known as the National Nurses United (NNU).[68] These four organizations formalized their alliance in the fall of 2008 by forming the umbrella organization The Leadership Conference for Guaranteed Health Care (LCGHC).

The LCGHC was formed in order to "have a visible impact in DC in the next year, to show the *H.R. 676 movements'* great diversity and strength."[69] While Healthcare NOW, PDA, PNHP, and CNA were considered to be the "four partners"[70] of this new mobilizing structure,

[65] Dr. Steve B, Single Payer to HCAN: We Will Not NOT Be Listened to, posted July 19, 2008, www.pnhp.org.

[66] See Chap. 4 for details.

[67] National Nurses United (NNU) had 170,000 members in "every state," 31 State and Local Chapters in 15 states. http://www.nationalnursesunited.org/pages/about.

[68] This is a unification of California Nurses Association/National Nurses Organizing Committee, United American Nurses, and Massachusetts Nurses Association occurred in the winter of 2009.

[69] Tom, Healthcare NOW Conference Call, Sept. 2008.

[70] Ibid.

importance was also placed upon encouraging other multi-issue organizations that had supported single-payer in the past (i.e. NOW, Unitarian Universalists, etc.) to join this coalition and actively push for single-payer. While many of these multi-issue organizations supported single-payer theoretically (as illustrated through resolutions passed and official policy recommendations), most favored actively supporting organizations, such as HCAN, that supported more general principles for healthcare reform rather than a specific policy, because single-payer was still not defined as "politically feasible."[71] Others supported this new umbrella organization in more practical, but less action oriented, ways. For example, during this cycle of healthcare reform debate, the United Methodist Church provided the LCGHC with office space in Washington D.C. This was an excellent resource for movement leaders, who began focusing on the beltway political issue of encouraging more congressional support for single-payer because it became

> clear that we must target Congress particularly at the Congressional District Level. We need new Congressional Targets—identify key actors in the House with leadership roles in Key Committees—new targets who need to be identified and added to the much stronger and expanded national coalition.[72]

The LCGHC also encouraged local groups to take advantage of the grassroots opportunity presented to them by focusing on "Outreach, Lobbying, Media, and Fundraising."[73]

The development of internet-based mobilizing structures, such as websites and social media networks, facilitated the efforts of local and national groups to participate in these efforts. Another significant difference from Clinton era of healthcare reform was that single-payer organizations active during the Obama era had ready access to material culture, via the internet, that would allow them to share their counter-narratives with a larger segment of the public. Many organizations had already begun to network via social media sites such as Facebook, and a few, such as Healthcare NOW, had developed YouTube channels. These new internet-based

---

[71] Unnamed caller, Healthcare NOW conference call, Sept. 2008.
[72] Tom, Healthcare NOW Conference Call, December 2008.
[73] Ibid.

mobilizing structures were also integral to the development of the more radical tactics that became important during the end of this era.

The existing mobilizing structures formed a well-developed infrastructure for the SPM prior to the Obama period of healthcare reform. This enabled single-payer activists to take advantage of the opportunities that existed during this period. This in itself is an issue important to grassroots opportunity. It allowed single-payer activists to mobilize a wider audience and adapt more quickly to the ever-changing conditions within the environment of opportunity—including the opportunity that changing economic realities represented.

The 800-Pound Gorilla: Economic Crisis or Economic Opportunity?

> The economic crisis is the 800 lb. gorilla that will impact whatever we do on a national and local level. We have to respond to this crisis by linking the bailouts of Wall Street and the refusal to deal with Main Street. We must be bolder and offer solutions that are going to show the hypocrisy of Congress and our leaders.[74]

The economic crisis that the United States was just starting to address during the first year of the Obama administration (2009) also became defined as a source of grassroots opportunity. The Obama administration chose to act on the economic crisis as an opportunity to go forward with healthcare reform.[75] Economic turmoil can often encourage the public to question the supremacy of hegemonic economic narratives.[76] While this economic crisis could have been, and was by a minority within the SPM, defined as a negative aspect of the environment of opportunity because it could become "another excuse, for politicians, why we can't afford to do this for everyone,"[77] the dominant conclusion of this narrative of economic opportunity was that it represented an opportunity to mobilize a public that would become disenchanted with for-profit health care, to convince political agents (through effective uses of grassroots opportunity) that the best

---

[74] Josephine, Single Payer New York, Online Interview, Nov. 25, 2008.

[75] Jacobs, Lawrence, and Theda Skocpol. 2010. *Health Care Reform and American Politics: What Everyone Needs to Know.* Oxford University Press.

[76] Amenta, Edwin. 2006. *When Movements Matter: The Townsend Plan & the Rise of Social Security.* Princeton University Press.

[77] Linda, New Mexico for Single Payer, Online Interview, Nov. 25, 2008.

solution to the crisis would be to implement a cost-saving single-payer plan, and to "make a better economic case for reform."[78]

The economic crisis represented the opportunity for grassroots mobilization because single-payer activists believed that it would encourage the public to question the hegemonic economic narrative that came to the forefront of American politics following the Clinton era of healthcare reform and during the development of the "Contract With America." According to this opportunity narrative, the "Government response to the crisis could improve the chances of public looking more favorably on involvement of government."[79] Single-payer activists began to argue that "the economic crisis is opportunity"[80] that would "open some doors for Healthcare NOW,"[81] and concluded that they should take advantage of this opportunity in any way possible. In his address to the gathered activists at the 2008 annual Healthcare NOW meeting, Dr. Arthur MacEwan summarized the issue in this way,

> The most important opening created by current crisis is that it discredits the ideology and the idea that free markets are the only way to go in finance and in general. The end of the argument changes—government involvement is no longer bad—Laissez Faire is over. You know that something is different as a result of the events of the last year or so. What's happening with finance—what's happening with the automobile industry is that that ideology doesn't work. When crisis exists in the economy—there are possibilities for political change that weren't there before. We should certainly take advantage of that. We can be preemptive about Baucus, Kennedy, and Obama. There is the possibility for pushing, now is the time.[82]

This period of economic crisis was defined by single-payer activists as a period in which the dominance of the free-market ideology would be questioned, and anti-government sentiment would lessen, within the public.

Single-payer activists began discussing ways in which they could garner support for single-payer by convincing the public, as well as politicians, that single-payer could, in part, solve the economic crisis. They worked to

[78] Richard, Executive Director of Vermont Citizens Campaign for Health, Online Interview, Nov. 25, 2008.

[79] Legislator from the South West and Single Payer Advocate, Online Interview, Nov. 25, 2008.

[80] Josephine, N.Y. Single Payer, Online Interview, Nov. 25, 2008.

[81] Male Single Payer Advocate—Eastern United States, Online Interview, Nov. 25, 2008.

[82] Fieldnotes: Healthcare NOW National Strategy meeting, October 2008.

"link comprehensive single-payer health care reform as a vital part of the reform package for economic recovery. Definitely civil rights/human rights but also the failure of the free market to benefit people and anti-corporate sentiment."[83] Many single-payer activists argued that they should focus on pointing out that "single-payer will actually save the US government and the US economy at least $350 billion per year"[84] and driving home the point that "healthcare is a significant part of our economic crisis. Real healthcare reform could lift all boats, make business more competitive, and provide relief for federal and state budgets."[85] In Maryland the plan was to "emphasize that going to a national/state single-payer universal healthcare plan will save BUCKETS of money! More people will fall into healthcare crises and the struggle will therefore become even more important".[86] Healthcare NOW included these assessments of the economic crisis in their funding solicitation emails for online donations. This time period did result in an increase in a material component of economic opportunity, donations to Healthcare NOW, which reached a new high in June of 2009 with almost 12,000 dollars being donated that month. The previous high had been 6,667 dollars in May 2009.

This narrative of economic opportunity became important in the SPM's criticism of the HCAN position on healthcare reform. The position of single-payer activists was that "incremental reforms help only a few and do not address the central problem, effectively delaying the ultimate requirement. It only benefits the insurance companies while the crisis and suffering remain," yet "HCAN is another diversion that takes single-payer allies away from the winning strategy."[87] The threat that HCAN could claim the grassroots opportunity that resulted from this economic opportunity was a very real concern for single-payer activists. However, some were also convinced that the economic crisis would "shut the door on the HCAN/ Obama Plan" which was still mired in the free market capitalist framework and that the public would realize that "it's now single-payer or nothing."[88]

Activists developed several tactics in order to act on this narrative of economic opportunity. While encouraging unions to join the SPM had

[83] Margaret Flowers M.D. Organizer for Maryland chapter of PNHP/then HCN board member/Online Interview, Nov. 25th, 2008.

[84] Aileen, then Vice President of United for National Health Care Bellingham Washington, Online Interview, Nov. 25th, 2008.

[85] Michele—Health Care for ALL Colorado, Online Interview, Nov. 25th, 2008.

[86] Jim, Maryland Healthcare NOW Chapter, Online Interview, Nov. 25th, 2008.

[87] Jim, Healthcare NOW Maryland and Veterans for Peace, Online Interview, Nov. 25th, 2008.

[88] Doug, Healthcare NOW New York, Online Interview, Nov. 25th, 2008.

long been a key factor in their movement building strategy, the economic crisis encouraged activists to increase their focus on union involvement. Kay Tillow, a Kentucky-based activist who had been working within the movement for decades, led a union involvement campaign through the organization "Unions for Single Payer Health Care"[89] that had already successfully persuaded "417 union organizations in 48 states including 107 Central Labor Councils and Area Labor Federations and 33 state AFL-CIO's"[90] to endorse H.R. 676, but this had not yet translated into the sponsorship of most national-level union organizations. The Labor Campaign for Single Payer (LCSPHC) was created in 2009, largely through the work of Healthcare NOW board member Mark Dudzic. The mission of the LCSPHC "is to increase and coordinate grassroots labor support for a Single-Payer Medicare-for-All healthcare system in America because we believe that health care is a fundamental human right and that the labor movement must take the lead in the fight for healthcare justice."[91] Convincing influential labor organizations, such as the AFL-CIO, to support single-payer became a central focus. Single-payer activists worked "to pressure the national , AFL-CIO from the grassroots up."[92] This strategy involved convincing local chapters of the AFL-CIO to endorse H.R. 676 and inspired a resolution campaign at the 2009 national meeting of the AFL-CIO. At this meeting, a resolution that stated "the task of establishing health care as a human right, not a privilege, will still lay before us. The single-payer approach is one the AFL-CIO supports and that merits dedicated congressional support and enactment"[93] was passed and it became "the policy of AFL-CIO to be the advocate of single-payer."[94] However, at the same meeting, a resolution was passed in support of the Obama administration's healthcare reform agenda.[95] Single-payer supporters at the meeting were adamant that "whoever speaks today, we have to say,

[89] For more info about this organization see: https://unionsforsinglepayer.org/.

[90] Kay, Healthcare NOW Conference Call October 2008.

[91] Labor Campaign for Single Payer Website "About" https://www.laborforsinglepayer.org/about/.

[92] Activist, Healthcare NOW Conference Call December 2008.

[93] Gaus, Mischa. "AFL-CIO Convention: Two health Care Solutions; Everybody's Happy" Posted on Sept. 15, 2009. https://www.labornotes.org/blogs/2009/09/afl-cio-convention-two-health-care-resolutions-everybodys-happy.

[94] Fieldnotes: Jerry, Healthcare NOW national strategy meeting, Nov. 2009.

[95] National Nurses Movement "AFL-CIO Endorses Single Payer Healthcare" Posted on Sept. 16, 2009. http://www.pnhp.org/news/2009/september/aflcio_endorses_sin.php.

passing a resolution isn't enough. All these unions pass single-payer reso-lutions. The AFL has to step up; the support has to mean something."[96]

Single-payer activists also further developed their campaign to acquire city endorsements of H.R. 676 in the context of the economic crisis through the development of the Win Win Campaign for Healthy Cities, which was spearheaded by Tom Knoche.[97] The Win Win Campaign, which was being developed as early as May 2008, was a "campaign to enlist local government officials, school boards and others in the campaign for pas-sage of H.R. 676."[98] The development of this campaign was based on the assessment that local government entities were also experiencing the eco-nomic crisis and should be informed of how much money they would save if the United States transitioned to a single-payer system. The campaign targeted,

> major employers, especially states, cities, towns, counties, and school boards—showing them how single-payer national health insurance would bring substantial savings in employee health care costs, and guarantee better coverage for all employees. In a time of economic crisis, national health insurance makes businesses more competitive, stimulates job creation, and helps those who have been hardest hit. HR 676 is a Win-Win that employers and workers can't ignore.[99]

This campaign was able to successfully acquire endorsements from 70 state and local governments,[100] as well as the endorsement of the American Conference of Mayors.[101]

[96] Rose Ann DeMoro, the California Nurses executive director quoted in Gaus, Mischa. "AFL-CIO Convention: Two health Care Solutions; Everybody's Happy" Posted on Sept. 15, 2009. https://www.labornotes.org/blogs/2009/09/afl-cio-convention-two-health-care-resolutions-everybodys-happy.

[97] As discussed in Chap. 4, the first city resolution was passed by University City in St. Louis Missouri in 2008, largely due to the work of Missourians for Single Payer.

[98] Healthcare NOW Conference Call June 2008.

[99] Agenda for 1/23/10 HCN Conference Call "Healthcare-NOW's HR 676 Win-Win Campaign" Available at: https://www.healthcare-now.org/docs/winwinnewres.pdf.

[100] Healthcare NOW Website "Win Win Campaign" http://www.healthcare-now.org/campaigns/win-win/.

[101] David Prensky, Quentin Young, and Alison Landes. "U.S. Conference of Mayors Backs Single-Payer National Health Insurance" Posted on June, 232,008. http://www.pnhp.org/news/2008/june/us_conference_of_m.php.

While it is clear that the SPM was able to use the economic crisis to successfully push for more endorsements from unions and local governments, it is less clear whether they were able to successfully use the narrative of economic opportunity in order to successfully address the grassroots opportunity that this time period also represented.[102] Their efforts to redefine single-payer as the only reform option that would successfully address the healthcare crisis in the eyes of the dominant healthcare reform organizations (HCAN) and dominant political agents in the healthcare reform debate were not successful. Instead, single-payer activists became progressively more marginalized within the movement for healthcare reform, and this, in combination with perceived grassroots opportunity, the opportunity presented by new forms of material culture, and the SPM's narratively affirmed identity as the "real grassroots," resulted in the use of more radical tactics in order to put single-payer "on the table."

ZOMBIES AND DIE-INS: RADICALIZATION OF SINGLE-PAYER TACTICS

None of us wants there to be no real reform (even if it is a first step) in 2009–2010!
But do not ignore us.
Do not tell us to shut up.
Do not tell us to go away.
Do not ask for our support after the fact.
So here is a deal ... You include single payer advocates at the table from the beginning, you leave single payer in as an option, and I (speaking just for myself, not necessarily PNHP as an organization) won't insist on it as the only option. This is just the beginning of the fight with AHIP, Pharma, the for-profit hospitals ... there's no need to take any of our chips off the table before real negotiations even begin. Let us organize and fight together.[103]

Directly following the election of Barack Obama to the presidency, single-payer activists began to focus on making sure that they had a seat at

---

[102] Although they were able to mobilize more grassroots funding resources—see funding chart (Fig. 5.1).

[103] Dr. Steve B. "Single Payer to HCAN: We Will NOT Not Be Listened To! July 19, 2008 www.pnhp.org.

the table during the debate surrounding healthcare reform. Single-payer activists were still cautiously optimistic that,

> His presidency provides an opening for real healthcare reform, but it means that HC-NOW will need to prove that there is a mandate from the public and that SP can be passed by Congress. Best courses of action are expanded grassroots organizing, deeper and smarter Congressional District lobbying, emphasizing cost savings, and exposing problems with incremental proposals.[104]

Although the public support of single-payer was still an important factor in the single-payer narrative and mobilizing the grassroots was viewed as a vital objective, the SPM initially focused on beltway politics. Partly because they expected "his presidency to provide a friendlier, more favorable atmosphere in the struggle for single-payer"[105] and partly because single-payer activists believed that they still had extensive political support, a beltway-centered strategy that used conventional tactics was initially deemed the best route to achieving single-payer.

This beltway-centered strategy included staffing an office in D.C., encouraging past H.R. 676 sponsors to re-enlist, pushing more congressional office holders to endorse H.R. 676, and forcing single-payer into the debate on healthcare reform. They organized letter writing campaigns based on congressional districts in an attempt to meet Obama's requirement of a "mandate" that could put single-payer on the table. When single-payer politicians were not invited to the Health Care Summit organized by President Obama in March of 2009, single-payer activists organized a nationwide call in day, which, according to the action narrative of this mobilization effort, successfully resulted in Representatives John Conyers and Dennis Kucinich being invited to the forum at the last minute.

Single-payer activists also held rallies and lobbying days in D.C., as well as demonstrations at local congressional offices.[106] On June 30th, 2009, Medicare's 44th birthday, I attended a single-payer day of action in Washington D.C. I spent the morning with Representative Eric Massa (D–NY) touring the capitol building—I even got to take a ride in "Nancy

---

[104] Josephine, N.Y. Single Payer, Online Interview, Nov. 25th, 2008.
[105] Jim, Healthcare NOW Maryland and Veterans for Peace, Online Interview, Nov. 25th, 2008.
[106] See Fig. 5.1 for a sampling of these activities.

Pelosi's private elevator."[107] I discussed with Massa and his legislative director, Ron Hikel, the process of healthcare reform that was ongoing in the halls of congress. Massa explained that he was doing everything that he could to insert the single-payer option into the debate, but he was experiencing pressure from more established Democrats to desist (this was Massa's first and only term). He said that he planned to persist and resist instead. Following this tour and discussion, I participated in a rally of over 1000 single-payer supporters. The energy and enthusiasm for single-payer was palpable at this rally. The gathered activists had spent the morning visiting the halls of congress and delivering "cupcakes and birthday cards to honor Medicare to every member of Congress."[108] They continued to lobby congress throughout the day. At the rally, which took place at Upper Senate Park, several influential leaders of the movement spoke—including Donna Smith, Representative John Conyers (D-MI), and Senator Bernie Sanders (I-VT). They all encouraged the crowd to continue the fight for single-payer because the general consensus was that "this is the time—the time is NOW."[109] Sanders urged the gathered activists to continue the fight saying,

> You are fighting a system. The moral issue is that healthcare is a right and not a commodity ... The truth is that it should not just be progressives that are for a single-payer system it should be conservatives ... The reason is that for every dollar that you put into a system you want as much of that dollar as possible to do what it is supposed to do ... So, what we've got to do not just today or tomorrow, but every single day, is to go back to all of our 50 states and rally millions and millions of people, so when the current absurd system fails, to move us toward a single-payer system.

[107] Eric Mass (D-NY) while on capitol tour. Nancy Pelosi was then speaker of the house and the elevator used was designated for the use of the speaker according to Massa.

[108] Healthcare NOW blog "Report of Medicare's 44th Birthday" July 2009. https://www.healthcare-now.org/blog/report-on-medicares-44th-birthday-july-30-2009/.

[109] "Dr. David Scheiner, Obama's personal physician of 22 years who is calling for President to enact Medicare for all, State Senator Jim Ferlo who gathered over 100 signatures from fellow state legislators in support of HR 676, Terry O'Neil, President of National Organization for Women, Rep. John Conyers, Sen. Bernie Sanders, Tim Carpenter (National Director of PDA), Medea Benjamin (Code Pink and Global Exchange), Donna Smith (California Nurses Association and co-chair of PDA's Healthcare NOT Warfare Campaign) and Baucus 8 arrestees: Mark Dudzic (Labor Party), Dr. Margaret Flowers (PNHP) and Katie Robbins (Healthcare Now!), and various union leaders." Ibid.

Following the rally, the crowd marched across the quad chanting "Everybody In! Nobody Out!" after which many of the activists continued to engage in citizen lobbying by visiting the offices of their congressional representatives.

Single-payer supporters had also been attending town hall meetings held by President Obama in an effort to insert single-payer into those discussions. At the town hall meeting held in Rio Rancho, New Mexico, on May 14, 2009, it became clear to single-payer activists that the Obama administration would not accept single-payer as a valid option. At this meeting, Obama responded to a question regarding single-payer saying that it would be an option only if they could "start from scratch" but that he would focus on maintaining and expanding the current employment-based system because,

> The only problem is that we're not starting from scratch. We have historically a tradition of employer-based healthcare. And although there are a lot of people who are not satisfied with their healthcare, the truth is, is that the vast majority of people currently get healthcare from their employers and you've got this system that's already in place. We don't want a huge disruption as we go into healthcare reform where suddenly we're trying to completely reinvent one-sixth of the economy.[110]

Single-payer activists began to understand that they would need to work extremely hard to have a seat at the table. At the Medicare birthday rally, which followed this town hall, Representative John Conyers explained that,

> That's why this rally is important. The more members that know that there are more and more people coming to this position, it makes it easier for them to come to this position. And that's the whole idea—that's what the rally is about. To wake up our colleagues to understand that we know what's going down. And reading a thousand-page bill is not what's going down. ... The public option is being modified and compromised ... they tell me that's going on in Waxman's committee right now. The senate has already announced—no public option period. Well, then what are we doing? We're facilitating the insurance company industry even more now—by now making it a law that you've got to get insured even if you don't have any money.[111]

[110] President Barack Obama, Town Hall Meeting, New Mexico, May 2009. https://www.koat.com/article/transcript-obama-s-rio-rancho-town-hall-meeting-on-credit-card-reform/5030242.

[111] Video interview posted by Bill Hughes on YouTube, July 30, 2009. "Rep. John Conyers Jr. on HR 676, at Capitol Hill Rally." https://www.youtube.com/watch?v=5120xwMCPfs.

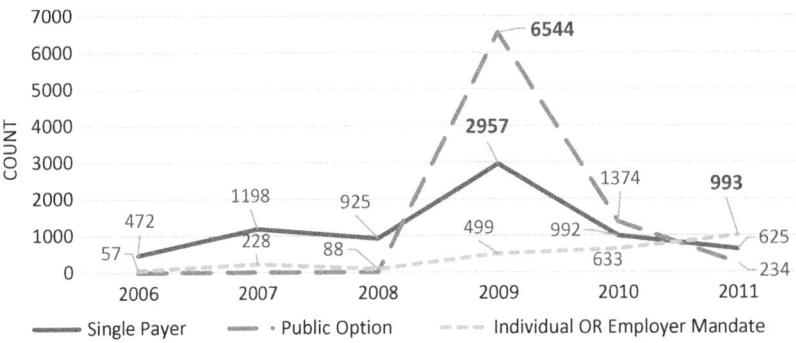

Fig. 5.2 Single Payer in Newspapers during the Obama era

Political leaders of the SPM continued to urge grassroots single-payer activists to push for single-payer as it became more obvious to them that even the compromised position of creating a public option would fail.

In addition to critiquing the political establishment for not including the single-payer option in the discussions dealing with healthcare reform, single-payer activists also critiqued the media "blackout"[112] that they were experiencing when their efforts to shape the debate and gain a seat at the table were not reported in mainstream news media. As illustrated in Fig. 5.2, my own analysis of news media coverage of single-payer during this period shows that while there was an increase in coverage of single-payer, the discussion of single-payer was significantly less extensive than the coverage of the public option at this time. However, it is interesting that both the public option and single-payer were discussed more frequently than individual and employer mandates combined, coverage of which peaked later in the period.[113]

Although they were already participating in many actions around the country, including demonstrations in front of insurance companies and candlelight vigils for those who had died due to the for-profit healthcare

[112] Healthcare NOW conference call Oct. 2008.

[113] Figure 5.2 is based on the comparison of three searches limited to newspaper articles within the Nexis Uni database system using the search terms, ""single payer"" AND (""healthcare"" OR ""health care""), "Public Option" AND (Healthcare OR ""Health care""), and (""Individual Mandate"" OR ""Employer Mandate"") AND (Healthcare OR ""Health care"").

system, according to this narrative these actions were not being covered by mainstream media. Through Fairness and Accuracy in Reporting (FAIR), activists started an online "petition to **ABC**, **CBS** and **NBC**, demanding that single-payer be a part of their coverage of the healthcare debate."[114] The SPM also used alternative media forms, including YouTube, with increased vigor. Most actions were recorded and then posted to one of the YouTube channels[115] in an effort to increase the audience for these actions and to provide evidence to the public that there was a vibrant grassroots movement in support of single-payer. These alternative media forms became progressively more important as activists began to commit to more non-conventional forms of activism.

Non-conventional forms of activism are more costly than institutionalized forms, such as citizen lobbying, or more conventional forms, such as sponsoring educational programs. Direct action requires more participants to be effective—it only takes one or two activists to lobby a politician or conduct an educational program, but a rally or demonstration with "less than 500 people is just not worth it."[116] Radical forms of non-conventional activism also come with a higher risk of legal repercussions.

Radical tactics, such as acts of civil disobedience, also require a higher degree of performance than other types of institutionalized actions. Although it has been argued that all activism requires some degree of performance,[117] some actions are more performance oriented than others. Rachel V. Kutz-Flamenbaum[118] calls this type of political activity "performance activism" when the performance activity is highly structured. According to Kutz-Flamenbaum, in order to be labeled a performance an action must include one or more of the following characteristics—costumes, skits, actions, song, dance, and "staying in character." I would add to this list of characteristics the importance of shared scripts and staging in

[114] Democracy in Action Petition. 2009. http://salsa.democracyinaction. org/o/592/t/9039/petition.jsp?petition_KEY=1993.

[115] For example, youtube channels; see http://www.youtube.com/user/healthcare-now4all, http://www.youtube.com/user/Singlepayeraction, http://www.youtube.com/user/singlepayermedia, http://www.youtube.com/user/singlepayer1.

[116] Fieldnotes: Don Bechler, Healthcare NOW National Strategy Meeting, Nov. 2009.

[117] Tarrow, Sidney. 1994. *Power in Movement*. Cambridge: Cambridge University Press.

[118] Kutz-Flamenbaum, Rachel V. 2007. "Code Pink, Raging Grannies, and the Missile Dick Chicks: Feminist Performance Activism in the Contemporary Anti-War Movement." *NWSA Journal* 19, no. 1: 89–105.

relation to an audience. Scripts are important to political performance because they give activist performers a unified narrative through which they state their position and attempt to change the frame of the discourse surrounding a particular issue. Although performance activism does not typically occur on a theatrical stage, the staging of the performance is no less important. The staging of a political performance is related to the intended audience for a particular action and affects the reach of the narrative that is told through the performance. Staging can also invoke greater, or less, audience participation depending on whether the audience is easily able to access the stage. All of these factors can make participation in performance activism more or less accessible for audience members. For example, an action that uses the street as a stage and involves minimal scripting, character development, or costuming is more permeable—or open to audience participation—than an action that takes place on an actual stage involving a more formalized production. All of these factors also make performance activism more costly than other types of activism due to the time required to develop the performance, and this cost increases as the performance becomes more structured. Consider the difference in the prep time required for a rally to which activists can just show up with a sign in comparison to a structured performance that requires the preparation of a script, the learning of that script by the activists, rehearsal time, and the time it takes to develop costumes and props.

These costs make reaching a wider receptive audience through the performance even more important in order to increase the benefits of the action. This is a key consideration for activists when they make decisions about the staging of a performance. An audience is an integral part and the primary focus of any performance. Performances are inherently interactive. The level of permeability between the audience and the activist changes depending on how structured the performance is[119] and what the organizational goals for the performance are.[120] Activist performers construct who their audience will be, assign meaning and value to this audience, and assess how influential audiences are, as well as how likely they are

---

[119] Ibid.
[120] Hern, Lindy (2018) "Derby Dames and Gender Games: Empowerment and Critical Gender Performance in the Derby Girl Revolution." In *Critical Perspectives on Gender and Sport*, ed. Curtis Fogel. Common Ground Publishing.

to be influenced.[121] The audience's understanding of movement narratives, the increased involvement of the audience, and the degree to which a collective identity is formed during the performance are measures that are also important to the assessment of a political performance.[122]

When social movement actors perceive that there is public interest in and support for their goals (grassroots opportunity), but less political interest or support, non-conventional activism using performance becomes more likely.[123] However, if the social movement activists are not able to reach this wider receptive audience, the costs of performance may outweigh the benefits. Ideally, performance activity would encourage the coverage of mainstream media, but as performance became a common aspect of political organizing, it also began to draw less media attention.[124] Single-payer demonstrations that involved some degree of performance were still subject to the "media blackout" experienced by movement activists at this time. But, new forms of internet-based media allowed single-payer activists to share their performances, and their narratives, with a wider audience.

The combination of perceived grassroots opportunity in form of public support for single-payer, cultural opportunity in the form of decentralized media outlets, and negative political opportunity during the debate surround healthcare reform resulted in single-payer activists taking on progressively more non-conventional performance-based tactics. The breadth of these tactics cannot be unpacked here, and notable activities will not be covered (such as the actions of the Mad As Hell Doctors).[125] However, the following activities are representative of this issue and the progression to more radical performance-based tactics that occurred during this period.

---

[121] Blee, Kathleen, and Amy McDowell. 2012. "Social Movement Audiences." *Sociological Forum* 27, no. 1: 1–20.

[122] Rupp, Leila, and Verta Taylor. 2003. *Drag Queens at the 801 Cabaret.* Chicago: University of Chicago Press.

[123] Grodsky, Brian. 2007. ""Resource Dependency and Political Opportunity: Explaining the Transformation from Excluded Political Opposition Parties to Human Rights Organizations in Post-Communist Uzbekistan."" *Government & Opposition* 42, no. 1: 96–120.

[124] McAdam, Doug, Sidney Tarrow, and Charles Tilly. 2001. *Dynamics of Contention.* Cambridge: Cambridge University Press.

[125] Mad as Hell Doctors (MADH) is a group of "Physicians and Advocates" from Oregon and California who mobilized in August 2009 and set out on a 3-week caravan to Washington D.C.—stopping at single-payer rallies and events along the way. They visited "30 towns and cities in 15 states" and "attracted 6000 participants." http://madashelldoctors.com/about/.

THE BAUCUS 8[126]

When Senator Max Baucus (D-MT), who was then the chair of the senate finance committee, held "health care roundtables" in the spring of 2009, single-payer was once again left off the table. While Baucus claimed that the round tables would address all perspectives in the debate on healthcare reform, the single-payer perspective was excluded. This incensed single-payer activists and made the "blood of single-payer supporters boil."[127] According to the single-payer action narrative of these roundtables,

> Senator Baucus, chair of the Senate Finance Committee, convened the May Roundtable to kick off the public consideration of the 111th Congress' legislative proposals for healthcare reform. The Leadership Conference for Guaranteed Health Care, a coalition of nurses, doctors, labor, faith, health advocate and community groups representing over 20 million people nationwide, sent a request to the Finance Committee for one of their leaders testify. When this was denied, thousands of single-payer supporters across the nation contacted the committee to request that single-payer be included. "Despite the outpouring of requests," said Katie Robbins of Healthcare-Now.org, "we were clearly told that we would be excluded. This cemented our growing impression that the healthcare debate was at best, political theater, and that we would have to try a different tactic in order that the only really affordable health reform solution, that addresses the real health care needs of 100% of our nation be heard."[128]

Several single-payer activists did not accept the exclusion of the single-payer perspective and decided to take the more radical action of "disrupting" the roundtables by forcing the case for single-payer into the discussion. These activists became known as the "Baucus 8," although several additional protestors also participated in this tactic.

The Baucus 8 were "all trying to find ways to make sure that this time when Congress and the White House addressed health care reform, that we actually had an open and honest debate about health care reform,

---

[126] Also sometimes referred to as "The Baucus 13."
[127] Helen Redmond for Counterpunch, "I Prefer Single-Payer, But ...." July 28, 2009 Single Payer News. www.healthcare-now.org.
[128] "Probation Ends for Baucus 8" Healthcare-NOW! Updates, January 8, 2010. https://www.healthcare-now.org/blog/probation-ends-for-baucus-8/.

about what was best for the people of our nation."[129] When Baucus invited "around 43 people or so to testify, not one of which represented what we wanted, what we believed the majority of the American people wanted,"[130] these activists took direct action in order to bring the single-payer perspective to the table. It became essential for these activists to "pierce the veil and let everyone see what's really going on,"[131] which was defined by single-payer activists as "political theater."[132] The hearings were "really conversations of interest groups, and the interest groups that weren't there were the patients and the providers. And that offends. It offends! Such a misrepresentation of democracy is so troubling, it's really worth getting arrested for."[133] The troubling nature of this hearing process, along with the potential to reach a supportive public by "lifting the veil," made this action worth the heavy cost and risk of arrest associated with acts of civil disobedience.

Several elements of performance were present in the actions of the Baucus 8. Although this action did not utilize elaborate costumes, there was an element of costuming for the Baucus 8. This included wearing single-payer accoutrement (i.e. buttons, t-shirts) and red articles of clothing, along with their otherwise professional attire. Disrupting the roundtables also involved a short script. The Baucus protesters understood that they would peacefully repeat the phrase "We (single-payer supporters, patients, providers) want a seat at the table." They were asking to have the voices of patients, providers, and healthcare activists be valued and heard as part of the discussion. Rather than complying with this request, Baucus is quoted as saying "We need more police."[134] Each of the single-payer supporters that spoke out at the roundtables was arrested and dealt with the consequences. Supporting them through their arraignments and court dates became a rallying point for other single-payer activists.

[129] Margaret Flowers M.D. Video transcript. "Baucus 8 One Year Later: Path to Victory." http://www.youtube.com/watch?v=aMdwK3R3iok&feature=plcp&context=C46b3c41V DvjVQa1PpcFPY_sGg5dz8qrcs5j99FM5C0zzXPnUH0ys%3D.

[130] Russel Mokhiber, Esq. of www.singlepayeraction.org, ibid.

[131] Kevin Zeese, Esq. of www.prosperityagenda.us, ibid.

[132] Katie, Organizer for Healthcare NOW, ibid. It is important to note that I am not using the term political performance or performance activism in the same way that Katie is using the term "political theater," which refers to the perceived farcical or fake quality of the roundtable proceedings.

[133] Pat Solomon-Rodriguez M.D. www.pnhp.org, ibid.

[134] Healthcare NOW Blog "Baucus 8 Update." http://www.healthcare-now.org/baucus-8-update-single-payer-in-the-news/.

Another key aspect of this political performance is the importance placed upon staging in relation to a particular audience. The staging for this action was oriented toward multiple audiences. The Senate Finance Committee, including Senator Baucus, was one audience, but perhaps not the most important one. The emphasized audience in the action narrative of this activity was not Baucus or the committee, but the American public that was defined as supportive of "real reform," but unaware of the biased nature of the proceedings. This made it imperative that the action reach a wider audience beyond those who were present at the proceedings. The actions of the Baucus protestors "received great media coverage from Bill Moyers, Ed Shultz, and other mainstream media outlets."[135] Single-payer activists were also able to distribute this performance tactic to an even wider audience by sharing videos of the action and interviews with the activists online through YouTube channels and organizational web pages.

Although only a small segment of the SPM actually participated in this action, the individuals who participated and were arrested due to their participation became folk heroes within the single-payer narrative. They were asked to give lectures about this experience to single-payer groups around the country. Supporting them during their legal battles and court dates became a rallying point for further single-payer activity. Their actions during this early period of the debate on healthcare reform had a lasting impact on the single-payer narrative and single-payer activities.

A few of these folk heroes of the SPM also became semi-public faces within the debate on healthcare reform. Katie Robbins, head organizer for Healthcare NOW and a member of the Baucus 8, became a key public face of the SPM. An article, in the Vows section of the February 18, 2010, issue of *The New York Times*, discussed Katie's support for single-payer, as well as her involvement in the protests of the Finance Committee hearings, and explained that she had finally married her long-time partner "For love and health,"[136] because she had insurance coverage and he didn't. Single-payer activists were enthused when Dr. Margaret Flowers, another

[135] Katie, Healthcare NOW Conference Call June 2008—See also See Crowley, Cathleen. 2010 "Doctor Arrested Twice in Bid for Reform" The Times-Union (Albany, NY), February 5, 2010 Friday, CAPITAL REGION; Pg. D4/Eggen, Dan. "Backers of 'Single-Payer' Insurance Challenge Democrats," *Washington Post*, June 7, 2009 Pg. A01/Curtis, Abigail. "South Thomaston activist arrested at Senate Session," *Bangor Daily News*, May 15, 2009 pg. A8/. http://www.pbs.org/moyers/journal/02052010/profile3.html.

[136] Abbey Ellin, "Vows: Katie Robbins and Philip Swift," *New York Times*, February 18, 2010.

folk hero of the SPM, was asked to explain her experience as a member of the Baucus protestors for NBC's Frontline special "Obama's Deal" which aired on April 13, 2010. However, single-payer activists were disappointed that when the program aired the single-payer perspective was cut from the discussion. According to Dr. Flowers,

> The producers at Frontline carefully cut single-payer out of the film. When the host, Mr. [Michael] Kirk, interviewed me for "Obama's Deal," we spoke extensively of the single payer movement and my arrest with other single-payer advocates in the Senate Finance Committee last May. However, our action in Senate Finance was then misidentified as "those on the left" who had led a "counter attack" because of "liberal outrage" at being excluded.[137]

The narrative of the performance action—that single-payer was being left off the table—was reframed as "the power of the insurance lobby and showed how activists like Dr. Flowers were excluded from the debate over the bill."[138] According to Ken Dornstein of PBS, the single-payer perspective was left out of their coverage of the debate because,

> Obama's Deal" was centered on the political process that led to the final reform bill, and on what that process revealed about the president and his style of governance during his critical first year in office. While there is much to say about the merits of the single-payer idea—and about the politics of why it did not, in the end, figure significantly in this past year's debate—this issue ultimately fell outside the scope of this single hour of television. This is not "censorship," as Dr. Flowers argues, it's the work of journalism to report widely on a topic, then find the sharpest focus for his or her reporting, unfortunately leaving out much strong material along the way to shaping the clearest communication possible in the time or space allowed.[139]

While this might be true, the PBS Ombudsman, Michael Getler, received "almost a thousand critical e-mails"[140] that dealt with this program. Getler concluded that,

---

[137] Margaret Flowers M.D. in "Frontline Disguises Single-Payer Advocates as Public Option Promoters" By Peter Hart for FAIR, April 21, 2010.

[138] Michael Kirk—Obama's Deal producer—response to criticisms of Dr. Flowers in "Single-Minded about Single-Payer: The Ombudsman Column by Michael Getler of PBS.

[139] Ibid.

[140] Ibid.

while the hard-nosed journalistic decision may be to focus on the real options and debate, it seems to me that to ignore something that was out there and popular with millions of people and thousands of health-care professionals but not really on the table, was a mistake. Although obviously tight on time, the producers should have found 30 seconds to take this into account because many Americans support it, yet the deal makers never mention it nor is the politics of discarding it addressed.

This analysis of how coverage of the Obama era of debate ignored the activities of the SPM *even when using interviews with single-payer activists who discussed single-payer* further illustrated the importance of using other forms of decentralized media to share the single-payer narrative.

While the actions of the Baucus protestors were not successful at getting single-payer a seat at the roundtables, it was uninformed for anyone to argue that the actions of single-payer activists were not an important part of the story of healthcare reform. As Getler pointed out, single-payer was not "a typical throw-away or easily cast aside idea."[141] Even Senator Baucus, who was successfully persuaded to meet with single-payer supporters in late May of 2009, after the roundtables had concluded, admitted that he had perhaps made a mistake by leaving single-payer supporters out of the discussion. This was defined as "concrete movement" by Dr. David Himmelstien, who also cautioned that "he announced no intention of opening up the hearings on single-payer in the future and we will therefore need to continue to press him."[142] This call to action was taken seriously by the grassroots segment of the SPM, which had defined this action as a success saying "the dynamics have changed since the arrest. People have been coming out of the closet for single-payer."[143] Single-payer supporters, such as Katie Robbins and Dr. Margaret Flowers, were also invited to testify at the congressional hearings on healthcare reform held later in the year. While the actions of the Baucus protestors were not successful at putting single-payer on the table, it does represent an activity that was successfully able to act on the grassroots opportunity that a receptive public represented and the cultural opportunity that new forms of social networking and digital video sharing presented. Single-payer activists began discussing the next stage of the debate and how they could act at the

[141] Ibid.
[142] Carrie Dudoff "Baucus Soothes Single Payer Backers" in Politico, posted on healthcarenow.org, June 3, 2009.
[143] Katie, Healthcare NOW conference Call, June 2009.

healthcare forums that Obama was "calling for"[144] in order to insert single-payer into these discussions.

ZOMBIES FOR SINGLE PAYER VS. THE TEA PARTY

During the current health care debate, one option is curiously being left out: a single-payer system. Because it would eliminate the profits of the health insurance industry, their lobbyists have effectively pushed it off the table. We need to organize demonstrations to force single-payer back onto the table. And what better way to do that than with a zombie march?[145]

In the spring of 2009, Organize for America, the grassroots group that formed in relation to the Obama campaign, began a "Listening Tour." This became a focus for grassroots organizing for many progressive and conservative grassroots organizations. The official purpose of this listening tour was to retain and build support for the newly elected President's agenda. It represented the new administration's continuing concern for the "grassroots." According to their website,

In many ways these small (and sometimes not so small) gatherings echo the same type of meetings that took place in diners and homes in the early days of the campaign, over two years ago. This time however, the focus is not on any one election, but on how to build support for the President's agenda on a wide range of issues, and how to bring about the change that so many of you worked so hard for. The campaign brought an unprecedented number of new voices into the process. Our goal now is to make sure those voices remain at the center of the debate as the President and Congress move forward to address the challenges we face.[146]

This listening tour represented another opportunity for grassroots organizations to express their perspectives to the new administration and, as indicated in the above excerpt, make their voices part of the debate. These listening tours inspired many grassroots groups to mobilize, on the left and the right, and the opportunities that they represented encouraged the development of somewhat radical performance-based tactics.

[144] Ibid.
[145] Universal Single Payer Health: the Only Way to Stop the Zombie Apocalypse! Public Facebook Group. 2009.
[146] BarackObama.com "Listening Tour" https://my.barackobama.com/page/content/listeningtour (no longer active).

Single-payer activists quickly realized that the "Organizing for America listening tour can be an effective tool to use in reaching people about single-payer."[147] They began to mobilize in and around these events in fairly conventional ways. They attempted to insert the single-payer perspective into the discussions that the Obama administration and the political elite were "listening" to,

> activists targeted Baucus when he came home on recess after the finance committee hearings. Single-payer healthcare supporters were a visible and vocal presence at town hall meetings across Montana. Baucus canceled personal appearances, sending instead a video and a representative for this "listening tour." A "buy back our senator" campaign is in the works.[148]

These town hall forums provided single-payer activists with another opportunity to confront politicians and to act on the grassroots opportunity that they concluded still existed in a public that was supportive of a truly universal healthcare system. Another "grassroots" group would challenge the opportunity to frame the discussion by reframing it in ways that were contrary to the single-payer perspective.

The emergence of the Tea Party in the spring of 2009 resulted in another shift in grassroots opportunity. Although the Tea Party identified as "grassroots," evidence shows that it was initially an astro-turfed organization to which "conservative leadership organizations provided resources, direction, and standardized messages that were crucial in instigating and sustaining Tea Party protests."[149] Although single-payer activists and Tea Partiers differed greatly in their goals for the healthcare system, they were both "energized by a feeling that their ability to influence the policy process is limited and the legitimacy of the political process is in question."[150] As single-payer activists began to mobilize in relation to the listening tour, they also had to develop ways to deal with "tea baggers" who would

---

[147] Rebecca, Healthcare NOW Conference Call August 2009.

[148] Laura S. Boylan "Fighting to Cure a Sick System" Healthcare NOW blog. http://www.healthcare-now.org/fighting-to-cure-a-sick-system-single-payer-advocates-take-unconventional-approach-to-healthcare-reform/.

[149] Lo, Clarence Y.H. 2012. "AstroTurf Versus Grass Roots: Scenes from Early Tea Party Mobilization," chapter 4 in Larry Rosenthal and Christine Trost, eds., *Steep: The Precipitous Rise of the Tea Party*. Berkeley and Los Angeles: University of California Press.

[150] Courser, Zachary. 2012. "The Tea 'Party' as a Conservative Social Movement." *Society* 49:43–53 PG 47.

"show up and are told to be disruptive."[151] The videos recorded of single-payer activities at these events make clear the confrontational relationship between single-payer activists and the Tea Partiers who, according to the single-payer narrative, acted with "destructive rage"[152] and fabricated "'death panels' scares to the traumatized seniors urging legislators to keep the government's hands 'off my Medicare,'" which caused the healthcare debate to "lurch[ed] off the rails."[153] Although most single-payer activists confronted these town halls through fairly conventional tactics (i.e. tabling, rallying, and joining the inside discussion), a small segment of the SPM developed a fairly radical performance activism tactic—the Zombie's for Single Payer.

The "Zombies for Single Payer" segment of the SPM developed a unique performance-based tactic rooted in the symbolic narrative of the zombie apocalypse. Zombie narratives have represented various societal fears in different historical periods[154] and have often been used as a "safe" avenue through which to discuss these fears.[155] This ***strategy enhancing symbolic narrative*** dramatically illustrated the fear of and concern about a dysfunctional healthcare system by connecting it to the culturally salient narrative of an epidemic that would end civilization as we know it. According to the single-payer zombie narrative,

> The Zombie hordes are upon us. As the undead shamble across our world, devouring humans and spreading their disease, we find the private health insurance companies to be woefully inadequate in preventing the Zombie outbreak from spreading to apocalyptic proportions. Only a universal single payer health care system would stop the Zombie Apocalypse. Under the private insurance companies, many people who are bitten by Zombies, cannot afford to see a doctor who would be able to treat the bite and prevent that person from becoming a Zombie. It seems that the Undead Panels are

[151] Leona, Health Care NOW conference call, August 2009.

[152] Update: Join the Mad As Hell Doctors on September 30th in Washington D.C., Campaign News, http://www.healthcare-now.org/update-join-the-mad-as-hell-doctors-on-sept-30th-in-washington-dc/, Sept. 24, 2009.

[153] Rose Ann DeMoro. http://www.healthcare-now.org/lets-get-back-to-what-health-care-reform-should-be-about/.

[154] Drezner, Daniel W. 2010. "Night of the Living Wonks." *Foreign Policy* no. 180: 34–38.

[155] Saunders, Robert A. 2012. "Undead Spaces: Fear, Globalisation, and the Popular Geopolitics of Zombiism." *Geopolitics* 17, no. 1: 80–104.

the Billing Departments of the Insurance Companies, denying care to the poor simply because they cannot afford it.[156]

This narrative was the basis for performance activism that involved culturally salient costuming, staging, and script. The zombies explained that,

> we are calling on the victims of the Zombie virus, and the victims of the Health Insurance Industry, to stand up and speak out in support of single payer universal health care. Organize Zombie rallies, picket at Town Hall meetings in full zombie garb, forward this to your friends and organize for equal healthcare for all![157]

The zombie garb that made up the zombie costumes for these actions illustrated the zombie's support of single-payer, with single-payer often written across the chests of ripped t-shirts in what resembled blood. While the script for this performance mostly consisted of zombie speak (i.e. Arghhh), in videos of these events, subtitles inform the audience that the zombies are supportive of single-payer. This is illustrated in the following transcript.

Reporter: Zombies. The undead, intent on feasting on the living, and wreaking havoc on society, or perhaps just another misunderstood and underrepresented demographic in our society, not unlike libertarians or the Irish. (to Zombie) Is there a particular form of health care reform that you favor?
Zombie: Aiuuuu, Urgh, Argh, (etc.)
Subtitle: "One that really addresses cost control and provides true health care parity."
Reporter: Ah. So a single-payer system is what you're advocating for?
Zombie: ERRR ARGHHHH
Subtitle: "Of Course."[158]

Although this particular activity was not a mass mobilization activity sponsored by large national single-payer organizations, the Zombies

---

[156] Miami Independent Media Center, August 2009, http://miami.indymedia.org/news/2009/08/13656.php/MiamiIndependentMediaCenter/stopthezombieapocalyps.com.
[157] Ibid.
[158] Zombie March, Health Care Town Hall, 8-31-09, Skokie IL, aired on Chicago Independent Television. http://www.youtube.com/watch?v=KfPKld1nsQI.

did continue to march for single-payer and then later on Wall Street[159] and in California for "The Horrors of Corporate Health Care: April Ghouls Day").[160] Zombie marches occurred in several places around the country and the zombie narrative was shared with hundreds of people who attended healthcare town halls or viewed recordings of these actions on YouTube. It is notable that while still not a core tactic in the SPM, zombie marches that involve "people dressed as grisly ghouls taking to the streets. But instead of eating brains, organizers are raising awareness on the fight for a single payer healthcare system,"[161] still occur around the country, which highlights the ongoing salience of this symbolic narrative.

The zombie narrative, and the single-payer message within it, was shared with a wider audience than those who were actually present at the town halls. These actions were staged so that they could be shared with a larger audience through digital film sharing. Many[162] of the zombie marches were recorded, edited, and shared on YouTube or through independent television. This is another example of the ways in which the decentralization of media, including the advent of digital filmmaking, and internet distribution technology, represented significant cultural opportunity for single-payer activists. The zombies for single-payer were not only able to share their narrative with a wider audience through digital technology, they also utilized social media networking sites as their primary venue for organizing the zombie marches. One Facebook page, for the Twin Cities Zombies for Single-Payer, explained that "the plan is to use this group to begin organizing for events. Anyone who wants to see this happen, get active!"[163] The Zombie's for Single Payer were able to use social networking sites in order to organize and mobilize.

Although the Zombies for Single Payer seemed to be an energized segment of the SPM and represented a constituent population that the

[159] "Wall Street Zombie March." *New York Daily News*, YouTube Channel. Posted on Oct. 4, 2011. http://www.youtube.com/watch?v=RMsgN2WF0-M.

[160] PNHP California "Zombie March." http://pnhpcalifornia.org/zombie-march/.

[161] Galli, Joe. "Liberal Groups holding a Medicare for all Zombie March Saturday" San Antonio News 4 Posted on April 2, 2019. https://news4sanantonio.com/news/local/liberal-groups-holding-a-medicare-for-all-zombie-march-saturday.

[162] That is, Chicago 2009, Atlanta 2009, Minneapolis 2009, Skokie 2009, Washington D.C. 2015, Houston 2017, San Antonio 2019.

[163] Twin City Zombies for Single Payer Facebook Group. https://www.facebook.com/group.php?gid=135768649967.

movement wished to mobilize (young adults), this performance activism did not become an aspect of the dominant single-payer action narrative. I had not heard of the Zombies for Single Payer through my work with the national single-payer groups (i.e. Healthcare NOW or LCGHC) and discovered them randomly in the fall of 2009 as I searched for videos and news coverage of the SPM. I, a fan of zombie lore, became excited about what I saw as an interesting and creative way to attract a younger population to the movement. I knew that the zombie narrative was culturally salient and already had a large subcultural following. I, much like the CDC eventually would in connection to disaster preparedness,[164] saw it as a way to draw attention to the issue and mobilize a new constituency to act. However, when I mentioned my discovery to leaders of the core single-payer organizations, they were just as surprised, but not as excited, as I was about the activity. They seemed to think that it was an amusing, but not productive, avenue for mobilization. Although zombie activities did garner "mainstream" news coverage, there was *not a single* report at that time about the zombies on the Healthcare NOW or the national Physician's for a National Health Program websites other than a brief notation of a news article about a zombie march. This begs the question as to why the core single-payer organizations did not act on the grassroots and cultural opportunity that the zombies represented.

Although the core single-payer organizations did use progressively more radical tactics that acted on grassroots opportunity during this time period, these tactics were still conventionally oriented toward beltway politics. While the actions were more risky and more radical, they were still encased in the realm of "legitimate" radical activity that has been used in the past to work for social change. The greatest risk of the zombie performance activism was that it could possibly delegitimize the SPM in the eyes of the political and economic elites who were still constructed as the primary target of grassroots mobilization, regardless of the importance placed on grassroots opportunity. At this time, even radical activity was only viewed as legitimate if it worked to mobilize the grassroots in relation to these elite entities in order to encourage the support of political actors. Other activities were not constructed as legitimate in the same way. The most traditionally risky, in regard to the cost of arrest, activity of this time

---

[164] CDC Center for Preparedness and Response "Zombie Preparedness." http://www.cdc.gov/phpr/zombies.htm.

period was rooted in the legitimacy of the Civil Rights Movement and in the SPM's identity as the "real grassroots."

DIE-INS, TEACH-INS, AND SIT-INS: MOBILIZING FOR HEALTH CARE FOR ALL

Patients! Not Profits! Medicare For All![165]

America deserves better, and that's why we voted for change. But the insurance companies are spending millions to confuse and scare the public to keep us from ending their grip on our health and our money. When the civil rights movement faced serious challenges in the struggle to end segregation, nonviolent civil disobedience moved the nation and made reform possible. **Just like the lunch counter sit-ins did for the civil rights movement**, we have to make it impossible for the media and our country to ignore how outrageous the status quo of private insurance is for the American people.[166]

Early in the Obama era of healthcare reform, single-payer activists in several areas began using direct action as an avenue through which to insert the single-payer perspective into the debate, but this did not become a widespread mobilization effort in the form of civil disobedience until the fall of 2009. While single-payer activists had been using "conventional" forms of direct action, such as rally's and protests, they did not start using disruptive forms of direct action on a mass scale until the fall of 2009. High levels of public interest and support in conjunction with low levels of political support for a particular group often result in more radical and disruptive tactics being used.[167] The support of political officials for a particular challenge, or the development of a "brokerage" relationship, may result in increased grassroots mobilization using conventional tactics, whereas low levels of political support may result in increased grassroots mobilization using disruptive tactics.[168] In the fall of 2009, the single-

---

[165] Chant used at Insurance Company Sit-ins. "Aetna Sit-In for Single Payer, Medicare for All, September 29, 2009. Posted on healthcarenow4all youtube channel. http://www.youtube.com/watch?v=xOB1zOBr7IM.

[166] Mobilizeforhealthcare.org "About."

[167] Saikia, Pahi. 2011. "Political Opportunities, Constraints, and Mobilizing Structures: An Integrated Approach to Different Levels of Ethno-Political Contention in Northeast India." India Review 10, no. 1: 1–39.

[168] Sherman, Daniel J. 2008. ""Disruption or Convention? A Process-based Explanation of Divergent Repertoires of Contention Among Opponents to Low-level Radioactive Waste

payer tactics became increasingly focused on forms of nonviolent civil disobedience due to a decline in political opportunity, while grassroots,
cultural, and economic opportunity were still defined as positive. This
focus facilitated a movement building strategy rooted in increasing public
support for single payer.

Although single-payer still had many supporters in the halls of
Congress—most notably Representatives Eric Massa (D-NY), who con-
tinued to be a stalwart defender of the single-payer position, and Anthony
Weiner (D-NY) who introduced a single-payer amendment to the House
Bill 3200 that would replace it with H.R. 676, as well as Representative
Dennis Kucinich (D-OH) and Senator Bernie Sanders (I-VT) who both
introduced single-payer amendments that would allow for states to
develop single-payer systems, the political opportunity that confronted
single-payer activists was defined as progressively more negative. While
Senator Ted Kennedy (D-MA) was not as supportive of the single-payer
option as he had been in the past,[169] and he was defined as a "colossal
failure"[170] by some single-payer activists, his death on August 25, 2009
resulted in a significant shift in the political opportunity for healthcare
reform as it resulted in the Democrats losing their super majority of 60
senators.[171] While many activists were critical of the Obama administration
for compromising from the outset of the healthcare reform debate, the
loss of Senator Kennedy, and of the super majority, was defined as a shift
that would result in even further compromise—even of "half measures"
such as the public option. Single-payer was even farther away from having
a seat at the table.

This decrease in political opportunity was occurring at the same time as
a narratively defined increase in grassroots opportunity was perceived
because more supporters of universal health care and of single-payer were
realizing that the actions of Congress would not result in a "real" change
of the healthcare system. "Real" change would mean creating a system
based on "care not profit" that removed for-profit insurance from the
healthcare delivery system. While the House Bill, HR 3200, did initially

Disposal Sites."" Social Movement Studies 7, no. 3: 265–280.

[169] See Health Security Act of 1971.

[170] Helen Redmond "The Lion Sleeps Tonight." 2009. http://www.healthcare-now.org/
the-lion-sleeps-tonight/.

[171] Although Jacobs and Skocpol (2010) argue that the upset election of Tea Party favorite
Scott Brown to fill the vacant Kennedy seat actually served to strengthen health care reform
and the final version of the reform bill.

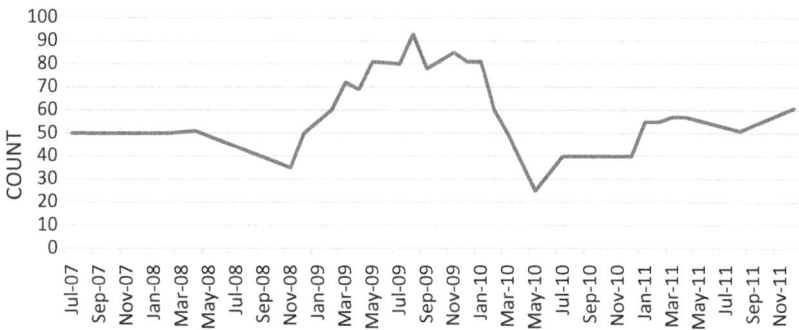

Fig. 5.3   Healthcare NOW Conference call attendance (July 2007 to Oct. 2011)

include a public option that would provide care for a very small percentage of the population, even this weak version of the stated goal was written out of the final legislation.[172] This period was defined by activists as being a positive period for mobilization of the public. The positive grassroots opportunity experienced by the SPM is also quantifiable and visible with the increased participation in monthly organizational conference calls as an indicator of interest (see Fig. 5.3). The participation of larger amounts of people facilitated the use of a wider range of tactics and a rising focus on strategizing outside of beltway politics. This also facilitated the development of a strategy of widespread and collective civil disobedience oriented toward disrupting the operations of for-profit insurance companies, as well as disrupting the hegemonic economic narrative that profits should be allowed factor in health care.

In the spring of 2009, Russell Mokhiber and Jason Kafoury of the Daily Citizen Inc. formed Single Payer Action (SPA) which didn't "do inside the beltway politics," would "never compromise on single-payer," and did "direct action."[173] According to Healthcare NOW, this new group supported,

> direct action targeting members of Congress and the health industry's corporate agents. They believe in using creative actions to get press attention, e.g. belly dancers for single payer in West Virginia, and burning health insurance bills at the AHIP [America's Health Insurance Plans] meeting in DC.[174]

[172] Jacobs, Lawrence, and Theda Skocpol. 2010. *Health Care Reform and American Politics: What Everyone Needs to Know.* Oxford University Press.
[173] Single Payer Action "About" http://singlepayeraction.org/about.html.
[174] Katie, Healthcare NOW Conference Call, May 2009.

This groups' strategy of direct action outside of beltway politics became the direction toward which other single-payer groups moved as the process of political maneuvering and compromise occurred in D.C. By the fall of 2009, the leaders of SPA were suggesting a uniform strategy of nationwide disruptive direct action or civil disobedience.

Civil disobedience is an even riskier radical tactic than other performance-oriented activities because it moves beyond conventional forms of direct action, to disruptive forms of action that can be defined as illegal.[175] Civil disobedience has been used by many of the most important and influential social movements that have resulted in significant social changes in American politics.[176] One particular act of civil disobedience that has had a resounding effect on American political culture is the act of sitting in. The "sit in" is a tactic that was developed and utilized by student organizations during the Civil Rights Movement and was effective at encouraging increased participation in and awareness of the movement.[177] The origin story of Healthcare NOW connected it to the earlier Civil Rights Movement and supported the SPM's identity as the "new civil rights movement."[178] This connection was also invoked when single-payer activists began planning to "sit in" at the headquarters of insurance companies around the country.

Single-payer organizations, most particularly Single Payer Action and Healthcare NOW, joined efforts in a new strategy called "Mobilize for Health Care." This strategy invoked the sit-in movement of the 1960s and was oriented toward growing public support for single payer. In the promotional video for this campaign, the narrator stated that "we have to do the same thing for the civil rights movement of today."[179] In this promotional video, concerned parties were encouraged to continue to organize, because "many who believed our chance to win universal health care had finally come are losing hope, but now is not the time to turn back or give

---

[175] McAdam, Doug, Sidney Tarrow, and Charles Tilly. 2001. *Dynamics of Contention*. Cambridge: Cambridge University Press.

[176] Piven, Frances Fox, and Richard Cloward. 1979. *Poor People's Movements: Why They Succeed: How They Fail*. New York: Vintage Books.

[177] Polletta, Francesca. 2006. *It Was Like a Fever: Story Telling in Protest and Politics*. University of Chicago Press.

[178] For a more lengthy discussion of this origin story, see Chap. 5 of Hern, Lindy. 2012. *Everybody In and Nobody Out: Opportunity, Narrative, and the Radical Flank in the Movement for Single Payer Health Care Reform*. Dissertation. University of Missouri. ProQuest Dissertations and Theses.

[179] Mobilize for Health Care Promotional Video at Mobilizeforhealthcare.org.

up."[180] They were encouraged to take on the "real villain" of reform, which is defined as insurance companies although all politicians "Democrat and Republican, are standing against reform, on the side of the insurance companies that fund them, rather than the people who elect them."[181] This digitally enabled promotional video was used to recruit activist participants around the country.

Although the stage for this act of performance activism was to be the headquarters of insurance companies in "major cities" around the United States, the intended audience was much larger. Activists planned to directly confront insurance companies and demand that they provide care for those in critical need of it.

> We hope that we can save the lives of some of the people who are being denied critical care for life threatening conditions today, but we know we can save the lives of millions of people in the decades to come, by dramatizing just why our health care system is broken and demonstrating the fierce urgency of fundamental change.[182]

Although the actions would ideally entail directly confronting the heads of these insurance companies, the participants would through their "sacrifice ... speak beyond them to the conscience of our nation and call on our fellow Americans, to demand real reform—Medicare for All"[183] by "dramatizing" this situation. In order to reach this wider intended audience, it would be necessary to record, edit, and distribute footage of the actions themselves via digital media. Posting video of all demonstrations "within 5 hours"[184] of them taking place as a way to ensure that the activists were not just "talking to ourselves"[185] was solidified as a movement tactic. This was a central component of the Mobilize for Health Care strategy that took activists out of the beltway and into the domain of public interaction with for-profit insurance.

The possibility of being arrested was a significant part of the script for this performance action. The first sit-in took place at the headquarters of Aetna health care in New York City and resulted in 16 arrests. This was an

---

[180] Ibid.
[181] Ibid.
[182] Ibid.
[183] Ibid.
[184] HCN Conference Call Notes Sept. 2008.
[185] HCN Conference Call Sept. 2008.

intended outcome of this activity, as illustrated by the Mobilize for Health Care promotional video.

> Imagine, with the whole country watching, people willingly going to jail and even staying there, because private insurance companies refuse to cover the care their patients need. Our actions will put the healthcare reform media spotlight where it belongs, on the problem.[186]

The act of being arrested has been a useful tactic for social movements to garner attention for their goals and to illustrate their commitment to the cause.[187] The arrests of the activists who were committed to sitting in (many more demonstrated outside of the building on public sidewalks) figured prominently in the videos that were edited and shared widely through YouTube, social media, and organizational websites. Activists were shown being forcefully removed from the headquarters with their wrists in plastic handcuffs while still chanting "Patients, not profits, Medicare for All."

In addition to the planned staging and scripts, participants were also instructed to wear low-key costumes for these actions. At the first Aetna sit-in, participants wore t-shirts that said "Victim of For Profit Insurance" on the front and "Medicare for All" on the back. Variations of this costume were used at the following sit-ins. While wearing these costumes, activists presented a unified front as they linked arms while sitting in a semi-circle in the lobby of the headquarters and chanted "Aetna Profits, People Die! Medicare for All." Another key aspect of this performance activism was the incorporation of the "teach-in" tactic that was developed in the anti-war movement of the Vietnam era[188] with the "sit-in" tactic of the Civil Rights Movement. The sit-ins of the Mobilize for Health Care campaign often also involved an informational lecture about the healthcare system performed by one or more of the activists involved—making them teach-ins. These short lectures were also featured in the videos of the events that were distributed digitally.

These informational aspects of the sit-in mobilization also countered the narratives created and supported by other grassroots organizations involved in the healthcare reform debate. By narratively reframing the issue and solidly putting the blame for the healthcare system on for-profit

---

[186] Mobilize for Health Care Promotional Video.

[187] Piven, Frances Fox, and Richard Cloward. 1979. *Poor People's Movements: Why They Succeed: How They Fail*. New York: Vintage Books.

[188] Gamson, William. 1990. *The Strategy of Social Protest*. Second edition Wadsworth Publishing Company.

insurance companies, single-payer activists countered the "death panel" narrative that Tea Party activists and conservative politicians so often used in their argument against the Obama agenda for healthcare reform.

> We are just here because of the many people that we know who die because the insurance companies put profits before people's care. The myths about government death panels are a lie. The reality is that the death panels are the people who are paid every day to deny care to people. That's their job.[189]

In this statement, Mark Milano directly confronted the "death panel" narrative and developed a counter-narrative which argued that the "reality" of the situation is that death panels do exist, but within the for-profit insurance industry not within state-financed healthcare systems. Activists further illustrated this by transitioning from sit-ins to "die-ins," during which activists would lay on the floor and pretend to be dead—holding signs that explained statistics or specific examples of those who had died due to being un, or under, insured. Further, this *strategy enhancing counter-narrative* also rejected the hegemonic economic narrative that resulted in a for-profit insurance system. The narrative told through this performance action not only constructed insurance companies as primary offenders in the healthcare crisis experienced by millions of Americans, but it also targeted the hegemonic economic narrative of the free market which privileges profits over patients as activists stridently chanted "Patients. Not Profits. Medicare for ALL!"

While the Mobilize for Health Care website initially requested that 100 activists commit to sit-in to the point of being arrested in order for the strategy to be effective, many more committed (700) to this than planned. A total of 150 activists were eventually arrested due to this mobilization effort. The action narrative of the outcome of this tactic uses this figure to define it as a success. However, the video of the first sit-in at Aetna in New York City ends with the statement "we are here to say that we will not rest until every person that needs care in America gets it and the way to get that care for everyone is Medicare for All."[190] While this tactic did continue to be useful for several months, with sit-ins taking place in 30 cities around the country, they did not continue until the passage of Medicare for All as the above statement indicates was the overall goal (see Fig. 5.4 for a visual representation of the narrative practice of this era).

---

[189] Mark Milano at Aetna Sit-in NYC, Sept. 29th, 2009.
[190] Mark Milano ibid.

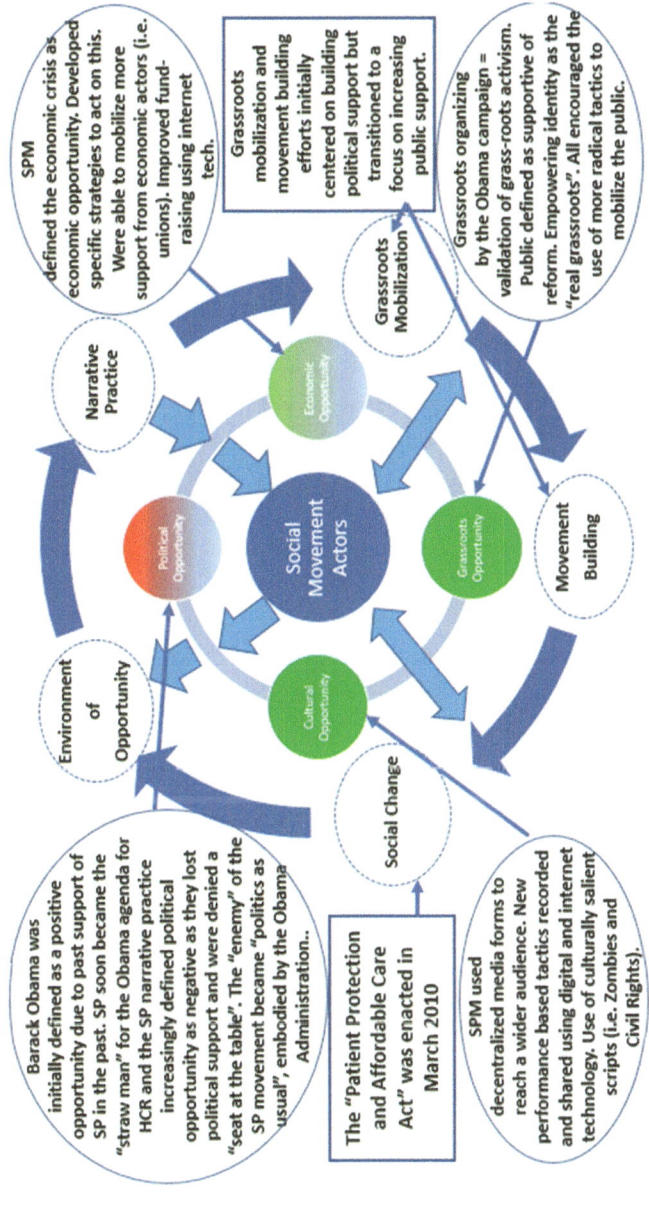

Fig. 5.4   Obama era narrative practice

The passage of the Patient Protection and Affordable Care Act and the signing of this act by President Obama on March 23, 2010 would result in another reorganization of the SPM's strategy and movement building orientation. The radical performance activities detailed above acted on perceived grassroots opportunity, were facilitated by the cultural opportunity that the decentralization of media represented, and were oriented toward shifting the debate that was occurring in D.C. at this time. The passage of PPACA/ACA was viewed by many as the end of the debate on healthcare reform. In defiance of that conclusion, single-payer activists constructed this as the beginning of a new era for the SPM. In this new era, they would act on the grassroots opportunity that followed the enactment of the ACA and focus on "building the movement" rather than on beltway politics, or "politics as usual" which became narratively defined as the "enemy" of the Single Payer Movement.

CHAPTER 6

"War with the Whitehouse": Redefining the Enemy During the ACA Era

The energy and enthusiasm at the 2009 Healthcare NOW annual strategy meeting is palpable. I, along with the other participants of Missourians for Single Payer (MoSP), am particularly excited because this is the first time that the meeting is being held in St. Louis Missouri. While welcoming the 150 or so activists who have traveled to St. Louis from all over the country, Mimi—the legislative chair of MoSP, explains that Missouri is a great place for the meeting because the Missouri based movement is one of the longest and continually active state-based movements in the country—having both an active organization and state level bill since the early 1990's. Mimi also explains that MoSP has been working with Healthcare NOW since its conception and that "we are energized by you and hope that you will be energized by us." While the gathered activists are energized by each other and enthusiastic about the work that they are committed to doing, they are also figuring out how to do this work following the loss of their leader—Marilyn Clement—the founder of Healthcare NOW. Marilyn had recently passed following a long battle with illness. Donna Smith explains to the group that at their final meeting before her death Marilyn had told her that, "You all know what you need to do, you don't need me to tell you" and had encouraged Donna to remind other activists that "we are not always going to agree. Our agenda won't always be the same. But, we need to have the courage to fight together and not restrict others ideas and intentions." While the gathered activists were determined to work together to achieve their goal, they were feeling less confident about their work with other potential allies—particularly those within the political sphere. The process of health policy

© The Author(s) 2020
L. S. F. Hern, *Single Payer Healthcare Reform*,
https://doi.org/10.1007/978-3-030-42764-1_6

reform that was ongoing on capitol hill had alienated single-payer supporters.[1]
Throughout this process they had,

"learned that legislators are not movement leaders—they will sacrifice principles if they think it's needed to pass the bill. We also learned that we were actually at war with the White House for the past year—we thought that we could convince him (Obama)—'we know that the President will have us at the table'—instead they excluded us and fought us every step of the way. They did not want to be tainted as a government run bill—so they had to distance themselves from single-payer. This resulted in an undeclared war with the White House. We lost the debate on government run healthcare—the right wing became the defenders of Medicare! I was involved in the Clinton year health care fight. Single-payer was taken off table in a way that would make your head swim—in those 15 years we began to build a movement, we didn't let it go away.

We are a movement with many tactics but one objective. That objective will continue to be at the forefront of our movement."[2]

Following the enactment of the Affordable Care Act (ACA),[3] single-payer activists were dismayed that they had never been provided the "seat at the table" that they so desired. During the implementation period of the ACA (2010–2014), single-payer organizations continued to find ways to mobilize by building alliances with a more diverse audience through narrative-based tactics and the use of the Human Rights Repertoire[4] in order to "build the movement" for single-payer. This orientation arose following a turn against "politics as usual." This turn encouraged single-payer activists to focus on building a movement with the strength to change the political context by challenging establishment politics.

The enactment of the ACA signaled the denouement of this cycle of healthcare reform for political actors on Capitol Hill. However, for single-payer activists it represented a disruption in the story of healthcare reform rather than a resolution. Rather than praising President Obama for enacting the ACA, single-payer supporters were critical of the outcome of his strategy for achieving reform. Dr. Quentin Young stated,

[1] Fieldnotes, Healthcare NOW Annual Strategy Conference, St. Louis MO, November 2009.
[2] Fieldnotes: Michael, CNA organizer and HCN board member, Healthcare NOW annual strategy conference, public address, Nov. 2009.
[3] Note: The Patient Protection and Affordable Care Act is typically now typically shortened to Affordable Care Act or referred to as Obamacare.
[4] Hagan, Margaret. 2010. "The human rights repertoire: its strategic logic, expectations and tactics." *International Journal of Human Rights* 14, no. 4: 559–583.

I don't have any sympathy for the idea that the president had to compromise because his opposition was strong. Winning is not always about winning the election. Winning is making a huge fight and then taking the fight to the people—re-electing people who are supporting your program and defeating those who aren't.[5]

In this quote, Dr. Young critiques the strategy of starting from a position of compromise. Young also highlights the turn toward a focus on changing the political context by emphasizing the centrality of electoral politics to the process. Single-payer supporters were dismayed that, from their perspective, Obama reneged on his promise of hope and real progressive change. This reform cycle convinced single-payer activists that "legislators are not movement leaders—they will sacrifice principles if they think it's needed to pass the bill" and that this period involved an "undeclared war with the White House."[6] The moral of this single-payer narrative warned activists that they should not ally themselves with any particular political party or politician because "politics as usual," embodied by the Obama administration, was the "enemy" of real healthcare reform. Due to this narrative practice, the strategy of the SPM shifted in focus to building a grassroots movement that would be large enough to change the political context and force politicians to support "real" progressive healthcare reform.[7]

THE ACA CONTEXT: RESHAPING THE SPHERE OF POLITICAL OPPORTUNITY

At the Healthcare NOW national strategy conference in November of 2009, the gathered single-payer activists representing many organizations discussed their status as "the only group of health care reform activists who are meeting and not celebrating this bill," while "3000 people met at

---

[5] Dr. Quentin Young served as the national coordinator of Physicians for a National Health Program from 1992–2014 and continued to be an active supporter of single-payer until his death in the spring of 2016. Quoted in, http://healthoverprofit.org/incrementalism-ppt/.

[6] Fieldnotes: Michael, then a National Nurses United organizer and Healthcare NOW board member—HCN National Strategy Conference—November 2009.

[7] See also, Hern, Lindy. 2019. "Resisting 'Politics as Usual': Examining the Rise of Anti-Establishment Politics by Comparing the Narratives of Opportunity Used Within the Single Payer Movement During Two Presidential Eras." *Journal of Historical Sociology* 1:18.

the capitol to celebrate this bill."[8] While single-payer activists were developing their strategy for the coming year, the Senate Finance Committee had already passed their healthcare reform bill (The Healthy Future Act) to the floor of the Senate and the House had already passed H.R. 3962. This reality forced single-payer activists to conclude that they had not successfully won a seat at the table. Single-payer activists continued to work with some of their political allies in order to push through single-payer amendments to these bills. For example, Senator Bernie Sanders (I-VT) introduced amendment 2837 which "would have instituted a Medicare-for-all single-payer program." Movement forward with this amendment would have "been the first time in American history that a Medicare for All single-payer bill was brought to a vote before the floor of the Senate."[9] Representative Anthony Weiner (D-NY) introduced a similar amendment to the House bill (HR 3962) that would have replaced the text of that bill with the language of H.R. 676—Representative John Conyers (D-MI) pre-existing single-payer bill.[10] While single-payer activists saw votes on these amendments as important opportunities to highlight the political support for single-payer, they were realistic in their assessment that they probably did not have a chance of passing. However, a vote on either the floor of the House or the Senate would have been a historic opportunity to insert single-payer into the debate surrounding the final stages of development for the bill that would eventually be enacted. These amendments to the House and Senate bills were viewed as their last opportunity to bring single-payer "to the table" and activists were encouraged to call their Representatives and Senators because "the time draws short to weigh in clearly with your Senators. And with a yes vote on this amendment, Senators send us the message that they heard us, that they will keep fighting with us until the day when this nation no longer leaves the weak, the sick and the poor behind in the delivery of its most basic human rights."[11]

[8] Fieldnotes: Michael, National Nurses United organizer and Healthcare NOW board member—HCN National Strategy Conference—November 2009.
[9] Senator Bernie Sanders (I-VT), Floor Speech on Single-Payer Amendment, December 16, 2009—see full transcript of this speech here, https://www.sanders.senate.gov/newsroom/press-releases/floor-speech-on-single-payer-amendment.
[10] PNHP Resources "Urge your rep to vote Yes for single payer!" http://www.pnhp.org/amendment/.
[11] Healthcare-NOW "Urgent: Call Senators Today to Support Sanders Single-Payer Amendment" https://www.healthcare-now.org/blog/urgent-call-senators-today-to-support-sanders-single-payer-amendment/.

Both amendments were prohibited from either hearings or votes on the floor of either chamber. Representative Weiner eventually withdrew his amendment following pressure from Democratic leadership because "given how fluid the negotiations are on the final push to get comprehensive health care reform that covers millions of Americans and contains costs through a public option, I became concerned that my amendment might undermine that important goal."[12] Although the Sanders' Amendment did make it to the Senate floor, debate or a vote over this amendment was prohibited when Senator Tom Coburn (R-OK) insisted that the 700-page amendment be read in full before debate could begin. This delay tactic was supported when Senator Max Baucus (D-MT) told Sanders that his only option, other than reading the 700-page document, was to withdraw the amendment. Donna Smith, who was watching this unfold from the gallery, explained that,

> The Republicans seemed to be pleased with the procedural maneuver. Periodically one of the Democratic leadership would walk over to Coburn and chat. He'd smile and lean on his stack of documents—everything being very well staged for the C-SPAN cameras. I thought how cold and callous it all looked from the gallery—healthcare is not a laughing matter for millions of us. This crisis has killed thousands of our fellow citizens and bankrupted millions more. I fail to find any of that remotely funny or something over which any Senator ought to feel pride as he or she blocks progress towards a better healthcare system.[13]

Donna's personal account of this particular event highlights the role that "Democratic leadership" played as an opponent to the SPM within single-payer narrative practice. Once again, the establishment had prohibited open debate over a single-payer solution. Although these political maneuvers were successful at prohibiting a debate about a single-payer solution, they were not successful at decreasing the support of activists or politicians who were committed to this solution. Of this experience, Sanders said that he was still optimistic that a "Medicare-for-all single-payer bill will eventually prevail" not only because it is the best option but because,

---

[12] PNHP Press Release "Rep. Weiner withdraws single payer amendment" Posted on Nov. 6, 2009. http://www.pnhp.org/news/2009/november/rep_weiner_withdraw.php.

[13] Donna Smith "Sanders Says Single-Payer Day Will Come as He Withdraws Amendment." https://www.healthcare-now.org/blog/sanders-says-single-payer-day-will-come-as-he-withdraws-amendment/.

The day will come, although I recognize it is not today, when the Congress will have the courage to stand up to the private insurance companies and the drug companies and the medical equipment suppliers and all of those who profit and make billions of dollars every single year off of human sickness. On that day, when it comes—and it will come—the U.S. Congress will finally proclaim that health care is a right of all people and not just a privilege. And that day will come, as surely as I stand here today.[14]

Single-payer activists were also quick to point out how the fact that these amendments had almost resulted in floor votes was a sign of movement success because "nobody, particularly the President, expected our single-payer option to be alive in the Congress for so long. As you know, they attempted to keep it 'off the table' from the very beginning," and "the fact that single payer got so far along in the House is a testament to the strength of our single-payer movement."[15]

Single-payer supporters used these experiences as indicators that single-payer was not being stymied by a lack of public support but rather by the direct actions of Democratic establishment leadership. Sanders, who identified as an Independent, was outside of this leadership circle and was viewed as a challenge to it. Although Sanders had been relevant to the SPM in the years preceding this exchange due to his active support for single-payer, other political figures, such as Representative John Conyers (D-MI), were viewed as the political leaders of the movement due to the movement's emphasis on supporting H.R. 676. Following this exchange in the senate, Sanders became more centered as a political leader of the movement within single-payer narrative practice, while establishment politicians were defined as the "enemy" of single-payer.

Defining the Enemy

The narrative of opportunity that arose during this era redefined the relationship between the SPM and establishment politics as a "war" which pitted single-payer activism against "politics as usual." This initially resulted in the movement redirecting its focus to a grassroots strategy oriented toward "building the movement" through increasing public

[14] Senator Bernie Sanders (I-VT), Floor Speech on Single-Payer Amendment, December 16, 2009.
[15] Comment by Ida Hellander, M.D., Executive Director, Physicians for a National Health Program. http://www.pnhp.org/news/2009/november/rep_weiner_withdraw.php.

support, rather than on a beltway strategy oriented toward redirecting the political debate by increasing the support of political agents. The goal of this era became challenging "politics as usual" by building a movement that could change the political context. A key aspect of this process involved defining the enemy of the SPM before, during, and after the implementation of the ACA.

While the Medical Industrial Complex—including insurance and pharmaceutical companies—was still defined as a powerful enemy of the SPM during this era, their relationship to political leadership following the enactment of the ACA was a more important focus of the single-payer narrative during the ACA implementation years (2010–2014). "Corporate legislators and the private health insurance industry" were together defined as "the true enemy"[16] at this time. Activists were encouraged to focus on opposing "corporate democrats," who were defined as "DINO's" (Democrats in Name Only) or "PINO's" (Progressives in Name Only). Activists concluded that they could not "trust the Democrats" and realized "that this is our movement and it's our responsibility to make it happen. Movements have made politicians move."[17] Activists developed tactics that would challenge the position of these legislators. Rather than only utilizing tactics that would encourage them to support single-payer legislation, single-payer supporters considered tactics that would remove non-single-payer politicians from office.

This definition of the enemy was influenced not only by experiences within the SPM but also by the evolving narratives of those involved in the larger movement for healthcare reform during this era. Richard Kirsch, who had led Health Care for America NOW (HCAN) in its support for the public option, discussed this at length in his account of the HCAN mobilization period. Kirsch explained that although HCAN had built massive grassroots support for the public option, he was told by the Obama administration that an "outsider strategy" would not play a major role in the reform process and that the "insider strategy" would be the main focus. This insider strategy brought many contributors from the healthcare industry to the table while excluding grassroots activists.[18]

---

[16] Fieldnotes: Paul Song M.D., One Payer States Annual Strategy Conference, 2014.
[17] Kevin, Healthcare NOW Conference Call, April 2010.
[18] Kirsch, Richard. 2012. *Fighting For Our Health: The Epic Battle to Make Health Care a Right in the United States.* NY: Rockefeller Institute Press.

These movement stories fed into the conclusion that the enactment and implementation of the ACA was the result of "politics as usual" which included insiders in the policy process but excluded outsiders. Tensions developed as the ACA moved through the implementation process due to the rise of what was often referred to as the "Obama Era protection racket" through which "closet" single-payer supporters "were effectively gagged by Obama and the Democrats from openly criticizing Obama's law."[19] According to single-payer activists, this phenomenon limited the amount of insider critique of Obama era policies that would be tolerated, such as critiques by politicians who had previously supported single-payer, and outsiders, such as those who had supported the ACA through participation in organizations such as HCAN. Single-payer activists worked within a context in which they concluded that "in their hearts, they want single-payer. But they can't say it, because they are engaged in an Obama Protection Racket. Got to bust that racket before we move on to protecting the American people. Onward to single-payer."[20]

Focus transitioned to challenging the "racket" which was, according to the single-payer narrative, a symptom of the enemy of single-payer—the "politics as usual" that turned corporations and establishment democrats into allies. Single-payer activists began to "fight back against this corporate bullshit, by going after the corporate democrats—they are the ones who stand in the way of progress—corporatists in sheep's clothing," in part by building "the broadest coalition possible."[21] Activists operated on the conclusion that it was "not enough to have the policy argument" but they must also "take on power that is opposed to us."[22] Activists concluded that "social change doesn't happen because those in power wake up one day and say I'm going to make things easier. NO that happens because activists organize, and work, and demand, and win."[23]

---

[19] Russell Mokhiber "Single Payer Supreme Court and the Obama Protection Racket" March 28, 2012. https://www.singlepayeraction.org/2012/03/28/single-payer-supreme-court-and-the-obama-protection-racket/.

[20] Ibid.

[21] Fieldnotes: Paul Song M.D., Keynote Address, One Payer States National Conference, 2014.

[22] Fieldnotes: Michael Lighty, Single Payer National Strategy Meeting, Chicago, October 2015.

[23] Fieldnotes: Laurie Wen, Healthcare NOW National Strategy Meeting, Philadelphia, November 2010.

These events forced single-payer supporters to reconsider their relationship with traditional beltway politics. This narrative of political opportunity redefined their relationship with the Obama administration, and with establishment politics in general, as an overt conflict. Some prominent single-payer leaders even defined this relationship as a "war." While they were at "war with the Whitehouse," entities that were previously defined as the enemy of single-payer—insurance and pharmaceutical companies—were viewed being in a much less contentious relationship with the Obama administration because they were offered a seat at the table. This resulted in legislation which included policies that would reaffirm the role of private insurance in the U.S. healthcare system—such as the individual mandate to purchase private insurance that they so dreaded. Unlike their experience of alienation from the political process during the Clinton era, which they shared with the medical industrial complex, single-payer activists were particularly alienated during the Obama era in which the Obama administration had used single-payer as a "straw man" in order to distance itself from government-run healthcare. Because of this, single-payer activists warned that they should not ally themselves with any particular political party. The reality that most of the progressive Democratic representatives who had co-sponsored H.R. 676, including the original sponsor of H.R. 676, Representative John Conyers (D-MI) had abandoned single-payer and instead voted in favor of H.R. 3962, affirmed this assertion. To add injury to insult, the most stalwart supporter of single-payer in the House of Representatives who refused to vote for anything that was not single-payer, Representative Eric Massa (D-NY), resigned from congress in March 2010 due to allegations of sexual misconduct with a male staffer at a wedding reception. Massa resigned before the pending House Ethics Committee investigation took place, but later argued that there was a concerted effort by establishment Democrats to oust him because he was voting against the healthcare reform bill moving through congress.[24] This narrative further confirmed the critique of and challenge to "politics as usual" within the SPM.

Due to these conclusions, the strategizing within the SPM was redirected toward how they could best build a grassroots movement that would be large enough to force politicians to act in the best interest of the public, or even change the political sphere in more generalized ways. In

[24] Condon, Stephanie (March 8, 2010). "Eric Massa Details Alleged Harassment, Blames Health Care Debate for Resignation." CBS News.

order to do this, single-payer activists had to make decisions about how they would interact with the new healthcare policy context, which shaped the environment of opportunity within which they continued to work. They had to determine if and how they would continue to focus on single-payer, or specific single-payer bills, within the ACA context.

THE IMPLEMENTATION OF THE AFFORDABLE CARE ACT

During the ACA implementation years (2010–2014) **the unwavering support of H.R. 676 became a point of debate and discussion.** The perceived abandonment of this legislation by both the original sponsor, Representative John Conyers (D-MI), and most H.R. 676 co-sponsors who had instead supported the enactment of the ACA, resulted in some movement activists raising the question "should we focus on HR 676 at all."[25] This discussion resulted in some division within single-payer organizations, such as Healthcare NOW. Prior to this point, the national SPM was primarily focused on increasing political sponsorship of H.R. 676, even calling themselves the "H.R. 676 movement" at times. While some activists adamantly believed that the focus of the movement should continue to be on H.R. 676, others argued that focusing on one piece of legislation was too limiting for the movement in the new ACA context. Activists who had experienced the Clinton era of healthcare reform in the 1990s, which resulted in a shift away from single-payer and the death of the national movement, were adamant in their assertion that a focus on single-payer must be maintained. In order to preserve organizational unity, the Healthcare NOW board passed a motion that they continue

> to support HR 676 and its advocacy for improved Medicare for All, along with supporting our individual members and affiliates in the diversity of tactics expressing the principles and movement-building for single-payer (including but not limited to other national legislation, state legislative efforts, healthcare is a human right, divestment, strike debt, etc.) and engaging in those efforts with the strength of our network where it is strategic and we have capacity to do so. ... This is a strong recommendation to continue to use HR 676 as tool to educate people on what we mean by single-payer, but we are not limited to it as the only tactic for our work.[26]

[25] Fieldnotes: Activist, Healthcare NOW board meeting, October 2013, Nashville TN.
[26] Ibid.

This resolution highlights the need to affirm their support for single payer through support of H.R. 676 while also emphasizing the need for "movement-building" within the new ACA context. Instead of H.R. 676 being identified as the core goal of the organization that will be achieved by mobilizing political support by adding co-sponsors to the bill, it is referred to as a tool that can be used to explain single-payer to an uniformed public in order to build the public support for single-payer that could change the political context into one that would be open to progressive healthcare policy (see Table 6.1 for a comparison of H.R. 676 and the Affordable Care Act).

Single-payer supporters were also divided in their assessment of how the SPM should interact with the ACA. This resulted in roughly four camps within the movement:

1. Those who did not want to shift any focus away from single-payer in order to address the ACA.
2. Those who wanted to directly challenge specific aspects of the ACA in order to halt its implementation.
3. Those who wanted to "make it work" and do what they could to support the implementation of the ACA.
4. Those who wanted to use critiques of the ACA as a way to talk about single-payer.

These perspectives dealing with how the SPM should react to the ACA were tied to slightly differing narratives of opportunity centered not only on what the implementation of the ACA would mean for the SPM but also on the possible effects of the failure or success of this policy on the future of the movement. These narratives of opportunity were open-ended, with different hypothetical conclusions. These predicted conclusions shaped the movement building decisions made by single-payer activists in each camp. This highlights how movement adaptability is shaped by possible narrative endings as well as current opportunities.

Those who wanted to continue focusing on specific pieces of legislation, such as H.R. 676, and not spend energy addressing the ACA, were a vocal minority within the movement. This group was concerned that any shift away from a focus on specific single-payer bills would result in the same type of movement death that had occurred following the Clinton era. This narrative of opportunity did not construct the ACA as an opportunity for mobilization but rather as a change that could kill the SPM if it was allowed to become a focus within the movement. A few of these

Table 6.1   Comparing the Affordable Care Act and H.R. 676

ACA era policy	The Patient Protection and Affordable Care Act (ACA)	H.R. 676
General approach	Mandatory Insurance via Employer and Individual Mandates = Play or Pay	National Health Insurance/Single Payer
Federal administrative role	Increased regulation of private insurance market and plans. Provides federal level exchange if not provided by the state. Administers tax-based penalties.	Establish Medicare for All Trust Fund Establish National Board of Universal Quality and Access Establish Office of Quality Control Appoint Director of Program
State administrative role	Create state-based American Health Benefit Exchanges and Small Business Health Options Program (SHOP) exchanges. Provide oversight of health plans. Increase Medicaid coverage.	Establishes Medicare for all regional offices "for the purpose of distributing funds to providers of care." State Directors coordinate funding, billing, reimbursements, assessment, health planning, global budgets, and so on.
Employer role	Employer mandate requires employers with 50 or more employees to provide health insurance coverage for employees working 30 or more hours per week or pay penalties.	Finance the system through payroll taxes.
Employee (patient) role	Individual mandate requires U.S. citizens and residents to have healthcare coverage—tax penalty imposed if individual does not comply.	Finance system through taxes.
Financing	In addition to premiums, insurance purchased through the exchanges is subsidized by federal government. Includes increased federal funding for state Medicaid expansion.	Establishes Medicare for All Trust Fund—funded by current federal funding mechanisms (medicare tax), progressive income/payroll tax, tax on capital gains income.
Benefits	Creates benefit tiers—Bronze, Silver, Gold, and Platinum—that involve the provision of different levels of services and cost-sharing. All provide "essential health benefits."	Comprehensive services such as hospital care, primary care, preventative care, long-term care, prescription drugs, mental health care, eye care, and dental care.

(continued)

Table 6.1 (continued)

ACA era policy	The Patient Protection and Affordable Care Act (ACA)	H.R. 676
Cost-sharing	Provides premium credits to those who purchase insurance through an exchange. Premiums, deductibles, and co-payments still active, but creates limits. Provides some subsidies to small business through tax credits. Reduces out-of-pocket expense limits up to 400 percent of poverty.	No deductibles, premiums, or copayments. No balance billing.
Payments	Payments depend on the private or public insurance plan but are subject to federal regulation and state oversight.	Negotiated reimbursement rates with physicians, and prices for prescription drugs, equipment, and so on. Global budgets for hospitals allowed. Payments made from Medicare for all Trust Fund.
Role of private health insurance	Mandated participation in the private insurance market for most individuals and businesses.	Prohibited by the state if payment by private insurance would duplicate payment made by state program.

individuals reduced their participation in established single-payer organizations in order to create new organizations that would reaffirm their support for specific single-payer legislation. For example, Dr. Margaret Flowers established Health Over Profit for Everyone (HOPE), which was rooted in a mission statement that included the assertion that "we believe that a National Improved Medicare for All system, as embodied in HR 676, is the best way to achieve this goal."[27] Activists in this camp were critical of any incremental healthcare reform measure and warned that incrementalism was "an obstacle to improved Medicare for all."[28] HOPE, for example, designed trainings dealing with how to resist incrementalism by "challenging the current talking points being used by 'progressives' to promote an incremental approach to healthcare reform."[29] Although

[27] Health Over Profit for Everyone "Our Mission" http://healthoverprofit.org/our-mission/.
[28] Health Over Profit for Everyone "Incrementalism as an Obstacle to Improved Medicare for Al and How We Resist It." http://healthoverprofit.org/incrementalism-ppt/.
[29] Ibid.

incremental measures change, many of the talking points that support them such as "we have to do what is politically feasible"[30] are relevant regardless of the time period or the specific incremental change being proposed. While this camp, HOPE included, was critical of many single-payer organizations that rooted themselves in a differing perspective, rather than conflicting with these established single-payer organizations, this new organization, as well as others, became important members of the single-payer network and further strengthened the mobilization potential within the movement.

The perspective of single-payer activists who mobilized to directly challenge the ACA in order to stymie its implementation, most notably the organization Single Payer Action,[31] was rooted in a narrative of opportunity that also constructed the ACA as a change with the potential to deflate the SPM and halt progress toward single-payer. The conclusion of this narrative was that, if successful, the ACA would close the door to future reforms for many years. Therefore, it became imperative to not only critique the ACA for its shortcomings but to actively mobilize against its implementation. This camp initially decided to focus on challenging the individual mandate component of the ACA by supporting a Supreme Court brief, written by Oliver Hall, that questioned the constitutionality of the individual mandate and encouraged the implementation of a Medicare for All system. This brief, which was signed by 50 doctors, did not receive a hearing, but briefs submitted by right-wing entities that similarly challenged the individual mandate component of the ACA did. This focus on the individual mandate resulted in single-payer activists unexpectedly finding some common ground with right-wing organizations, such as the Tea Party, who were also challenging the ACA through supreme court briefs.

The right-wing challenges to the ACA also occurred via state-based initiatives designed to overturn mandates at the state level, the first of which was Proposition C in Missouri. This was discussed as an opportunity by some single-payer supporters.

> Kevin in Houston: Obviously we don't want to align with the Tea Party. But the Missouri vote brings up a challenging opportunity for the movement.

---

[30] Ibid.

[31] Single Payer Action is a project of Daily Citizen Inc. founded by Russell Mokhiber. https://www.singlepayeraction.org/about/.

The vote is targeted against the individual mandate by the right. But it's hard for SP supporters because it sort of lines us up with them against the mandate, but we need to distinguish ourselves from the right.[32]

Because the first of these initiatives would be voted on in Missouri, where I was still located at that time, I was asked by national movement leaders to analyze Proposition C, the "Missouri Health Care Freedom Bill," and report back. I concluded that the short text presented on the ballot (which had drawn the attention of single-payer supporters) was misleading because the full text of the bill resulted in different conclusions. In my policy brief I stated that,

> After this reading of the text, it is clear that Proposition C works against the single-payer agenda. It is a good thing that Prop C is not binding. While the actual vote could still be interpreted as a public speaking out against mandates to buy specifically private insurance, because most of the public has only read or heard the condensed ballot text, and that this could be a good indication of the discontent that the public has with private insurance—the actual implementation of this measure would work against our goals for a publicly financed system.

Single-payer activists used this, and analyses of similar initiatives in other states, to conclude that while they might share critiques of the individual mandate with right-wing organizations, those critiques were rooted in opposing frameworks; thus the solutions to those critiques were incompatible. This, as well as a Supreme Court decision on June 28, 2012, that affirmed the individual mandate component of the ACA by concluding that it was a tax and therefore well within the scope of the powers of congress established in the constitution,[33] prohibited any further discussion of possible connections with right-wing organizations based on this issue.[34] This supreme court decision, which also struck down the Medicaid component of the ACA that required states to increase Medicaid coverage

---

[32] Healthcare NOW Conference Call Notes 2010.

[33] See also the full text of the SCOTUS decision here, https://assets.documentcloud.org/documents/392159/supreme-court-health-care-decision-text.pdf.

[34] For further discussion of this, see Hern, Lindy (2016) "Navigating the Borderland of Scholar Activism: Narrative Practice as Applied Sociology in the Movement for Single Payer Health Care Reform." *Journal of Applied Social Science* 10(2): 119–131.

because it was a violation of states' rights,[35] encouraged more alliance activities with left-leaning organizations working to both protect and expand Medicaid.

While it is true that many single-payer supporters were mobilized in support of the ACA and that these individuals or organizations continued to support the ACA, including Medicaid expansion, during its implementation, within the active single-payer organizations this perspective was rare and, in some ways, unwelcome. Those who wanted to "make it work" were a less vocal minority who were concerned that

> if ACA fails, it's inconceivable to me that anyone will want to touch HCR for 100s of years—generations to come. We are stuck in a world where our dysfunctional system cannot work—hopefully at some point 10 or 20 years, someone's gonna look up and say, why don't we just do Medicare, but that's not gonna happen if the ACA fails. We have to make it work.[36]

The narrative of opportunity supporting this perspective concluded that the failure of the ACA would mean the death of healthcare reform and thus the death of any possibility to move toward a single-payer system. This perspective encouraged single-payer activists to support aspects of the ACA, such as Medicaid expansion, while also inserting single-payer into the conversation. This was not incompatible with the dominant conclusion that a majority of the single-payer organizations, such as Healthcare NOW and PNHP, came to. Although they "balked at the idea of incrementalism,"[37] they knew that "we have to take certain incremental measures"[38] and decided to use critiques of the incremental changes stemming from the ACA as a tool for increasing grassroots support for single-payer. They could do this while also supporting the success of aspects of the ACA, such as Medicaid expansion. Later, when other challenges to the

---

[35] This decision removed the requirement to expand Medicaid to those at or below the threshold of 133 percent of poverty in order to receive federal funding for state Medicaid programs. Following the ruling, states could now opt in or opt out of the option to expand Medicaid with increased federal funding.

[36] Fieldnotes: Activist, Healthcare NOW National Strategy Meeting, Nashville TN, October 2013.

[37] Ken, Healthcare Now National Strategy Conference—Workshop on the ACA Five Years Later—October 2015.

[38] Ben, Healthcare NOW National Strategy Conference, October 2013.

ACA arose, the "make it work" contingent also adamantly worked to protect the ACA.

Most established single-payer organizations decided to continue to focus on building the movement, rather than on challenging or supporting the ACA directly or limiting their movement building to the support of any particular piece of legislation. Within this opportunity narrative, the ACA and the process of implementing it became a location for continued mobilization for single-payer and for building alliances with individuals or groups who did not previously support single-payer. This opportunity narrative concluded that the ACA was just one more step on the path toward single-payer and regardless of what happened to the ACA, single-payer activists must continue on that path. They did this not by ignoring the ACA or by directly challenging it but by inserting the single-payer option into discussions dealing with the ACA. For example, Healthcare NOW decided to insert single-payer into the public debate surrounding challenges to the individual mandate through the "Never Mind the Mandate Campaign." This campaign encouraged "members to send emails to Congress and the President with the message, 'No matter the outcome of the Supreme Court hearings, we still need single-payer healthcare.'" According to Healthcare NOW, almost 3000 people participated in this action, which was an important sign that there was still grassroots interest in single-payer. While this perspective was similar to those who wanted to "make it work" in that they used aspects of the ACA, such as the fight for Medicaid expansion, to mobilize for single-payer—unlike the "make it work" contingent, their primary focus was not on supporting the implementation of the ACA but on using this process as a way to move toward single-payer. So, when challenges to the ACA did occur, this contingent used those challenges to talk about the better option that would be "inevitable" if the ACA failed—a single-payer healthcare system. Single-payer activists were cautious about this assertion of inevitability,

You may have seen **dozens of articles and news clips claiming that if the Supreme Court strikes down the Affordable Care Act** in June, Democrats will have **no choice but to turn to single-payer** as the necessary alternative to healthcare reform. **"It's inevitable,"** they say. It thrills us to see single-payer in the limelight, **but claiming that single-payer is inevitable should the ACA go down misses a central component: you.** Your hard work lifted single-payer, improved Medicare-for-all, to the widespread consciousness we're now seeing. With your support we can push improved Medicare-for-all beyond talk and make it a reality. No matter how the Supreme Court rules in June, **we need to make sure single-payer healthcare remains a visible option for reform**. If the ACA is dismantled, the Democrats could, after all, decide to do nothing. Let's not let that happen.[39]

This perspective, that it would be best to use the activity surrounding the ACA as an opportunity for mobilizing in support of single-payer, became the dominant perspective in the movement during the implementation period, but it was not unchallenged.

Developing a unified and healthy way to mobilize within the new ACA context was not an easy process. The implementation of the ACA created "tension within the movement" as activists made decisions about how to approach the new context which was a "reality now" that activists were "going to have to engage with."[40] A hope-producing narrative arose from this debate and eventually became a unifying force for the SPM. Rita summarized this narrative when she concluded that the "ACA is here and everyone is moving around it, it's an incredible movement and organizing opportunity"[41] at the 2013 HCN national strategy conference. As the ACA was implemented, more openings for its critique and for alliance building connections with other organizations developed, leaving one activist to argue,

> this is our time. At the AFL-CIO conference, people were saying things about ACA that they were hesitant to say before—this is a time that we can be looking at new ways of organizing. Fight is not going away. In the 90's—Clinton put big hole in the Single Payer Movement. That's not happening now, we are too deep and too strong—we gotta be there and organize and move forward. Let's stay in the room and keep fighting.[42]

These conclusions encouraged single-payer activists to continue to "build the movement" for single-payer by forming relationships with other organizations working for social justice through progressive reform in multiple areas.

---

[39] Healthcare NOW Blog "Is Single-Payer Inevitable?" https://www.healthcare-now.org/blog/is-single-payer-inevitable/.

[40] Fieldnotes: Ben, Healthcare NOW National Strategy Conference, October 2013.

[41] Fieldnotes: Rita, Healthcare NOW National Strategy Conference October 2013.

[42] Fieldnotes: Mark, Healthcare NOW National Strategy Conference October 2013.

DEVELOPING INTERSECTIONAL GRASSROOTS SUPPORT FOR SINGLE PAYER

Single-payer activists defined the ACA implementation period as an opportunity to mobilize those grassroots activists who, working with groups like HCAN, had supported the Obama administration's reform agenda but were disappointed with the results. Single-payer activists hoped that due to the public option being dropped from the ACA, "HCAN and others may join the ranks of single-payer supporters."[43] According to this narrative of grassroots opportunity, these supporters of healthcare reform would now be "disenchanted" due to the lack of any kind of openly available publicly financed option in the ACA and thus would be more likely to participate in the mobilization for single-payer. Single-payer activists concentrated on taking advantage of this perceived grassroots opportunity by reaching out to these activists and organizations, while also diversifying their focus by taking on other causes that would ally them with these groups—such as defending public hospitals against closure and working with immigrant rights groups. The rise of other social movements during this period, such as Occupy Wall Street and Black Lives Matter, became a significant focus of the narrative practice of the SPM. Although the ideological background and goals of these movements varied, they shared similar critiques of "politics as usual" exemplified by "establishment politics." Their primary goal did not transition away from single-payer, but activists did shift their focus away from mobilizing political actors and toward mobilizing the public, in order to change the political context in which healthcare reform must occur.

Reconnecting with Old Friends

Single-payer activists worked to act on perceived grassroots opportunity by connecting with "old friends." Although the enactment of the ACA indicated to single-payer activists that there was less opportunity for the mobilization of political support, this was also defined by single-payer activists as an event that would increase the grassroots opportunity that the SPM would now face. Single-payer supporters believed that the enactment of a bill that did not even provide a public option would encourage single-payer supporters, who had redirected their energy toward

---

[43] Activist, Healthcare NOW Conference Call September 2009.

supporting the Obama administration's reform agenda, to once again support single-payer. Lynn in California explained how **"moveon vigils have provided good opportunities to push single-payer**—my experience is that 90% of attendees support single-payer. Going to these events is worth the effort,"[44] and Ken in Texas expressed hope that because the public option was dropped, "HCAN and others may join the ranks of single-payer supporters."[45] This narrative constructed the disappointment of public option supporters as an opportunity to mobilize these forces in order to build the SPM.

Disappointment over specific aspects of the bill did indeed encourage the re-commitment of some influential organizations to the cause of single-payer. Prior to enactment, the inclusion of the Stupak Amendment in the House bill, which imposed "tight restrictions on abortions that could be offered through a new government-run insurance plan and through private insurance that is bought using government subsidies,"[46] "incensed"[47] the National Organization for Women (NOW). Although the amendment was not included in the final language of the ACA, President Obama enacted a compromise through an executive order that reinforced the Hyde Amendment policy which prohibits the use of federal funds to pay for abortion procedures. NOW, which had originally voted to support single-payer in 1993,[48] recommitted to the goal of single-payer and prepared to "roll out a national action campaign in support of single-payer health care."[49] While NOW had recommitted to this goal as recently as 2004,[50] they had also redirected their focus to shaping the Obama administration's agenda during the healthcare reform period. NOW had,

> long argued that single-payer health care is the best way to achieve the goal of universal, comprehensive and affordable care for everyone. We believe

[44] Healthcare NOW Conference Call September 2009.

[45] Ibid.

[46] Herszenhor, David M. and Jackie Calmes "Abortion Was at Heart of Wrangling" New York Times online Posted on Nov. 7, 2009 See the text of this amendment here: http://documents.nytimes.com/the-stupak-amendment.

[47] National Organization for Women Press Release Posted March 2010 http://www.now.org/press/03-10/03-21a.html.

[48] National Organization for Women "Issues—Health" http://www.now.org/issues/health/052204owl.html.

[49] Fieldnotes: Terry O'Neill, NOW President, at Health Care NOW annual strategy meeting September 2009.

[50] Ibid. http://www.now.org/issues/health/050504vives.html.

single-payer will give doctors and patients, not the government and not a profit-driven industry, the power to choose the best medical care for each patient. At minimum, any health care reform package must contain a strong public option, while also allowing states to create their own single-payer plans.[51]

When it became obvious that the ACA would not have a public option and that it would not ensure reproductive choice for women, NOW once again recommitted to pushing for *national* single-payer instead of other options. This was a significant legitimization of the narrative of grassroots opportunity that single-payer activists constructed during the early implementation period.

Developing alliances with groups like HCAN was also discussed as a possibility. This created a significant tension within the drive to build the movement. Participants in HCAN were sometimes viewed as traitors to the cause because,

> their job is to channel people away from fundamental reform and the abolition of the insurance industry. That's what I'm arguing against HCAN—that is what they did. They never supported single-payer, and they siphoned off people who would have supported single-payer. In that sense, we are in opposition to them.[52]

While suggestions of alliances with HCAN resulted in tension, they also resulted in discussions about who was really involved in HCAN and the possibility of pulling them into the SPM. Francesca, who was the national organizer/executive director of Healthcare NOW in 2012, explained that,

> we're looking at two things: individuals we are trying to organize who may or may not know about single-payer and who we want to motivate to take action, and then there are the monolithic organizations for lack of a better term that are institutions who take public positions on the issue. And I think these are two separate things. Because the leaders of HCAN may not necessarily represent their membership. And I don't think it helps us to not reach out to individuals who may have been slightly informed on healthcare issues—and thus who may have been organizing for HCAN in the past—but who don't know anything about single-payer. Because these are individuals

---

[51] Ibid. http://www.now.org/press/09-09/09-10.html.
[52] Helen. Healthcare NOW conference call. July 2012.

who are much more likely to understand the nuances of our argument and become single-payer supporters rather than people who don't know anything about healthcare reform at all.[53]

Here, Francesca highlights the difference between the organization and the individual participants, which emphasized the possibility of mobilizing HCAN participants even if Healthcare NOW did not form an alliance with HCAN as an organization. Single-payer supporters were encouraged to "bury the hatchet" because,

> I'll tell you that the folks at HCAN, they are not your enemy folks—your enemy are the folks that I used to work for. Know who your common enemy is. For all who wanted to preserve the status quo—their enemy was ACA. ... Most at HCAN share views that single-payer is the ultimate goal. I know those people, they are wonderful folks and they do want the same thing. In my view, their ultimate goal is universal coverage for every American, there are different road maps that people will have to go to get there. ... I apologize if I got into sensitive areas. HCAN, I would be doing a great disservice if I didn't mention it. I'll tell you that you need some tough fuckin talk sometimes, or else you'll be here next year with no progress. United we win, divided we fall. They look for ways to divide you. So, just take my word for it, they are good people.[54]

Here, Wendell Potter is encouraging single-payer activists gathered at the One Payer States national meeting in 2012 to consider changing their relationship with HCAN into one of alliance instead of opposition. This was a difficult idea for some single-payer supporters to accept, but perhaps they would have come around and worked to develop this relationship with HCAN. However, HCAN discontinued operations before any meaningful alliance could develop. When the ACA was almost fully implemented in 2014, HCAN disbanded because their work of supporting the Obama administration's reform agenda was done. This was viewed as yet another opportunity because,

> It means there won't be a highly financed organization that is calling for something else as a progressive solution to the health care crisis. It gives us

---

[53] Francesca, Healthcare NOW conference call, July 2012.
[54] Wendell, One Payer States National Strategy Meeting, Keynote Address, Philadelphia, 2012.

an opportunity to reach out to groups that worked with HCAN. I think it's really important that we address it and how much more work there is to do. People probably have thoughts about this, but it's important we address it.[55]

The cessation of HCAN activities resulted in less competition for grass-roots resources and was defined as an opportunity to mobilize the membership that had supported this organization. For the most part, single-payer activists agreed that "a lot of people at the end of that process would say we're really for single-payer, but it's not possible right now. Gathering up those grassroots people will be important. I'm proud we're still standing."[56]

In addition to developing their alliances with grassroots organizations, single-payer activists concentrated on further developing their alliances with professional organizations, such as the Labor Campaign for Single Payer (LCSPC). In addition to the economic resources garnered from these alliances, which were sorely needed during the period of decreased funding directly following the enactment of the ACA, single-payer organizations learned and developed new movement building tactics through these alliances. One movement building tactic involved creating "Everybody Institutes" which was a method that had been used by labor organizations for some time. Mark Piotrowski, who is a labor organizer that sits on the Healthcare NOW board, introduced this tactic in the fall of 2013. Everybody Institutes were designed as regional training sessions that would train the public to be grassroots activists for single-payer. The goal of these institutes was to increase action-oriented grassroots support for single-payer, which would involve walking the walk as well as talking the talk. This focus on getting more support in action, and not just in theory, also played a role throughout the process of mobilizing labor support for single-payer. While labor unions had long been a location of support in theory, through the passage of resolutions and, economically, through donations to grassroots organizations, during the ACA implementation period, the emphasis transitioned to union activism. Single-payer activists were no longer satisfied with resolutions (which were often used primarily to encourage the support of political actors) or donations, they now wanted "boots on the ground" support from unions who indicated their theoretical support of single-payer through resolutions and

[55] Katie, Healthcare NOW conference call, January 2014.
[56] Rita, Healthcare NOW conference call, January 2014.

donations. Cindy Young, Healthcare NOW board member, CNA organizer, and NNU member, explained that,

> First someone will say you can't beat the medical industrial complex. Yes, we can beat them, but we have to be focused and willing to pony up that kind of money *and put our troops on the ground.* We have been focused on trying to bring the labor movement to the table—we can't bargain out of this. The ACA has helped us with this—nonunion employers are now going to have an advantage and unions are angry about that ... this is an opportunity to make the case—you can't fix this at the bargaining table, you need to come with us. No financial barriers to come with us—we want your people power and access to your membership—we have to build relationships and short-term stuff to show that we are partners.[57]

Cindy explains that the implementation of the ACA, which in some ways further reduces the autonomy and power of labor unions, is an opportunity to mobilize more unions in support of single-payer. She also indicates that it is important that this mobilization should involve actual "troops on the ground" which would reflect historical union activism in which "union meant social movement."[58] The process then turned to getting the "607 that have signed resolutions" to "translate into some action at the local level."[59] The new Labor Campaign for Single Payer, which was created in part through the work of Healthcare NOW board member Mark Dudzic, was designed to do this and became an important ally to grassroots single-payer organizations, such as Healthcare NOW. In fact, in August of 2014, Healthcare NOW and the Labor Campaign for Single Payer held their first joint national strategy conference in Oakland, California, which was also sponsored by National Nurses United and the One Payer States Association. This was the first of many successful joint conferences with allied organizations that were to follow.

---

[57] Fieldnotes: Healthcare NOW National Strategy Conference, Nashville TN, Oct. 2013.

[58] Fieldnotes: Kurt, OH Auto Workers Union, Fieldnotes: Healthcare NOW National Strategy Conference, Nashville TN, Oct. 2013.

[59] Fieldnotes: Pete, Healthcare NOW National Strategy Conference, Nashville TN, Oct. 2013.

Single Payer in the States

While national single-payer organizations remained committed to supporting legislation at the federal level, some, like Healthcare NOW, were also committed to supporting their old friends in the ongoing state-based movements around the country. While some previously successful movements, such as the one in Hawaii,[60] lost traction following the enactment of the ACA, others, such as the movement in Vermont, became more successful and thus a focus of the narrative practice and grassroots efforts of the SPM at large. In fact, a key aspect of the ACA—State Innovation Waivers—supported a renewed focus on state-level change. Ideally these waivers, which could also be tied to federal grants, would facilitate the development of transformational programs, such as single-payer. The "One Payer States" association was formed in order to connect state-based movements so that they could share lessons learned, as well as resources, in their efforts to enact state-level single-payer systems. I could write an entire book solely dealing with state-based movements for single-payer, but do not have the time or the space in this text to unpack every example. So, here I will examine the state-based movement that took the most central place within the single-payer narrative practice during the ACA implementation period—the movement in Vermont. Two of the central lessons learned through the state-based movement in Vermont were how to successfully use the "healthcare is a human right" frame to push for single-payer and also how, even if enacted, progress toward single-payer can be stopped during the process of implementation.

The human rights framework has long been used by social movements to fight for social change. Although this frame had also been used within the SPM for decades, examples of its use also exist in the Clinton era[61]; this frame really came to the forefront of single-payer narrative practice at the state level during the Obama era of healthcare reform (2007–2010) and, at the national level, during the ACA implementation period (2010–2014).[62] State-based movements had previously used the human

---

[60] A more extensive discussion of the Hawaii based movement can be found in Hern, Lindy (forthcoming) "Aloha Health: Examining the Impact of the Affordable Care Act on Health Care Policy Implementation in Hawai'i."

[61] See Chap. 2.

[62] Finnegan, Amy C. and Shelley K. White (2016). Vermont and Healthcare Reform Organizing: Human Rights Promise and Praxis. *Journal of Human Rights Practice* 8(1): 148–170.

rights framework when fighting for amendments to state constitutions that would affirm that health care is indeed a human right that should be protected by state policies. These efforts were critiqued by some because they "didn't really do anything." At an event at the tail end of the 2004 election season, Julia explained that,

> I'm about action, less talk more action. Groups who are trying to do that are trying to change the perceptions about healthcare in the United States. Most people now think that if, and only if, you can pay for it, then you should have it. They are using this amendment to make people think of it more like education, as a human right. Then maybe the way we fund healthcare can change.[63]

At that time in the early 2000s, the dominant framing used by single-payer proponents involved talking about how expensive health care in the United States was and how single-payer really was the economically conservative option that could reduce costs. This was a response to the dominance of the "contract with America" narrative and its effect on political economic policy. These frames discussed universal healthcare as a public good and focused on the assertion "that it is for the common good economically for everyone to be covered."[64] It's interesting that groups focused on economic inequality were some of the first to reject the economy-based frame in favor of the human rights frame. In 2008, Nicole, of the Women's Economic Agenda Project, explained why "the human rights framing is so important for this movement. This is the strategy that we should use and it is doable and is effective. We will convince people to mobilize and then pass legislation—based on principles not just a piece of legislation."[65] Here, Nicole highlights the relationship between this frame and a transition in strategy, from a focus on passing a "piece of legislation" to a focus on movement building. At this same meeting, Ethel Long-Scott, the executive director of WEAP,[66] led a panel detailing their work on health care as human right. WEAP had held Teach-Ins and Truth Hearings while also working with the Poor People's Economic and Human Rights Coalition to educate poor people on their right to

[63] Fieldnotes: Julia, MoSP "Victory Party," November 2004.
[64] Fieldnotes: Mimi, Healthcare NOW National Strategy Meeting, Chicago IL, 2006.
[65] Fieldnotes: Nicole, WEAP, Healthcare NOW National Strategy Meeting, Chicago, 2008.
[66] Women's Economic Agenda Project http://www.weap.org/.

healthcare. The National Health Care for the Homeless Council (NHCHC),[67] under the leadership of John Lozier, also began using the human rights frame very early. The Divestment Campaign for Healthcare Not Wealthcare educated and organized "to end all investment in health insurance companies" and sought to "make health care a human right through a publicly funded, national single-payer, improved Medicare-for-all system that assures all medically necessary care to everyone."[68] Activists "tied healthcare is a human right with ending poverty,"[69] which also highlighted the intersectional reality of the issue. The utility of the human rights frame was becoming more and more apparent to single-payer activists all over the country. It was viewed as an "approach that can unite us. All social movements have been successful because they were based on human rights."[70]

During the ACA implementation period, the primacy of the use of the economic "public good" frame was critiqued more extensively and the need for more transformational frames discussed. "We need to shift discourse from commodity to human rights frame—from market based to publicly financed. Look to colleagues from Vermont for example. Incredible success there using this."[71] Here, Anja critiques the use of a framework couched in a capitalist ideology that treats health care as a commodity and focuses on the cost of health care. This is set in juxtaposition to the human rights frame, which contradicts the idea that health care is something to be bought and sold on the market because, unlike a commodity, health care is a human right which "are inseparable and inalienable" from the human condition.[72] They are not rights that are granted, they are rights that exist and should therefore be protected through the social contract with the state. The Obama administration was also critiqued for "touting the major success of passing the ACA when it clearly falls so far short of the human rights guidelines."[73] The Obama administration was encouraged to "show their commitment to health care is a

---

[67] National Health Care for the Homeless Council https://nhchc.org/.

[68] Healthcare NOW "Divestment Campaign for Healthcare" https://www.healthcare-now.org/campaigns/divestment/.

[69] Fieldnotes: Ethel, Healthcare NOW national conference call, April 2010.

[70] Fieldnotes: Anja: National Economic and Social Rights Initiative. Report on the human rights movement in single-payer. Healthcare NOW national conference call. June 2009.

[71] Fieldnotes: Anja, Healthcare NOW National Strategy Conference, Chicago IL, 2010.

[72] Fieldnotes: John L., Single-payer National Strategy Conference, Chicago IL, 2015.

[73] Fieldnotes: Mary, Healthcare NOW national conference call, March 2011.

human right" by telling "each of the states that they will support their efforts to support universal health care and their commitment to health-care is a human right."[74] Single-payer activists hoped that the human rights frame could be successfully applied at the state level.

Healthcare is a Human Right campaigns had started in a few states during this era, with the most notable effort taking place in Vermont. This was a grassroots campaign created "basically to make health care reform politically possible in Vermont. There have been many efforts over past couple decades to enact single-payer, and they have all failed. In order to get change we want, we need to amass more political power."[75] This was a challenge to the idea that single-payer was not politically feasible and it worked to move single-payer "from being not politically possible to becoming a political priority."[76] The narrative background to this frame involved an analysis of the failures of single-payer mobilization efforts in the past. The conclusion formed from these action narratives was that top-down approaches, meaning a focus on mobilizing political support through conventional tactics directed toward political actors, had not been valid means to the end goal of implementing a single-payer system. This encouraged Healthcare is a Human Right campaigns to take a "step back from legislative work and focus on grassroots organizing."[77] This entailed a focus on building the movement from the ground up before focusing on legislation—which was a transition away from past efforts that started with legislation and had primarily worked to build political support for specific bills. In that past scenario, building public support was a secondary focus as a means to the end of building political support for a particular example of single-payer legislation.

There were two primary organizations within the Vermont movement. These organizations had the same goal, but different ideas about getting there. Vermont Health Care for All "framed healthcare as a public good, looked at economic and moral aspects, would cover everyone and save money," "focused on health professionals and businesses,"[78] and utilized

---

[74] Ibid.

[75] Fieldnotes: David Kriendler, Policy Committee Vermont Worker's Center, "Vermont single-payer update," Healthcare NOW conference call, June 2010.

[76] Vermont Workers Center "About" http://www.workerscenter.org/about-vermont-workers-center/history.

[77] Fieldnotes: Eric, Healthcare NOW national conference call, March 2012.

[78] Meeting Minutes: Deb, Healthcare NOW board discussion with Vermont/VWC activists, Healthcare NOW board meeting, Vermont Workers Center, August 2011.

more conventional methods directed at increasing the support of political and economic actors. The other organization, the Vermont Worker's Center (VWC), was grounded in the framework "Healthcare is a Human Right." This developed into a movement building model which empowered participants through grassroots organizing. Within this model, one didn't "have to just sit there and listen" because "that's counter to the HCHR model."[79] The human rights model required active participation, from the ground up. VWC activists asserted that "our continued success is largely a result of our grassroots organizing strategy combined with our human rights analysis."[80] Later, the VWC conducted human rights model training, which included lessons on both messaging and grassroots tactics, with national organizations.

The Vermont movement was influential because it did successfully enact single-payer legislation. First, in 2010, Act 128 was enacted. Act 128 "committed the state to design a new health care model for Vermont" and "allocated $300,000 to the Health Care Reform Commission to hire consultants to design three plans—a 'pure' single-payer plan through a public or private single-payer, a multipayer system with a 'public option,' and a third option that the consultant was given free rein to design." Quickly following this, in 2011, was Act 48, which "declares that healthcare is a public good and should be grounded in human rights principles"[81] and had the intended outcome of creating a single-payer system called "Green Mountain Care" in the state through a "three-stage implementation of a publicly-financed universal health care system, the point of which is a cost-saving single-payer financing mechanism," which was "designed to meet federal requirements of the Affordable Care Act, to take advantage of federal monies targeted for Vermont's insurance exchange and to petition for federal waivers that would streamline Vermont's reform."[82] According to the VWC's action narrative of this period, "after organizing in communities across the state to build a groundswell of grassroots

[79] Fieldnotes: Matt M., Healthcare as a Human Right Workshop, Single-payer National Strategy Conference, Oakland, August 2014.

[80] Meeting Minutes: David, Healthcare NOW board discussion with Vermont/VWC activists, Healthcare NOW board meeting, Vermont Workers Center, August 2011.

[81] Online Petition "Vermont can lead the way" http://www.workerscenter.org/vermontcanleadtheway.

[82] Vermont Health Care for All "Why Single Payer in Vermont?" http://www.vermontforsinglepayer.org/why_single_payer_in_vermont.

power," they had "proven that universal healthcare is politically possible."[83] Not only this, but the narrative dealing with how this success had been achieved through a human rights model became an important touchstone within single-payer narrative practice.

As Act 48 moved toward implementation, the VWC called for more active participation and support from the national SPM. Vermont activists explained that,

> Giant healthcare profiteers and other big monied corporate interests have begun an all-out fight to derail the effort. "Astroturf" front groups such as Vermonters for Health Care Freedom and Campaign for Vermont have already begun to take their message of fear to the airwaves as they easily buy up Vermont's small media market. They want to confuse and scare people in Vermont so they back away from actual implementation of this ground-breaking healthcare plan. … We will never be able to outspend these groups in an air war. But, we can out-organize them on the ground! We can over-come their messages of fear with the hope and promise of a transformed healthcare system, based on human rights.[84]

Connected to this was the assertion that if single-payer could be successful in Vermont (or California, or Hawaii, etc.), then it could be a model for the nation—Vermont could "lead the way!" National organizations responded to the call for national support and worked to support the implementation of Act 48 in several ways, including hosting national meetings in Vermont and sponsoring grassroots organizing activities in Vermont and around the nation, which was similar to the healthcare summer that happened in California during the Clinton era of the 1990s.

Earlier statements made by Vermont Senator—Bernie Sanders—had affirmed this state by state strategy. Previously, Sanders had said that "the quickest route toward a national health care program will be when individual states go forward and demonstrate that universal and non-profit health care works, and that it is the cost-effective and moral thing to do."[85] Senator Sanders, who had also supported a Vermont-based movement in

[83] Vermont Workers Center "Healthcare is a Human Right Campaign." http://www.workerscenter.org/healthcare.

[84] Online Petition "Vermont Can Lead the Way." http://www.workerscenter.org/vermontcanleadtheway.

[85] Senator Sanders' comments from the floor of the U.S. Senate, December 16, 2009. Quoted in http://www.workerscenter.org/vermontcanleadtheway.

the 1990s which had "organized all over state without internet" and "had 50 town halls that passed SP resolutions,"[86] continued to be supportive throughout the process of enactment and implementation of Green Mountain Care during the ACA period. This active support of the Vermont-based movement brought Senator Sanders even more into the center of narrative practice within the national SPM. Sanders' role in the Vermont state movement, as well as his role in national-level reform, made Sanders a key protagonist in the narrative practice of the SPM during the ACA implementation period.

While single-payer activists in Vermont were hopeful that some aspects of the ACA, such as the "state innovation waivers," would facilitate the development of a single-payer system in Vermont, the reality was much more complicated. Because Act 48 was enacted during the ACA implementation period, its own implementation was necessarily complicated by the process of implementing the ACA in Vermont. The enactment of Act 48 did not release the Vermont state government from the task of establishing a state-level exchange on which patients could shop for healthcare insurance. In Vermont, they "had to go through an exchanges setup first"[87] before they could focus on implementing Green Mountain Care. This process created problems for the implementation of Act 48. The first problem was that implementation of Act 48 was pushed back in order for the state to focus on implementing the ACA. While the financing mechanism for "Green Mountain Care" was supposed to be introduced in 2013, this was pushed back to 2015. Not only were the steps of the implementation process delayed, but problems with the implementation of the ACA resulted in Vermonters raising questions about the validity of state-centered approaches to healthcare financing. Vermont, like many states, "had a lot of problems with the state exchange. This has created some political challenges and undermined credibility of the government to administer health programs."[88] While this was viewed as a negative result that could stymie the implementation of Act 48, on the positive side, single-payer activists asserted that it had also "shown the problem of treating health care as a commodity in the exchanges."[89] The opposition was

---

[86] Meeting Minutes: Deb, Healthcare NOW board discussion with Vermont/VWC activists, Healthcare NOW board meeting, Vermont Workers Center, August 2011.

[87] Activist, VWC, Healthcare NOW national conference Call, April 2014.

[88] Ibid.

[89] Ibid.

"also trying to get together and work in a unified way, like we are." This opposition included

> the full spectrum: the loud tea party groups formed over the last couple of years, such as 'Vermonters for Health Care Freedom.' They're the mouthpiece, get a lot of money and will take out ads. But the real powerbrokers opposing this are the chambers of commerce, the hospital association, the insurers, business roundtable.[90]

Vermont single-payer activists worked to redirect the focus to Act 48 and encouraged its implementation as response to the shortcomings of the ACA.

This controversy came to an abrupt close when Vermont Governor Peter Shumlin, who had previously supported Act 48, "dropped a bomb shell by recommending that the Vermont state legislature not proceed with financing for universal, public health coverage for Vermont, stating that "now is not the time.""[91] Single-payer activists in Vermont, and around the country, were left to pick up the pieces and try to figure out exactly what had happened. The grassroots organizing training coming out of Vermont started to include an analysis of why Act 48, although enacted, was never implemented.[92] Important to this action narrative was the conclusion that a previously supportive political ally had given up and directed his support elsewhere. This further confirmed for the SPM that "legislators are not movement leaders" and that "politics as usual" would not allow for the development of a single-payer system.

Even though Act 48 eventually failed during the implementation phase, the national SPM continued to learn from the campaign in Vermont and their grassroots movement building strategy. The focus here was on boots on-the-ground training which involved going "door to door" in order to increase active public support for single-payer. National leaders viewed the Healthcare is a Human Right model as a "powerful tool" that "puts people first" and "challenged the austerity narrative and the narratives that

---

[90] James, Healthcare NOW national conference call, April 2014.
[91] Healthcare NOW "Webinar: Vermont at the Crossroads" https://www.healthcare-now.org/blog/webinar-vermont-at-the-crossroads/.
[92] Webinar "Lessons on the Vermont Movement for Healthcare as a Human Right" Jan. 22, 2015 ➔ https://www.healthcare-now.org/blog/webinar-vermont-at-the-crossroads/.

divide us."[93] Here, Ben explicitly ties the human rights frame to narrative practice by asserting that it is a direct challenge to the dominant narrative practice that was pushing for austerity measures at that time. Although, like the progress toward single-payer in Hawaii,[94] this movement toward single-payer that included the enactment of single-payer legislation was thwarted at the point of implementation, the national SPM continued to support them, as well as learn from their successes and failures. They continued to use the human rights frame because "the success of the Vermont Workers' Center's Healthcare is a Human Right Campaign has inspired others to replicate the VWC's model."[95] This also encouraged single-payer activists to work in organizations who were supporting human rights-oriented social change to address other, intersecting, social problems.

Making New Friends

The narrative of increased grassroots opportunity during the ACA implementation period encouraged single-payer activists to focus on the strategy of "building a movement" by connecting with organizations working on issues that intersected with health care. This strategy included a renewed focus on intersecting systems of oppression because "intersectionality is a very key concept, in terms of healthcare, SES is the most determinate indicator of health. This intersects with race and gender. We all have a stake in the outcome and organizing."[96] Single-payer activists focused on making new connections to and building coalitions with other grassroots organizations by specifically addressing more situational or located issues, while still maintaining their central goal of achieving a national single-payer system. Along with this focus on intersectionality came a concern for creating a more diverse movement. Single-payer activists were aware of the problem of diversity within the movement,

> This room is a little too white. That continues to be an issue in our movement. It's a challenge to figure out if we are going to win this, it's not some

---

[93] Fieldnotes: Ben Day, Executive Director of Healthcare NOW, Healthcare as a Human Right Workshop, Single-payer National Strategy Conference, Oakland, August 2014.

[94] See Hern, Lindy (Forthcoming), Aloha Health: Examining the Impact of the Affordable Care Act on Health Care Policy Implementation in Hawai'i.

[95] Healthcare NOW Work Plan, 2012.

[96] Fieldnotes: Michael L., Single-payer National Strategy Conference, Chicago IL, Oct. 2015.

people in and some people out is it? Everybody In, Nobody Out! We need to have our walk match what our words are saying. We are not always really great about talking about disparities around people of color, different economic divides—we want to talk about that today.[97]

Mechanisms to increased diversity were created, such as inviting participants with roles in a diverse array of organizations to speak at meetings or to even join the boards of single-payer organizations. Tied to this focus, single-payer activists were invigorated by emerging social movements dealing with a wide range of issues. They developed ways to act on the opportunities that these new movements presented.

Occupy Wall Street

The rise of Occupy Wall Street (OWS) in the fall of 2011 presented the SPM with another period of grassroots and economic opportunity—as this movement mobilized thousands of participants across the nation through grassroots activities in order to fight "back against the corrosive power of major banks and multinational corporations over the democratic process."[98] The critiques made by OWS challenged the supremacy of the free-market economic narrative and the role of corporations in the political sphere, both of which had stymied the progress toward single-payer in the past. Single-payer organizations did not immediately become involved in the OWS movement. There was concern about allying with a mobilization effort for which the goals were both unclear and multi-issue. In the fall of 2011 newsletter for Missourians for Single Payer (MoSP), Julia Lamborn discussed this issue in the "Message From Your President."

> As an organization should we support the Occupy Movement? As your President I am conflicted. I support peaceful demonstrations. Thousands will need to take to the streets to achieve Medicare for All. **We continue to be a one issue organization. That is why we do not join with most other organizations; no matter how we personally support the issue. In some ways, having one issue has hurt MoSP's growth and in other ways it has put us in the lead. MoSP is the only organization in Missouri (to**

---

[97] Fieldnotes: Pilar Schiavo Johnson—CNA organizer, Introduction to Plenary dealing with diversity within the SPM, Single-payer National Strategy Conference, Chicago IL, October 2015.

[98] Occupy Wall Street "About" http://occupywallst.org/about/.

my knowledge) that works for and educates for Medicare for All (improved and expanded). There is no confusion in our message. MoSP, the organization, will not support a different message.

At the national level, the support of OWS took on more active forms as single-payer organizations joined OWS marches and developed the narrative-based frame "Health Care for the 99 %." While the OWS movement is no longer as active and the occupations ended within a few years because it "was crushed in 2012,"[99] its critique of establishment politics, which was shared with the SPM, did have a long-lasting effect on political discourse in the United States.[100] Some of the practices of OWS, such as putting people on "stack,"[101] also filtered into the everyday practices of the SPM.[102] Single-payer organizations continued to work to mobilize supporters of OWS following its eventual departure from the public sphere and were able to intersect with these supporters via online social media platforms.

Black Lives Matter

The deaths of Trayvon Martin and Mike Brown resulted in the birth of a new wave of the racial equality movement. Black Lives Matter arose in 2013 when "three radical Black organizers—Alicia Garza, Patrisse Cullors, and Opal Tometi—created a Black-centered political will and movement building project called #BlackLivesMatter."[103] While the goal within BLM began with ending racialized violence, particularly the use of excessive or deadly force by law enforcement, it developed into a multi-faceted and intersectional effort to address human rights violations in multiple dimensions. This grassroots mobilization effort adeptly used both internet-based organizing, using the #blacklivesmatter platform, and on-the-ground organizing—notably mobilizing the "Black Lived Matter Ride" which converged on and supported the occupational protesting that had arisen

[99] Ibid.
[100] Calhoun, Craig. 2013. "Occupy Wall Street in perspective." *British Journal of Sociology*, 64 (1): pp. 26–38.
[101] This was a practice used in OWS in which individuals who wanted to raise a comment or question would be put onto a list—or stack. This became a common practice in the SPM and I first noticed its use at the 2012 OPS conference.
[102] Fieldnotes: One Payer States Conference, Philadelphia, June 2012.
[103] Black Lives Matter Website "Herstory" https://blacklivesmatter.com/herstory/.

organically after the murder of Mike Brown in Ferguson Missouri. This effort became formalized as the Black Lives Matter Global Network that currently has 40 chapters around the world in which "members organize and build local power to intervene in violence inflicted on Black communities by the state and vigilantes."[104]

Single-payer activists were also concerned about racial inequality, particularly within the realm of health care yes but also in its intersections with other social institutions and processes. Seven or so years before the rise of BLM, single-payer supporters, particularly Representative John Conyers and HCN Executive Director Marilyn Clement, who had both been active in the Civil Rights Movement of the 1950s and 1960s, had been purposeful in framing the SPM as the "New Civil Rights Movement" due to the intersection of racial, economic, and health inequality.[105] Several multi-issue organizations involved in the SPM, such as the Women's Economic Agenda Project (WEAP), also focused on other issues affecting racial and economic inequality. BLM became a focus of discussion at the 2014 Single-Payer Strategy Conference when Ethel Long-Scott, executive director of WEAP, gave a rousing speech about the intersection of the SPM with BLM which ended with a passionate chant involving all those attending affirming the movement by loudly chanting "Hands up. Don't Shoot."[106]

The intersection of BLM and the SPM was related to the focus on human rights. Matt, of the VWC, explained that "if we think that our struggles are not tied to Ferguson, then we are missing the point—that's one of the reasons to use the human rights framework instead of policy, we can unify under broader framework."[107] Single-payer activists worked to develop ways in which they could act on the opportunity to work with this intersecting movement. Single-payer supporters agreed that, other than their own movement, "Black Lives Matter is the most important

[104] Ibid.

[105] For a more detailed discussion of this, see Hern, Lindy S. F. (2012). "Everybody In and Nobody Out: Opportunities, Narrative, and the Radical Flank in the Movement for Single-Payer Health Care Reform." PhD thesis, University of Missouri Library Systems (Order No. 3530875).

[106] Fieldnotes: Single-payer National Strategy Conference, Oakland, August 2014.

[107] Fieldnotes: Matt M., Healthcare as a Human Right Workshop, Single-payer National Strategy Conference, Oakland, August 2014.

movement happening right now."[108] A creative mobilization effort for highlighting this intersection arose out of the Physicians for a National Health Program (PNHP), which created a "White Coats for Black Lives" tactic that became "a place to find that intersection"[109] with BLM. Tactics that focused on how "black lives matter in terms of healthcare and medicine"[110] became opportunities for intersectional grassroots mobilization. The issue of racial equality in health care was also important for another intersecting issue that had long been a focus of the single-payer narrative—that of immigrant rights.

Immigrant Rights: The Dreamers

Single-payer activists were, and are, committed to the goal—"Everybody In. Nobody Out." This specific aspect of their vision for an ideal single-payer system tied the SPM to the Immigrant Rights Movement. For most participants within the SPM, the ideal system would provide health care that is free at the point of service (meaning no deductibles or co-pays) regardless of immigration status. While the question of whether a universal system would really cover everyone, including undocumented immigrants, remains a contentious topic to this day, single-payer organizations continued to assert that for them, an ideal system would actually include everyone. Many agreed with the assertions that in order to stay true to this goal, it would be necessary to "work from ground up" and to not create any "policy without input from the immigrant community."[111]

The experience in Vermont was also a lesson in how difficult it would be to hold true to this aspect of the ideal. While it initially seemed as though everyone, including undocumented workers, would be included in Green Mountain Care because "there hasn't been the hostility that there has been in other parts of the country. The idea was that everybody was in, the consensus is that they should be covered,"[112] the reality was much more complicated. In fact, "a couple of senators added an

[108] Fieldnotes: Ben Day. "How Do We Build a Winning Social Movement." Single Payer National Strategy Conference. Chicago, IL. Oct. 2015.

[109] Fieldnotes: Katie. Healthcare NOW Board Meeting. October 2015.

[110] Fieldnotes: Marilyn. Single Payer National Strategy Conference. Chicago IL. Oct. 2015.

[111] Fieldnotes: Betsey, DREAMER and participant in the California based SPM, Plenary dealing with diversity within the SPM, Single-payer National Strategy Conference, Chicago IL, October 2015.

[112] Fieldnotes: Activist, One Payer States Conference, Oakland CA, August 2014.

amendment barring undocumented folks from the healthcare plan, Green Mountain Care," and "all political insiders said there was no possibility that the VWC could get this [amendment] repealed. The argument was that undocumented are barred from federal ACA anyway so why fight for this? Well, because universality means everyone."[113] This would continue to be an important focus within the SPM in the coming years—especially with the rise of authoritarian anti-immigrant politics on the right.

Single-payer activists worked to address all of these issues. But before moving forward too much, they had to assess what had happened during the ACA enactment and implementation period, how they could best respond to this, and how they could use this response to build the movement. Notably, strategies involving the direct use of narrative came to the forefront of the movement building tactics within the SPM. The focus transitioned to "winning the battle of the story, by developing our own narrative" because "the narrative of the mainstream is not our narrative— It is the narrative of the ruling class."[114]

NARRATIVE STRATEGIES: FRONT AND CENTER

Also necessary to movement building is a narrative about how we win that is believable and bold and lends people a sense of urgency. We ask, after stories, do you think if ordinary people come together, can working people come together and win? Make the "impossible" seem inevitable tomorrow? Nationally, people everywhere, whether state bills or not, need to have a movement narrative that allows people to feel they are part of a national movement that's winning. Need narrative that unites people around a single vision. That the ACA is not it, single-payer is.[115]

The first narrative tactic used by single-payer activists involved sharing the story of the Obama era of healthcare reform from a single-payer perspective. This tactic involved constructing and sharing a "Single-Payer Narrative" about this era of healthcare reform.

The idea behind the Single-Payer Narrative, is that we answer the question, "what happened to healthcare reform this year, and how do we get there

[113] Fieldnotes: David. Healthcare NOW board meeting with Vermonters.
[114] Fieldnotes: Matt M. "Healthcare is a Human Right" Workshop. Single Payer National Strategy Conference. Oakland CA, 2014.
[115] Fieldnotes: David—HCN board meeting with Vermonters. August 2011.

from here?" The idea is to tell the story, emphasizing the decision to leave single-payer out of the debate by the Democrats, and instead negotiate with the insurance industry. The strategic point to this is that, one of the things we were told is that single-payer isn't feasible. But the conclusion I draw from this year, because single-payer was off the table, it was inevitable that process would go the way that it did—into the hands of the insurance industry—and that real reform becomes impossible. A lot of people fell into the trap of the public option, and we need to tell them that the only way to go forward is with single-payer as the lead issue, because without it, you don't have much of a debate.[116]

The critique made by single-payer activists was that their perspective and experiences continued to be mostly excluded from mainstream coverage of the ACA era of healthcare reform. Thus, they concluded that they must create ways to share their own version of the story with a wider audience in order to encourage grassroots support and build the movement.

This narrative strategy resulted in the production of several "single-payer stories." One example is the film "The Vampires of Daylight" which was created by Helen Redmond and Marilena Marchetti, with the support of Healthcare NOW. This film is a

documentary film about health care [that] looks at the crisis from the perspective of ordinary people. It asks if they believe health care is a human right and if they support a single-payer, national health care system. It's also an unapologetic takedown of President Obama's fundamentally flawed health care legislation, the PPACA. The filmmakers argue that a mass movement must be built to abolish the for-profit health insurance industry. We document the fight in 2009 for single-payer that the mainstream media ignored.[117]

The filmmakers were able to develop this narrative, which counters the dominant narrative of the successful passage of "landmark" healthcare reform legislation, by utilizing the new forms of democratizing technology such as digital filmmaking and internet-based video sharing. They also drew on less material forms of cultural opportunity by connecting the narrative in the film with the pop-culturally salient and powerful narrative during that period of the "Vampires of Twilight." This film was shown for

---

[116] Ken, Healthcare NOW Conference Call March 2010.
[117] The Vampires of Daylight. 2012. Produced by Marilena Marchetti and Helen Redmond.

the first time on March 15, 2012, in NYC, and activists around the country were invited to attend via social media networking sites including Facebook. The creation of this resource illustrates the importance placed on this narrative strategy and the ability of the SPM to act on contemporary forms of cultural opportunity.

Several other documentary films were created by single-payer activists during this period. One particularly relevant film was created due to the efforts of business owner Richard Master when "he decided to tackle the problem of healthcare using best business practices … doing an in-depth analysis, finding the right diagnosis and then determining the fix,"[118] due to the enormous expense of providing insurance to his employees. This resulted in a film that makes the "business case" for single-payer, as well as follow-up films that tackle the role of *Big Pharma* and the *Big Money Agenda* in the U.S. healthcare system. While *Fix It* was originally distributed[119] or sold as DVDs, all of the films produced from this endeavor are currently available for free via online video streaming, which facilitates their use as organizing tools. Another filmmaking team, Laurie Simons and Terry Sterrenberg, produced two films during this period. The first film, *The Healthcare Movie*, is narrated by Keifer Sutherland and "provides the real story of how the health care systems in Canada and the United States evolved to be so completely different, when at one point they were essentially the same."[120] A follow-up film "NOW is the Time: Healthcare for Everybody" focuses specifically on the United States and "explores what single-payer healthcare is, how it saves money and what is being done in a growing movement to make it happen."[121] While these films were not made as freely available as the *Fix It* films, activists were encouraged to get copies of the films and share them with their communities in an effort to mobilize more grassroots support for single-payer.

In addition to these longer documentaries, single-payer organizations, such as Healthcare NOW, started producing short films that explained aspects of health policy, personal healthcare stories, or how to participate in the mobilization for single-payer. These short films were widely shared

---

[118] Fix It Healthcare "About" https://fixithealthcare.com/about/.

[119] Activists were given free copies of the film and supporting materials at the 2015 Single Payer Strategy Meeting in Chicago.

[120] The Healthcare Movie "About." http://thehealthcaremovie.net/home/about-the-film-2/.

[121] Now is the Time: Health Care for Everybody. Available at: https://vimeo.com/205116537.

via email, websites, and social media. Each time that I viewed a new film, I remembered the days in the mid-2000s when there was one short VHS tape film that explained single-payer, using a PROM analogy, that single-payer activists passed around. I was consistently amazed at how far the movement had come in its use of video and internet-based technology—from one VHS tape to thousands of videos online! Single-payer activists used all of these narrative tools to act on perceived grassroots opportunity.

As the ACA was implemented, the single-payer narrative concluded that the public was becoming more and more frustrated with this new policy. This was based on the assumption that due to glitches in the implementation process, "out of the ACA there's the narrative that the ACA Healthcare.gov is a disaster, so single-payer [or any government involvement in healthcare] is a disaster."[122] Single-payer activists worked to redirect this narrative by "trying to say that private insurance is the disaster and we're stuck with it right now, unfortunately."[123] A few tactics were developed as part of this narrative strategy including the "Health Insurance Watch" and "Healthcare Horror Stories" internet-based platforms. The Health Insurance Watch was intended to be an online platform providing analysis of the actions of private insurance companies within the ACA context—with data including insurance CEO pay, company profits, and healthcare outcomes. It was designed to counter the

> right-wing narrative about all these problems with the ACA, that government intervention is a bad thing. This is not just an attack on the ACA, but an attack on single-payer. We have to change the narrative, be able to be critical of the ACA in a way that is truthful, but also points us in right direction: public insurance is much more efficient, the humane thing to do would be to cover everyone. To change that narrative, we're going after the private health insurance industry, for things like this: limited networks, high overhead spending, high executive compensation. Send us your feedback on this campaign.[124]

Although this tactic was sponsored by Healthcare NOW, in practice it was intended to be developed as a wiki in which multiple participants could contribute to this data-based analysis of the health insurance industry. The "healthcare horror stories" tactic involved both training participants to

[122] Ben: Healthcare NOW national conference call, Jan 2014.
[123] Ibid.
[124] Ben, Healthcare NOW National Conference Call March 2014.

tell their stories in effective ways and giving them an online platform through which they could share their stories about healthcare problems within the ACA context with a wider audience. Both of these tactics were oriented toward revealing the ongoing healthcare system problems within the ACA context. While the health insurance watch was eventually abandoned due to a lack of resources for and participation in this particular tactic, as well as an increasing emphasis on using personal stories over statistics to garner support, the tactic of sharing healthcare stories continues to be used within the movement.

Specific narrative strategies were also used to encourage the support of particular groups of people. For example, the Healthy Artists Initiative was created to draw the support of young artists in order to get "young and creative people involved with this movement. ID artists who can contribute to this cause."[125] It was "founded on the idea that artists, creatives, and young people can play an important role in making a humane health care system a reality. Why? They have a special stake in the issue."[126] For this tactic, Julie Sokolow, a filmmaker in Pittsburgh, created short films in which artists talked "about their lives, work, and health care stories."[127] These short films were freely shared with a wide audience via the internet.[128] This tactic utilized the health care is a human right frame in order to attract a more general audience of artists (see Fig. 6.1 for a visual summary of narrative practice during this era).

BUILDING THE MOVEMENT: THE RISE OF A REVOLUTION

These developing narrative strategies were oriented toward building the movement in order to counter the negative aspects of the ACA context and mobilize a larger grassroots movement that would become powerful enough to challenge the political establishment and create a political context that would be forced to take the single-payer solution seriously. Activists critiqued the focus on debating the facts, both within the movement and within the larger discourse dealing with healthcare reform,

---

[125] Julie, Healthcare NOW national conference call, April 2014.
[126] Healthy Artists Initiative "Mission" https://healthyartists.org/mission/.
[127] Julie, Healthcare NOW national conference call, April 2014.
[128] Healthy Artists Initiative "Homepage" https://healthyartists.org/.

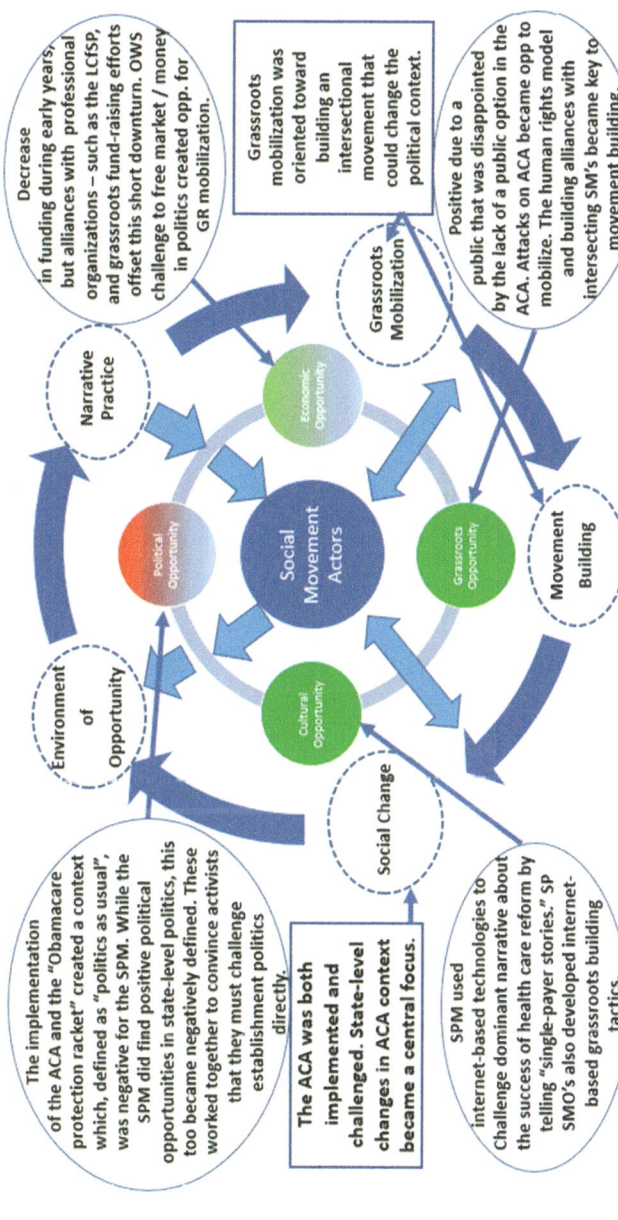

Fig. 6.1 The ACA era narrative practice

because they knew "that politics is based on emotion and narrative. The flood has come and many have drowned, many are still in the ocean. The lifeboat is single-payer, but they can't grasp it because they are afraid they will drown."[129] In the years leading into and during the Trump administration, single-payer activists focused on changing the political context from the outside in.

---

[129] Fieldnotes: Annette, Single Payer National Strategy Meeting, Chicago, October 2015.

CHAPTER 7

"Bernie Will": Narratives of Hope and Resistance During the Anti-Establishment Era

Sitting in my relatively new home in Hawai'i in January of 2017, I'm watching Nina Turner, past state-senator of Ohio and current progressive leader,[1] speak to hundreds of single-payer activists at the national single-payer strategy conference convening in New York City. This conference, which is the largest national single-payer conference to date, is being hosted by several progressive groups including Healthcare NOW and Labor Campaign for Single Payer. This is the first strategy conference that I have not been able to attend for about ten years and I am missing this opportunity to connect with the single-payer community. However, as I watch Turner speak, I am able to engage with other single-payer supporters by clicking "like", clicking love, or by leaving a comment to participate in the lively discussion surrounding the keynote address. Little thumbs up symbols or white hearts encased in a red circle float across the screen as Turner discusses the need to change the political environment into a context in which single-payer is not only possible, but probable. I express my appreciation through a heart emoji as the gathered activists in the room give Turner a standing ovation when she states that "we need a paradigm shift in this country, that people who run for elected office from dog catcher to President of the United States—mean what you say, say what you mean. Stand up for the people. Care more about the next generation than your next election—those are the kinds of people that we want elected."[2] I also contribute to the angry faced emojis marching across the screen when she mentions the recent election of Donald Trump to

---

[1] Turner is now President of Our Revolution and a co-chair of Bernie Sanders' 2020 presidential campaign.

[2] Nina Turner, Single Payer National Strategy Conference, New York, January 2017.

© The Author(s) 2020
L. S. F. Hern, *Single Payer Healthcare Reform*,
https://doi.org/10.1007/978-3-030-42764-1_7

the Presidency, his inevitable swearing in as the 45th President of the United States, and the likely consequences of this transition for national health policy, but express my solidarity with the gathered activists by clicking like when she states that regardless of the ascendency of Trump, they must continue working for single-payer because, "There is promise in the problem. We will surmount this challenge. We will get to single-payer. …The change that we need to get single-payer Medicare for all is not going to come from the grass-tops, it is going to come from the grassroots. It is going to come from people like you in this room. Soul force is what it's gonna take."[3]

A few months later, in June of 2017, from the same home in Hawaii, I'm watching the activities of the People's Summit that is taking place in Chicago. As activists from around the country discuss working for Medicare for All during a breakout session, I am able to comment and discuss this issue with other activists who are also participating via Facebook live. As Bernie Sanders discusses in a keynote address the need to "change the politics of what is possible", I contribute my own likes and hearts which add to the hundreds of likes and hearts being offered by others from around the country and around the world. There are several professional feeds—Our Revolution and The People for Bernie Sanders among others. But, I prefer the shaky camera coverage posted by my friend Pamela—it makes me really feel like I am there, in the thick of it, cheering with the crowd. I am filled with a similar sort of energy and emotion that encourages and invigorates me when I am able to attend these events in person.

You might say that these small actions, clicking like, leaving a short comment, or retweeting an image of a billboard that says "politics as usual won't guarantee healthcare for all. Bernie will,"[4] are not important—that they don't have any real political effect and can encourage supporters to click instead of taking action in other more instrumental ways. And, this may in fact be a legitimate criticism. You might also say that networking sites, such as Facebook, have played a role in creating the current political context through the diffusion of fake news, "alternative facts," or political propaganda. And given what we have learned about the systematic effort made to influence the outcome of the 2016 election by "Russian bots" via Facebook, this would also be a legitimate critique. There is tension in the promise of internet-based platforms—new technological innovations create opportunities for progressive mobilization, but they also create more ways in which oppositional forces can both constrain and motivate action. However, in my decade in the field as a scholar-activist, I have found that

---

[3] Ibid.
[4] National Nurses United (NNU) billboard in Iowa. Posted on Twitter by RoseAnn DeMoro, former executive director of National Nurses United. November 17, 2015.

one of the most important acts for producing the hope that change is possible is maintaining the type of communication that can foster ideas and energize action. For me, someone who made a move across an ocean for a dream job and was thus less physically connected to the activist community, finding ways to foster this communication has been extremely valuable. Facebook Live became one of those ways during the 2016 election season and it grew in importance during the period that followed. This, the possibility of building networks through communication platforms, is especially important during periods in which there is a rising call to action and increased energy to push for positive social change, periods like the one that followed the election of Donald Trump.[5]

While the election of Donald Trump to the Presidency of the United States seemed to be a definite blow to progressive social change, it actually inspired growth within progressive mobilization efforts. For example, while the push for the Affordable Care Act and the effects of its implementation initially resulted in some fragmentation within the Movement for Single Payer, this fragmentation ultimately resulted in the formation of new grassroots organizations in support of single-payer and increasing numbers of individual supporters—both of these factors served to increase the single-payer network and its mobilizing potential as it entered the Trump era. An important aspect of the resistance effort that developed following the election of Trump—a resistance effort that is focused on working for progressive social change while resisting regressive social change—is the ability of activists from all walks of life to communicate in empowering ways. Activists must adapt to changing technologies, as well as changing political realities, when working to mobilize for progressive social change.

In this chapter, I examine the narratives of opportunity that single-payer activists developed during what I refer to as the "anti-establishment era"[6] in which the rise of President Donald Trump and the popularity of Senator Bernie Sanders (I-VT) both played a significant role in single-payer narrative practice. During the Obama era, a critique of "politics as usual" rose to the forefront of the single-payer narrative. This critique

---

[5] Note: This was originally written as an analytical memo to myself, which I then published with Common Dreams—an independent news website—in June of 2017. You may find that earlier article here, https://www.commondreams.org/views/2017/06/16/power-personal-connections-dark-age-trump.

[6] I am not the only, nor the first, writer to use this term as a descriptive for the current era. But for me, this term is grounded in the data that I have collected during this period, not in the larger usage of the term.

arose due to many factors including the particular alienation of single-payer activists from the process of healthcare reform, the actions of "corporate" democrats during this process, and the impact of the new Affordable Care Act (ACA) context on single-payer activities. Lessons from state-based movements, such as Vermont, also informed this critique and the turn against establishment politics within the Single Payer Movement (SPM).[7]

IT TAKES A REVOLUTION: CHALLENGING THE ESTABLISHMENT WHILE GROWING A MOVEMENT

During the last years of the Obama administration, single-payer supporters focused on building a movement that could change the political context and developed several narrative driven tactics to do this.[8] During the 2016 election season, this push to change the political context resulted in some focus again shifting to the political opportunity presented by the Sanders campaign for the presidency. The dominant narrative of the current "Medicare for All Movement" presented in popular media, as well as some academic texts, seems to be that the Sanders campaign is the primary cause for a new wave of mobilization for single-payer. While the Sanders campaign was indeed a boon to the movement, the story of how the SPM arrived at this critical moment is much more complicated, and this story developed over several decades.[9] In fact, encouraging Bernie Sanders to run for the presidency was a key aspect of a political strategy designed to change the environment of opportunity, and specifically the political sphere, in ways that would make it more open to single-payer and other progressive causes. This "Outside / Inside" strategy was in development long before Sanders decided to become a presidential candidate.

Outside/Inside Strategy: Bringing the Outside Inside

I first heard the term "inside/outside" used at the 2007 Healthcare NOW National Strategy meeting in Chicago. In his keynote address, Congressman

---

[7] See Chaps. 5 and 6 for more discussion of this.
[8] See Chap. 6 for a detailed explanation of this.
[9] See Chaps. 1, 2, 3, 4, 5, and 6.

John Conyers (D-MI), the original sponsor of H.R. 676,[10] talked about what was happening with H.R. 676 on capitol hill, explaining that this was an "inside—outside game."[11] This strategy orientation emphasized the need to mobilize both support of political insiders and support of political outsiders in order to achieve a policy goal. Working to promote H.R. 676 in "an inside outside way" at that time included making sure that every congressional office was "flooded ... getting calls and calls and calls," which was intended to make politicians "focus like never before."[12] At this early stage, leading into the Obama era of healthcare reform, the "inside/outside" strategy mostly relied on outsiders being mobilized to encourage insiders to support single-payer, primarily by becoming co-sponsors of H.R. 676, by working to "bring the passion of the social movements inside the political arena."[13] Following the enactment and implementation of the Affordable Care Act (ACA), single-payer supporters, who were alienated from the policy process, narratively constructed "politics as usual," embodied by the Obama administration and exemplified by insider tactics, as the enemy of their goals as a social movement. Although Obama had emphasized an "outside" strategy during his campaign, once elected he rejected the involvement of outsiders during the process of healthcare reform.

Election periods were a way to bring outsiders into the political sphere and presented the SPM with both opportunities and constraints. Due to their tax status, most grassroots single-payer organizations are not able to directly support specific political candidates or parties—so their options are limited in comparison to other types of organizations that are specifically political or are professionally based (such as unions).[14] In addition to this, there is always the possibility that grassroots supporters and economic supporters of single-payer organizations will shift their resources toward campaign-driven organizations to support political candidates during an election season, which can mean less funding for or active participation in

[10] H.R. 676 was first introduced by Conyers in 2003 and was the central organizing legislation for the SPM until 2017.

[11] Fieldnotes: John Conyers—Address to the 2007 HCN National Strategy Meeting Chicago.

[12] Ibid.

[13] Fieldnotes: Tim Carpenter, Healthcare NOW National Strategy Conference, St. Louis Missouri, 2009.

[14] Unions typically have a 501 C 5 tax status, which allows for more political lobbying and support of political candidates.

single-payer organizations. At the same time, election periods also present single-payer organizations with an opportunity to reach more of the public by inserting their perspective into the discourse surrounding the electoral process. For example, Healthcare NOW often uses a tactic that involves critiquing the health policy proposals or past votes on health policy of each potential candidate. This critique is followed by an affirmation of which candidates would best support the single-payer agenda. Prior to the 2016 election season, single-payer supporters had primarily focused on an inside/outside strategy in which they reacted to the candidates in this way. This changed in the 2016 election season in which they participated in an outside/inside strategy that would involve an emphasis on bringing political outsiders to the inside of the political process through elections—primarily through the promotion of Senator Bernie Sanders (I-VT).

A transition to an outside/inside orientation really became apparent to me at the 2013 Healthcare NOW (HCN) National Strategy meeting in Nashville, Tennessee, three years before the 2016 election. At this meeting, activists often expressed their concern about the "polarization" that was occurring within the political sphere. Sociologist Frances Fox Piven—a champion of outsider politics—gave a rousing keynote address in which she told the gathered activists that this was a "time of big and tumultuous change in American politics." She explained that "there is madness in this country—there is. Not only at the bottom but at the top" and compared the conditions in 2013 with the conditions in the 1850s—in the years preceding the American Civil War. She warned that while there had been an expansion of democratic rights in the years since that horrible period, there had also been concerted efforts by economic and political elites to place "crippling limits" on those rights through "bureaucratic and procedure barriers," such as voter ID laws, the closure or under-resourcing of voting facilities, and the lack of an election day holiday. In addition to this, Piven said, other factors were lowering political participation or representation—such as the electoral college and the lack of transparency in the legislative process which made it "so difficult to understand what a contemporary government has done. This is why it is that Fox news can spread these lies about ACA and Obamacare—who can understand it? Legislation is difficult to read and extremely complicated." Piven warned that this was only becoming more troubling with the rise of the "tea party congress" that was continuing to gerrymander and commit a "full scale attack on voting rights." In the midst of all of this negativity, Piven indicated that there was still hope because "in moments of instability, progressive changes sometimes became possible." Piven encouraged the audience to work to "restore the promise of the U.S. and improve upon it."[15] I recall the feeling in the room after this speech, people were visibly shaken—there were even a few tears shed—but also motivated to act. Several comments were made about how "inspiring" the conference had been.

The conversation then turned to the need to build people power within the movement. The conclusion was made that old models, focused on growing support based on policy education, were no longer sufficient. Laurie, a single-payer activist from New York, summarized this saying, "there is education, and then there are power dynamics. The reason that we don't have single-payer is not because we don't educate, it's because we don't have power."[16] The conversation then turned to a possible outsider strategy that would involve massive disruption through various possible means such as sit-ins, strikes, and/or mass refusal to pay medical debt. Tim Carpenter, who was then the executive director of the Progressive Democrats of America (PDA), reframed this discussion a bit by bringing the focus back to an inside/outside strategy explaining that "Marilyn Clement took me under her wing, we talked about inside and outside organizing—working inside and outside of our government. We can make it and can do it collectively—she is a role model for all of us. I'm very proud to be part of this team."[17]

Tim Carpenter had worked for single-payer for many years and in many ways, the most prevalent being PDA's "Healthcare Not Warfare" campaign that initially connected a reduction in military spending to the promotion of single-payer health care. He "embraced an 'inside-outside strategy' that was designed to go around the party elites and link insurgent campaigns to grassroots movements" that emphasized "movement-guided politics."[18] Although Carpenter had emphasized at past meetings that the movement must work to elect candidates that support single-payer, this became a more significant focus for him following this Healthcare NOW meeting. PDA had been "an organization that works both inside and

---

[15] Fieldnotes: Excerpted from Frances Fox Piven's keynote address at the Healthcare NOW National Strategy meeting in Nashville TN, October 2013.

[16] Fieldnotes: Laurie. 2013 Healthcare NOW National Strategy meeting in Nashville TN.

[17] Fieldnotes: Healthcare NOW National Strategy Meeting, Nashville TN, October 2013.

[18] Written by John Nichols for The Nation magazine and found via https://www.health-care-now.org/blog/tim-carpenters-politics-of-radical-inclusion-in-the-streets-and-in-the-polling-booths/.

outside the Democratic party." They worked "inside the party to get Democrats to act like Democrats" and got "follow through on progressive legislation or projects." PDA also worked "outside the party by bringing candidates to the table who own the progressive agenda that we're pushing that is not necessarily what the traditional Democratic Party is pressing for right now."[19] In the years leading up to the 2016 election, Carpenter shifted more of this focus to convincing a progressive candidate to run for president through the Run Bernie Run Campaign.

RUN BERNIE RUN!!

By 2013, Senator Bernie Sanders already had a long history of working with the SPM. Although he had played a significant role in the Vermont movement of the 1990s and had proposed single-payer legislation in the House and then the Senate for several years, other politicians were viewed as the political leaders of the SPM—most notably Representative John Conyers (D-MI) who had sponsored H.R. 676, which was the bill at the heart of the movement for many years. While Sanders wasn't always at the center of the single-payer narrative, this changed during the Obama era of healthcare reform when his efforts to insert single-payer into the process through amendments to the senate bill became important within the single-payer narrative of that period. Sanders became even more central to the single-payer narrative practice during the ACA implementation period through his support of the Vermont-based human rights campaign for single-payer.[20] Sanders had believed for some time that a single-payer system would be linked to innovations at the state level, and the single-payer bill that he introduce in the Senate until 2016 promoted that model by letting states establish their own single-payer systems. Speaking with the activists on a 2014 Healthcare NOW conference call, Lori, a legislative aide for Senator Sanders, explained that "we believe that when single-payer happens, it's going to come from the states. Vermont's passage is a big deal. Other states will see how successful it is in Vermont and they'll want it too."[21] This is an important reason why Senator Sanders invested time and energy in supporting that state-based movement. When the Vermont

[19] Call Notes: Jeanne, PDA National Issue Team Coordinator, Healthcare NOW conference call June 2013.

[20] See Chaps. 5 and 6 for a more detailed discussion of this.

[21] Healthcare NOW conference call, February 2014.

movement ultimately failed at a point so close to implementation,[22] both Sanders and the national movement started refocusing on a way to bring single-payer back onto the national stage.

Tim Carpenter developed an idea for bringing the outside into mainstream American politics—through the 2016 presidential campaign season. Encouraged by Sanders' earlier critiques of the Obama administration, by a comment about a possible presidential bid that Sanders had made in a 2013 interview with the Nation,[23] and by the energy that he witnessed within grassroots organizations, such as HCN, Tim began developing his own campaign—one that would encourage Sanders to "Run Bernie Run!" This campaign to urge Sanders to run for the 2016 Democratic nomination for the presidency started with a petition.

Carpenter's plan was to collect thousands of signatures, mostly through an online petition, to present to Sanders in order to inspire his candidacy. Although "Sanders' name recognition was fairly low a month before he announced his run for president in 2015—76% of Americans had no opinion of him or had never heard of him,"[24] this petition drive was able to collect thousands of signatures online on the first day. The petition stated that,

> We, the Undersigned, make this call for a primary challenge in full recognition of the need to prevent the current crazed, mean, and dangerous incarnation of the Republican Party from seizing total power; and...We, the Undersigned, do declare that we will knock on doors, donate, make phone calls, use social media, and do everything we can to elect Bernie Sanders the next president of the United States.

Not only did the petition include encouragement for Sanders to run, but it also included a commitment made by the signer to participate in the Sanders campaign. Other grassroots, political, and professional organizations quickly jumped on board this Bernie train—with more online

[22] See Chap. 6 for a discussion of this.

[23] Nichols, John. 2014. "Democrat? Green? Independent? The 'Run Bernie Run' Jockying" The Nation Posted on May 12, 2014 https://www.thenation.com/article/democrat-green-independent-run-bernie-run-jockeying/.

[24] But more recently, that figure was down to 9%. See: McCarthy, Justin. "Americans Maintain a Positive View of Bernie Sanders" Gallup.com posted on October 5, 2018 https://news.gallup.com/poll/243539/americans-maintain-positive-view-bernie-sanders.aspx.

petitions, Facebook groups, and twitter accounts popping up. While HCN could not fully participate in the campaign due to its tax status, several other allied organizations, such as National Nurses United (NNU), did officially endorse Sanders and participate in campaign activities. NNU also used its political action committee—National Nurses United for Patient Protection—to raise funds to support the Sanders campaign. Some of these funds went toward establishing billboards in key primary states. One such billboard read "politics as usual won't guarantee healthcare for all. Bernie will," which directly reflected the critique of politics as usual that encouraged support for Sanders. Grassroots single-payer activists were able to participate in the Run Bernie Run campaign through these other organizations. While there was some disagreement within the progressive community about whether Bernie should run as a Democrat, Independent, or as a third party—most single-payer organizations, such as PDA, urged him to run in the Democratic primary. They wanted "him to know that there's enthusiasm for a run, and to run as a Democrat."[25] In addition to online petitions, Run Bernie Run campaigners showed up to Sanders events with signs and other campaign items—often chanting "Run Bernie Run!"

By the time that PDA held their 10 Year Anniversary Event on May 10th, 2014, in North Hampton, Massachusetts, they had already collected over 11,000 signatures via their petition. At the event, Sanders, who was the keynote speaker, was presented with the petition by author Jim Hightower who called him "our next President" and actress Mimi Kennedy—both PDA board members. In his keynote address, Sander's discussed "how we got to where we are and where we need to go." Rather than talking about a possible campaign for the presidency, Sanders told the audience,

> What we have to do, in an unprecedented way, is develop a strong grassroots network from California to Maine. It means that everyone in this room and not in this room has got to know that we are fighting for the life of America. That these are critical times. That ordinary people are going to have to become extraordinary people. We're gonna have to reach out and engage them in a political way. And I believe absolutely that if we educate, if we

[25] Mimi Kennedy: PDA board chair quoted in: Nichols, John "Democrat? Green? Independent? The Run Bernie Run Jockeying" The Nation. Posted on May 12, 2014 From https://www.thenation.com/article/democrat-green-independent-run-bernie-run-jockeying/.

organize, we are going to win this fight but it is not going to be easy—let me mention Tim again. Because the hard work that Tim did for his whole life is exactly what all of us have got to do. And it is hard work.[26]

Sanders eventually decided to start a campaign for the presidency, a decision that was affected by the Run Bernie Run mobilization effort,[27] but this statement made at the PDA event established the framework that would guide his campaign and its focus on grassroots organizing rather than insider politics.

The goal of the Run Bernie Run campaign, as well as the Sanders presidential campaign that followed, was not only to win the presidency but also to use the process of campaigning for the presidency as a way to increase the strength of the grassroots progressive network. Before Sanders even decided to run, the Run Bernie Run campaign became a way to develop solidarity within the progressive community.

> Just as many members of DSA have joined PDA and taken part in its campaigns, Tim Carpenter joined DSA out of solidarity. We worked together on compatible goals and out of a common heritage. We have welcomed and supported PDA's project of petitioning Bernie Sanders to run for president.[28]

The hole that could have been left within the progressive community following the death of Tim Carpenter just a few weeks before the 10th anniversary event for PDA at which Sanders was presented with the "Run Bernie Run" petition was filled instead with new connections, activity, and hope due to the efforts of Carpenter and other progressive activists.

"IT'S TIME FOR A POLITICAL REVOLUTION": THE SANDER'S CAMPAIGN

When Senator Sanders announced his candidacy informally on April 30th, 2015, first in an email to supporters and then in a press conference in Washington D.C., his chances of winning the nomination still seemed

---

[26] "Sen. Bernie Sanders, Keynote Speaker—10th Anniversary of PDA and Tim Carpenter" PDA YouTube Channel Posted on May 25, 2014. https://www.youtube.com/watch?time_continue=9&v=0Mwbhgq3MHk&feature=emb_logo.

[27] Sanders, Bernie. 2016. Our Revolution: A Future to Believe In. Thomas Dunne Books.

[28] Democratic Socialists of America. "Remembering Tim Carpenter" dsausa.org posted on, May 2, 2014 https://www.dsausa.org/democratic-left/remembering_tim_carpenter/.

extremely slim. Hillary Clinton had already announced her candidacy a few days before and was the favored candidate. But the goal of the Sanders campaign and those supporting it was not only winning but also to move the Democratic party left by building a progressive network that would continue functioning after the election was decided. For single-payer actors, stories about this campaign became not only examples of the political opportunity to finally win single-payer a seat at the table of mainstream politics but also of grassroots opportunity represented by the intense grassroots support of the Sanders campaign. The emerging grassroots network also highlighted the promise of opportunities yet to come.

To help Sanders win the nomination was the goal, but single-payer supporters also hoped that even if he did not win the nomination, the campaign would work to push the Democratic party left. Sanders supporters expected

> to see the two visions for America—the more corporate, neoliberal Hillary Clinton and the more populist, fighting-for-the-middle-class Bernie Sanders ... That's why having the two of them debate each other would be worth its weight in gold for progressive Democrats who really want to say, 'Hey, not all Democrats are the same here.' That would be a real example.[29]

According to this narrative of opportunity, the Sanders' campaign had the potential to create a more left-leaning Democratic party that would degrade the power of "corporate Democrats" in the party and introduce an era of democratic populism oriented toward the middle and working classes. They wanted the Democrats

> to become a party for the interests of working people and not be a corporate party. ... A Bernie Sanders campaign is part of that struggle within the Democratic Party. But it only moves the party as a whole to the left if there is an organized group that makes that a primary mission in addition to supporting Bernie [in the primary].[30]

---

[29] Conor Boylan, PDA's national deputy director quoted in Stangler, Cole 2014. "Run, Bernie Run—But as What?: Dems, Greens, independents and socialists are courting Vermont's junior senator" *In These Times* Posted on May, 21, 2014 C http://inthesetimes.com/article/16729/run_bernie_run_but_as_what.

[30] Michael Lighty, PDA/NNU/HCN organizer, quoted in Ibid.

Although Sanders did end up losing the nomination to Hillary Clinton, the goal of pushing the Democratic Party left was achieved to some degree. Indeed, Sanders "may have been the catalyst for socialist ideas percolating into recent political campaigns—at least 46 candidates backed by the Democratic Socialists of America have won primaries in federal, state and local elections"[31] in 2018. The network built during the Sanders campaign would continue to mobilize to achieve this particular goal long after the 2016 election was decided.

The "Run Bernie Run" campaign was always about more than electing a progressive president who would support goals like single-payer health care. It was also about building the progressive base that would create the political power to achieve those goals regardless of the outcome of the election. It was essential that the campaign be,

> run in such a way that it creates a democratic organizational network that continues past 2016. ... It is critical that something like that '86-'88 Rainbow Coalition phenomenon be created alongside of a Sanders electoral operation. Bernie needs to support it and help to lead it, but it also needs its own collective leadership not totally dependent upon Bernie or any one person. It needs to be a 21st century version of that late '80s Rainbow, with more participatory democracy, internet- and social media-savvy, a combination of from-the-top and bottom up leadership, all about popular education and leadership development, etc. As important as Bernie Sanders is right now, as much as he is the right person to lead us at this point in time, history teaches us that movements dependent upon one individual, even someone with credentials like Bernie's, are like a house built on sand. It may last for a while, but it will eventually be swept away.[32]

While grassroots activists were enthusiastic about the political opportunity that the Sanders campaign represented, they were also still cautious about relying on political actors or centering political opportunity in their movement building practices. The grassroots opportunity that the Sanders campaign presented at this time was perhaps more important than the possible

[31] McCarthy, Justin "Americans Maintain a Positive View of Bernie Sanders" Gallup News https://news.gallup.com/poll/243539/americans-maintain-positive-view-bernie-sanders.aspx October 5, 2018.
[32] Glick, Ted. "Run Bernie Run!" https://newpol.org/run-bernie-run/?print=pdf May 9, 2015.

opportunity that a Sanders win would mean. The Sanders campaign was on board with this orientation. They understood that

> we had to put together a strong grassroots movement in which people understood that of course it was important that we elect a progressive president, but it was equally important that we create a political revolution by involving millions of new people in the process, people who were prepared to stand up and fight back against a corrupt political and economic system. In other words, this was not going to be a typical campaign. It was not just about electing a candidate. It was the building of a movement. It was the understanding that no president alone could or should do it all. The working families and the young people of this country had to be involved.[33]

The Sanders campaign invested in grassroots organizing, building relationships with grassroots organizations, growing campaign finances from small grassroots donations, and encouraging the participation of newcomers in the political process. This worked. Several progressive organizations developed, including grassroots organizations such as Our Revolution and Political Action Committees such as Justice Democrats. These organizations joined the growing progressive network that continued to mobilize in order to change the political context following the 2016 primaries.

The Sanders' campaign came much closer to achieving the first goal—of winning the Democratic nomination—than anyone expected. Following the campaign, Sanders reminded his supporters that by,

> taking on virtually the entire political establishment, you helped us win primary and caucus elections in 23 contests and send nearly 1900 delegates to this Democratic convention. In a race in which everyone expected us to be outraised and outspent, you made more grassroots contributions than any primary campaign ever and proved that we could run a presidential campaign without begging millionaires and billionaires for money. Some of the wealthiest people in the world were prepared to spend billions of dollars to stop you.[34]

The promise of the narrative of opportunity which had concluded that a President Sanders would remain committed to implementing a

---

[33] Sanders, Bernie. 2016. Our Revolution: A Future to Believe Thomas Dunne Books pg. 85.
[34] Email from "Bernie Sanders for President"—info@berniesanders.com July 25, 2016.

single-payer healthcare system in the United States was not fulfilled. However, other campaign goals were. These continued to encourage grassroots mobilization. Sanders reminded his supporters that they had "built a grassroots organization that rivals anything seen before in our country, knocking on millions of doors, making tens of millions of phone calls, and building immense power in your communities."[35]

The end of the Sanders campaign was a hard loss for progressives, especially for single-payer supporters who still had very little trust for Clinton due to the Clinton era of healthcare reform in the 1990s.[36] There was tension between progressives and establishment democrats leading into and during the Democratic National Convention. Sanders reminded his supporters that,

> you have changed the policy platform of the Democratic Party and of Secretary Hillary Clinton's campaign. Because of our tireless work the Democratic Party has just passed the most progressive platform, by far, in the history of the party. Secretary Clinton now says that she will oppose the disastrous Trans Pacific Partnership trade deal. She has also embraced parts of our plan to make college tuition free—and if her new plan passes, it could revolutionize the way higher education is funded in our country. Secretary Clinton has also embraced the public option for health insurance, and now supports significantly increased funding for community health centers. She adopted these positions because of you and your organizing.[37]

While this action narrative relayed by Sanders to his supporters indicated that they had been successful in several ways, there was also a powerful narrative that the establishment had "rigged" the system against Sanders. This created some tension within the ranks of his supporters as well—between those who wanted to follow his lead and support Clinton and those who were angry that Sanders would even consider supporting a Clinton candidacy. This tension was exacerbated when DNC emails were released in July 2016, just before the Democratic convention. These emails showed bias against Sanders within the democratic establishment, particularly perpetrated by the then DNC chair, Debbie Wasserman Schultz. The friction grew even more pronounced when "Democrats

---

[35] Email from "Bernie Sanders for President"—info@berniesanders.com July 25, 2016.
[36] See Chap. 2 for more details.
[37] Ibid.

didn't even have the courage to put Single Payer in the platform!"[38] Sanders urged his supporters to vote for Clinton in the general election because "we must defeat Donald Trump, the worst presidential candidate in the modern history of our country."[39] This was a hard pill to swallow—especially for Sanders supporters who had endorsed him because of his outsider position in relation to the Democratic establishment.

Although some Sanders supporters refused to get on board with the Clinton campaign, many more remained committed to the grassroots organizing network developed during the Sanders campaign. This was viewed as a successful outcome of the period. In reflecting back on the original "Run Bernie Run" campaign period, the PDA had this to say,

> PDA has played a major role in expanding the range of ideas tolerated in public discourse. We have been a no-holds barred advocate for Medicare for All since our founding; and we were the first national organization to call upon a then-obscure Vermont Senator named Bernie Sanders to run for President. We launched our "Run Bernie Run" campaign in 2014, and we encouraged Bernie to enter the 2016 primaries. Bernie's remarkable campaign, in turn, inspired several exciting progressives to run for Congress![40]

Although Sanders did not win the nomination and Donald Trump was elected president, according to this narrative, the campaign had successfully built a grassroots network that could change the political context, which was even more important following the election of Donald Trump.

THE IMPACT OF THE TRUMP ELECTION

The election of Donald Trump, a Republican candidate who promised to repeal the ACA immediately after election, could be interpreted as a negative in relation to enacting progressive healthcare reform. However, the narratives of opportunity told by single-payer supporters in interviews, at movement events, and within organizational documents emphasized the opportunities represented by this election rather than the negative consequences. Through narratively defining this as a moment of opportunity, single-payer organizations were able to act on the opportunity prevalent

---

[38] Nina Turner, Keynote Address. Single Payer National Strategy Conference. New York. January 2017.

[39] Email from "Bernie Sanders for President"—info@berniesanders.com July 25, 2016.

[40] PDA Email Jan 13th 2019.

within the political and grassroots resistance to the Trump administration. This produced hope that the "chaos" created by the election of Trump would create "opportunity for change. The chips are in the air, it is our job to make them come down for single payer."[41]

According to this narrative, the predicted attacks on the Affordable Care Act (ACA) by the Trump administration would be a "good time to promote the Single Payer Movement"[42] because it would create an opening for single-payer to be brought to the table. This was based on a shared conclusion that "because he is trying to completely dismantle the ACA the Republicans are making the time ripe to push through Single Payer. The administration is causing many people to lose their healthcare and people are mad."[43] This challenge to the ACA would open up "new opportunities by threatening to repeal the ACA and thus highlighting the ongoing complexity, cost, and inefficiency of our healthcare system."[44] The SPM planned to use challenges to the ACA as opportunities to mobilize more grassroots support for single-payer.

The Trump election was also constructed as an opportunity to mobilize the public who were galvanized by the "Republican rule" that had prompted "citizen activism in numbers unseen since the 1960s... more than would ever have emerged during a Clinton administration," which meant that "the prospects of Medicare-for-All will surely be aided by the greater involvement and learning now taking place across America."[45] The conclusion that the Trump election had "inspired many new volunteers and new activists to join the movement"[46] was supported by the development of new organizational support for single-payer (such as by the new Sanders inspired organization—Our Revolution) and concentrated participation in movement activities. For example, the Single Payer National

[41] Respondent 32 Ohio based activist—member of PNHP, Healthcare-Now, SPAN-Ohio, Retirees for Single Payer Health Care—Online Interview.

[42] Respondent 2—Hawaii based activist—member of PNHP, APA, and HMA—Online Interview.

[43] Respondent 7—Maryland based activist—Online Interview.

[44] Respondent 28—Washington based activist—member of Unitarian Universalist Association, Northwest Unitarian Universalist Justice Network, Eastside Interfaith Social Concerns Council, Faith Action Network, Poverty Action Network—Online Interview.

[45] Respondent 32—Ohio based activist—member of PNHP, Healthcare-Now, SPAN-Ohio, Retirees for Single Payer Health Care—Online Interview.

[46] Respondent 28—Washington based activist—member of Unitarian Universalist Association, Northwest Unitarian Universalist Justice Network, Eastside Interfaith Social Concerns Council, Faith Action Network, Poverty Action Network—Online Interview.

Strategy Conference held in New York City directly following the Trump election resulted in the "record attendance" of "nearly 500 participants—including activists from not only the single payer movement, but also intersecting movements like housing first, undocumented rights, HIV/AIDs, and many others."[47] Both of these developments, as well as the emphasis on grassroots political revolution by the Sanders' campaign, indicated to single-payer supporters that there was more grassroots opportunity for single-payer than ever before. The "incredible momentum of the single payer movement last weekend, and the diversity of people and organizations committed to the fight" gave Stephanie, the Communications director for HCN, as well as others, hope that "the GOP will not have the last word on our healthcare!"[48]

While not all single-payer activists were as positive about the outcome of the election because it made single-payer seem to be "pie in the sky"[49] and "it shows us clearly how badly the cards are stacked against us,"[50] the dominant narrative concluded that "this is a golden opportunity for progressives to push for single payer as the BEST form of reform NOW and the only one which will provide quality universal care at lower cost."[51] A central aspect of this narrative was the continued critique of establishment politics which concluded that under Trump there would be "a greater opportunity for single payer than under Clinton, who was satisfied with the status quo and didn't want to change a thing."[52] This encouraged single-payer activists to continue to focus on building the movement because although the Trump election "makes things more difficult in the short run,… if we play our cards right, it could make things easier in the long run. It all depends on how we educate and mobilize people."[53] This conclusion persuaded activists to "plant seeds about Single Payer. Keep it in the conversation. Train groups of people about it and how to spread the word. Grass roots. Be ready for 2018 to bring it on when the epic fail that

[47] Stephanie Nakajima, Healthcare NOW email, February 3, 2017.

[48] Stephanie Nakajima, Healthcare NOW email, February 3, 2017.

[49] Respondent 15—Activist from Healthcare for All Pennsylvania—Online Interview.

[50] Respondent 24—Activist leader from Missouri—Online Interview.

[51] Respondent 8—member of PNHP New York Metro Chapter and NY Nurses Association, Online Interview.

[52] Respondent 36—Indivisible Activist—Online Interview.

[53] Respondent 14—California based Activist—Member of PNHP, Single-Payer NOW, and Healthcare NOW—Online Interview.

the GOP has cooked up occurs. We have a great shot at it then."[54] This narrative of opportunity would encourage a continued focus on movement building in order to "build power and change what is politically possible"[55] during the years that directly following the election of President Trump.

"Going on the Offense While Playing Defense"[56]

The narrative practice of the SPM during the first years of the Trump administration indicated that threats to existing policy—primarily the ACA—represented an opportunity to increase support for single-payer. Even single-payer supporters who suggested that the Trump era presented negative opportunity for single-payer also emphasized the effort that it took to achieve the ACA, which would now be threatened under the Trump regime, and the necessity to protect that policy. During the first several months of the Trump administration, focus for many shifted once again toward mobilizing political support for federal policy and resisting regressive efforts at the federal level. This included participation in citizen lobbying, rallies, die-ins, and marches that arose in defense of the ACA. Efforts also centered on mobilizing political support for H.R. 676 through national call in days and direct citizen lobbying.

Single-payer actors began to develop a defensive/offensive strategy even before Trump was sworn in as POTUS. Healthcare NOW

> helped convene a coalition meeting of almost 50 national unions, singlepayer groups, progressive organizations, and Bernie related groups, to launch a major campaign to fight back against the coming war on public and private health programs and commit ourselves to the most effective campaign for single-payer healthcare. ... this year, we cannot just defend the status quo: we must play offense while playing defense, and fight like hell for single-payer healthcare.[57]

---

[54] Respondent 21—Activist from California in Tri-Community Democratic Club, Indivisible, and Enact Single Payer CA—Online Interview.

[55] Fieldnotes: Ben of National Economic and Social Rights Initiative (NESRI), Single Payer Leadership Meeting Las Vegas Oct 2017.

[56] Ben Day, Healthcare NOW Executive Director, Email, Dec 2016.

[57] Healthcare NOW Email, Nov. 22, 2016.

This meeting led to the development of the "Campaign for Guaranteed Healthcare" because there was

> no viable "inside" strategy to stop attacks on virtually everyone's healthcare, or to fight for single-payer healthcare. After an exhausting election season, we need to quickly redirect our efforts towards a grassroots uprising of patients, healthcare providers, and other affected communities calling for healthcare justice. Fortunately, organizing such a movement is Healthcare NOW's mission! During the fight over the Affordable Care Act, we played a central role coordinating a national coalition demanding improved Medicare for All, up to and including civil disobedience targeting Congresspeople and health insurers across the country. We are now facing a bizarre mirror image of that political moment, with higher stakes and even greater need for national coordination.[58]

The Campaign for Guaranteed Healthcare was also created because single-payer supporters had concluded that they could not "afford to wait for them to make the first move"; therefore the Campaign for Guaranteed Healthcare needed to "be ready to activate people all over the country when the GOP launches its attacks on our healthcare."[59] This campaign was organized not only to defend existing programs but also to

> win improved Medicare for All—a single-payer healthcare system. Access to healthcare is basic to human dignity, and we will oppose any attempts to repeal, privatize, or undermine the healthcare of anyone anywhere in the United States. We see the movement for healthcare justice as a central component of a broader movement for social and economic justice that we stand in solidarity with.[60]

Organizations representing many different spheres of influence—grassroots, political, and economic—joined the campaign. Notably, the United Health Care Action Network, which had moved away from actively supporting single-payer following the Clinton era of healthcare reform, joined the campaign and reaffirmed its commitment to Medicare for All.[61] In the process of going on the defensive, guaranteed healthcare campaigners also

[58] Healthcare NOW Email, Dec 10, 2016.
[59] Healthcare NOW Email, Dec 26, 2016.
[60] Campaign for Guaranteed Healthcare "Our Mission" https://campaignforguaranteed-healthcare.org/our-mission/.
[61] For a detailed discussion of the 1990s era UHCAN—see Chap. 2.

interacted with non-single-payer organizations. Healthcare for America NOW (HCAN), for example, came out of hibernation in order to defend the Affordable Care Act from repeal. Single-payer activists interacted with HCAN supporters at events protesting the "repeal and replace" efforts of the GoP and worked to encourage their support of single-payer while also helping them to defend the ACA.

During the first two years of the Trump administration, the Republican party had control over both the House and the Senate in addition to having a republican president. This made the collective effort of an offensive/defensive strategy of outsiders even more important—mass mobilization was required to protect existing programs as well as create new ones. The first effort by the Republican-controlled federal government to repeal and "replace" the ACA was the American Healthcare Act, also commonly referred to as "Trumpcare," which was introduced in March of 2017. This bill would have replaced the ACA with a system that left some elements of the ACA intact—such as the protection for those with pre-existing conditions—but would have removed other key elements, such as the individual mandate to purchase private insurance and federal funding for Medicaid expansion. "Instead of providing 'health insurance for everybody,' it takes all of the weaknesses of the ACA and magnifies them while undermining essential public insurance programs and providing huge tax breaks to the rich and the healthcare industrial complex."[62] This would have caused a significant increase in the numbers of uninsured by repealing the insurance that many people had gained due to the measures of the Affordable Care Act. Mass mobilization efforts worked to stop the AHCA from being enacted—it was a "life and death" decision for many. While the original AHCA failed, there was a figurative shudder through the collective health justice movement when a "skinny repeal" effort—the Health Care Freedom Act—passed through the House and went to the Senate floor without any time for senators to read or comprehend the legislation being put forward for a vote. I vividly recall anxiously watching the debate and vote on the Senate floor on July 27, 2017—knowing that I had friends and family members who relied on the ACA programs for much needed coverage. I nervously awaited Senator John McCain's deciding vote and stood up and cheered when he gave a thumbs down—signaling his no

---

[62] Mark Dudzic, Six Ways Trumpcare Makes Healthcare Worse (and One Way to Make It Better) Mar 15, 2017, Common Dreams posted at https://pdamerica.org/six-ways-trumpcare-makes-healthcare-worse-and-one-way-to-make-it-better/.

246 L. S. F. HERN

vote on the measure. The mass mobilization that had occurred to stop the AHCA also gave me hope that there could be the kind of unity within the grassroots mobilization effort that would be needed in the continued fight for healthcare reform.

There was not complete agreement within the SPM about how to deal with the "repeal and replace" efforts, and there was continued division within the SPM in relation to how much effort should be expended in defense of the Affordable Care Act. Some organizations, such as HCN, decided to use participation in the defense of the ACA as a way to encourage support of single-payer while also emphasizing the ACA as a stepping stone toward that end. Other organizations, such as Health Over Profit for Everyone (HOPE) and Single Payer Action (SPA), decided to limit their participation in the defense of the ACA and to primarily use the efforts to repeal it as an opportunity to point out flaws within the ACA and stress that a single-payer system would address these flaws. They urged congress to "Repeal and Replace with Single Payer" because

> the time for fundamental health care reform is now. No more tweaking. No more incrementalism. No more 'political feasibility' arguments. It's time for Congress to stop putting the interests of private insurance and Big Pharma over constituent needs. It's time to make H.R. 676, Improved Medicare for All, the law of the land.[63]

These were not incompatible positions, but they were not without conflict.

A specific situation illustrates these divisions within the SPM. During the failed attempt to repeal the ACA, Senator Steve Daines (R-MT) proposed an amendment (340) which was almost a carbon copy of the single-payer bill introduced in the house—H.R. 676. Senator Bernie Sanders rejected this amendment as an attempt to discredit democratic senators in more conservative districts who were heading into a tough election season.

> Sen. Bernie Sanders had said before the vote that failure of Sen. Daines and other Republicans to vote for their amendment would demonstrate that this was a sham to be used to campaign against moderate Senators in the next election. When no Republican voted for it, most Democrats plus Independent Sen. Sanders voted Present. It is a sad commentary that the most important

---

[63] Dr. Carol Paris, quoted in "Repeal and Replace with Single Payer" by Russell Mokhiber of Single Payer Action—found here http://healthoverprofit.org/2017/01/25/repeal-and-replace-with-single-payer/.

health policy legislation ever introduced in Congress—legislation that would have brought health care justice to all—was used by the Republicans as a tool for political chicanery.[64]

In fact—there was no support from Democratic or Republican senators for this amendment, with 57 no votes, 0 yes votes, and many Democrats abstaining from the vote by simply choosing to vote "present." Leading up to the vote on this amendment, some organizations such as HCN followed Sanders' lead and decided not to push senators to support the amendment. This political theater convinced them that "This is war! Not the guns and bombs type of war but a war against man's inhumanity to man."[65] Other organizations, such as HOPE, urged their participants to contact their senators and encourage them to support the amendment, which was defined as an opportunity to show the political support for single-payer in the Senate. They were frustrated with the result, which was defined as a betrayal. They concluded that,

> Instead of taking a position in solidarity with the NIMA movement, Senator Sanders led the way by saying that he would not vote for the amendment and urging other Senators to join him by voting "present." This lack of courage to take a stance after campaigning so heavily on Medicare for All during his recent presidential campaign was disappointing to say the least. Senate Democrats chose political cover and party unity over solidarity with the movement for Medicare for All.[66]

For this segment of the SPM, Sanders' no vote was symbolic of his entry into the establishment as he was "fulfilling his new role as leadership in the Democratic Party."[67]

While specific repeal and replace bills were not successful, the Republican party was able to effectively retract the individual mandate aspect of the ACA through a provision in the Tax Cuts and Jobs Act enacted in 2017, which eliminated the tax penalty that was the enforcement mechanism related to the mandate to purchase private insurance. This controversy

---

[64] Email: Don McCanne. July 27, 2017 Senate defeats single payer amendment.

[65] Ibid.

[66] Margaret Flowers, Democratic Senators Chose Party Over People. Health Over Profit. July 29, 2017 http://healthoverprofit.org/2017/07/29/democratic-senators-chose-party-over-people/.

[67] Ibid.

over repeal and replace measures not only illustrates continuing divisions within the movement that began following the passage of the ACA but also highlights the growing need within the movement to develop leadership outside of mainstream political organizations.

CREATING LEADERS: FROM THE OUTSIDE IN

Developing leaders for the SPM from the grassroots base was not a new desire during the anti-establishment era. In fact, HCN had needed to develop innovative leadership strategies fairly early on due to the death of its original leader—Marilyn Clement—in 2009. At that point, HCN decided that while they would have a small paid staff to take on the day-to-day functions of the organization, the primary leadership mechanism should be made of volunteers representing differing constituencies within the SPM. While HCN already had an active board at that point in 2009, a decision was made to create a steering committee that would be available to HCN staff on a more frequent basis to help them make decisions when adaptations to changes in the environment of opportunity were needed or when problems arose. It was important to the HCN board that this leadership be representative of the diversity of perspectives within the SPM and also committed, as well as knowledgeable, enough to make decisions in support of the single-payer goal.

When focus shifted during the last years of the Obama administration to building a movement that could change the political context, this focus on leadership development from the grassroots up became even more central. Single-payer actors worked to develop mechanisms that would facilitate the development of grounded leadership within the movement. While this started with face-to-face tactics, such as "Everybody Institutes" that would involve intense leadership training over a few days, this effort soon developed into a more diverse array of training options within a new "Single Payer School" (SPS). While some aspects of this school would continue to take place at face-to-face events, a plan was hatched to create an online system that would become a platform for this project. Due to my experience teaching online courses and my expertise in healthcare politics, I was asked to be on the original committee that developed ideas for the creation of this single-payer school. At the SPS orientation meeting, it was decided that the new single-payer school would have two primary goals. The first goal was to create a space for people who were new to the movement to learn about policy issues, as well as movement history. This would be an asynchronous system involving several different tools. The hope was that newcomers could learn this information online so that when they came to face-to-face events, the background knowledge for strategizing and organizing would already be in place. The second goal was to create a space for the training of new leaders within the movement. This goal was rooted in the recognition that in order for the movement to grow, new organizations, and thus new leaders, would be needed around the country. This wing of the SPS would be much more interactive, involving real-time dialogue in addition to asynchronous discussion boards, and would provide training in movement building skills to students—such as grass-roots actions and organizational development. Healthcare now created a 501c(3) arm—the Healthcare NOW Education Fund—which was more restricted in political actions but able to collect tax exempt contributions specifically for education.

While the SPS was initially intended to cultivate leadership within the movement, it soon became necessary to develop movement leadership that could also take on positions in other spheres. In the final years of the Obama administration and the first years of the Trump administration, the SPM both lost and gained several leaders in the political sphere. Representative Dennis Kucinich, who had been a long-time supporter of H.R. 676 in the House, lost his seat when it was gerrymandered out of existence in 2012 and he was forced into a primary battle with another Democratic representative due to redistricting. Although H.R. 676 had the highest number of co-sponsors ever in the 2017/2018 legislative session (124), it lost its primary leader when Congressman John Conyers, the original sponsor of H.R. 676, resigned from his post after being accused of sexual harassment by former staffers.[68] The new Sanders single-payer bill (S 1804) was introduced in September of 2017 with sixteen co-sponsors—a vast increase from the zero co-sponsors that Sanders had on previous versions of the bill. However, one of the most vocal of these co-sponsors—Senator Al Franken (D-MN)—also resigned from his position due to allegations of sexual misconduct. For single-payer supporters, these events were reminiscent of Representative Eric Massa's (D-NY) resignation during the height of the Obama era of healthcare reform (see Fig. 7.1 for a visual depiction of changes in the co-sponsorship of single-payer legislation).[69]

---

[68] Representative Keith Ellison took over as sponsor of H.R. 676 for the remainder of the 2017 / 2018 session. H.R. 676 was replaced by HR 1384—introduced by Representative Pramila Jayapal—for the 2019 / 2020 session.

[69] See Chap. 5 for more information about this.

Although the SPM was experiencing more political support in theory than ever before, there was a concern within the narrative of political opportunity about how active this support was or would continue to be.

As single-payer grew in popularity in the political, public, and economic spheres—it was also met with more active opposition. In addition to the "repeal and replace" efforts in congress, the Partnership for America's Health Care Future (PAHCF) was formed in June of 2018 by the Federation of American Hospitals, America's Health Insurance Plans, and the Pharmaceutical Researchers and Manufacturers of America to directly counter the growing support for single-payer. This coalition started a campaign to convince Americans that "A one-size-fits-all government health insurance system like Medicare for All, Medicare Buy-In or the public option would threaten access to quality care for millions of Americans."[70] The PAHCF started a campaign against Medicare for All that included lobbying congress, running ads, and encouraging the public to sign a petition supporting its position on healthcare policy. While this well-funded organization became a negative material aspect of the environment of opportunity, within the single-payer narrative, it was a positive sign that they were making progress toward single-payer because "first they ignore you, then they laugh at you, then they fight you, then you win." This opposition indicated to single-payer activists that strong leadership would push them even closer toward the ultimate goal, even in the face of intense opposition.

Also, while the SPM had found a new political leader in Senator Bernie Sanders, they were hesitant to put too much of their energy and support on Sanders due to past experiences. They remained critical of Sanders, even to the point of declining to endorse his new single-payer bill until aspects such as cost-sharing mechanisms that were in earlier versions of his single-payer bill were eliminated and other provisions, such as coverage for long-term care, were added. To his credit, Sanders responded to these criticisms and revised some aspects of the bill because of these concerns. Many movement actors, such as HCN, endorsed the updated bill—S. 1129—introduced in the 116th congressional session (2019–2020) with 14 co-sponsors. They also continued to critique aspects of the bill, such as allowing for-profit healthcare facilities, because "For-profit health care facilities and agencies provide lower-quality care at higher costs than

[70] Partnership for America's Health Care Future. "Threat" https://americashealthcarefuture.org/threat/ Accessed on 2/6/2020.

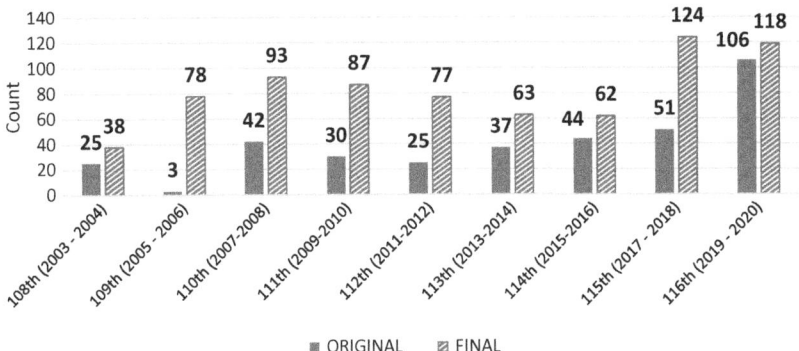

Fig. 7.1 H.R. 676 co-sponsors. (Source: congress.gov. Original = Co-sponsors at introduction; Final = Co-sponsors at end of legislative session. Note: 116th Congress is H.R. 1384: Final Count as of 1/2020)

nonprofits, resulting in worse outcomes and higher costs compared to not-for-profit providers."[71] The Medicare for All Act in the Senate became more central to the narrative practice of the SPM during this era.

Sanders' conclusion that grassroots leadership was necessary because it would "take a movement" to pass single-payer even with support within the political sphere also became influential within the narrative practice of the SPM. For this, and other reasons—single-payer activists worked with other organizations, such as National Nurses United, Our Revolution, and the Democratic Socialists of America, to cultivate leadership from the grassroots. One way that this happened was through tactics designed to force political leaders to move from talking the talk to walking the walk for single-payer. Efforts were made to encourage co-sponsors of the single-payer bills to state their support publicly either via their public materials such as websites or at public events. One tactic for encouraging this kind of support was "bird dogging." For this tactic, single-payer supporters were encouraged to attend public events held by elected officials, such as town halls, and ask the political leader to state on film their support for single-payer, as well as how they would actively support this goal. Bird dogging training was established in the single-payer school to facilitate this tactic.

[71] PNHP Statement about Bernie Sanders 2019 Medicare for All—SB1129. April 10, 2019.

Other successes occurred through efforts to bring outsiders into leadership positions within the insider political sphere. This strategy grew out of the experiences of the Sanders' campaign and focused on training grassroots leaders to run for office. Healthcare NOW realized that one of the things that was

> missing in our movement was a systematized way of identifying, recruiting, and training new leaders who can take on organizing roles in their communities. One of the things our movement needs to do to prepare for the end game is to grow our movement beyond the current participation we have now, reach more people, have deeper bases and roots in key areas, etc. And so HCN developed a leadership development program.[72]

A few of the individuals trained through this leadership development program within the SPS became candidates in the 2018 election cycle. The campaign of one of these individuals, Amy Vilela, was chronicled in the documentary "Knock Down the House." Although Vilela lost her campaign, she remains a key player in the mobilization around single-payer. Another woman featured in that documentary—Alexandria Ocasio-Cortez—did win a primary against a long-term Democratic incumbent and then a seat in the House of Representatives where she has become an outspoken champion of progressive causes, including single-payer.

These efforts to change the political sphere through movement building that results in outsider progressive leaders taking insider positions of power reflects the start of this era when the SPM hoped that an outsider would win his bid for the presidency of the United States of America. In addition to cultivating political and grassroots leadership, the SPM has also developed mechanisms to increase support and leadership within the economic sphere. The SPM began working with economists, such as Dr. Gerald Friedman, to develop economic analyses that would support progress toward a single-payer system through the careful analysis of the economic effects of such a system. These studies were often used to mobilize economic actors in support of single-payer. For example, the relatively new Business for Medicare for All organization worked to encourage business owners to actively support single-payer. Also, professional leaders such as the Physicians for a National Health Program targeted other key professional groups in efforts to encourage them to support single-payer. A recent

[72] Ibid.

action to pass a resolution to overturn the long-standing opposition to single-payer of the American Medical Association was narrowly defeated—with 47 percent voting to end the AMA's opposition to single-payer. In addition to this, the rise of "democratic socialism" in the political and grass-roots spheres encouraged the public to question the relationship between capitalism and democracy, and to consider other options for developing an empowering and just economic framework that would be oriented toward reducing economic inequality in support of the working class. The successful leadership development in the economic sphere was a boon to the movement during this period of movement building (see Fig. 7.2 for a visual representation of the SPM narrative practice during this era).

The SPM was able to act on opportunities in the political, grassroots, and economic spheres due, in part, to the availability of mobilizing structures present in online platforms. Rising single-payer leaders, such as Alexandria Ocasio-Cortez, who often represented the millennial generation of digital natives, were also more adept at using online resources than movement leaders of the past. Grassroots celebrity leaders, such as Ady Barkan,[73] were also able to reach a wider audience through these platforms. At the same time, issues such as conflicts over net neutrality and the emphasis within social networking platforms on capitalization through payments to "boost" group posts threatened to reduce the potential enabling qualities of these online resources. These resources increasingly required more economic resources for their effective use. The growing need for economic resources in the platforms was met, in part, through the fundraising contributions of cultural agents. For example, a famous director of comedy films gave a 15,000-dollar grant, and a popular rock band donated a percentage of the proceeds from their 2017 tour to a grassroots single-payer organization. Celebrity endorsers, such as Michael Moore, also became more visible in their public support of single-payer Medicare for All.

The rise of authoritarian politics within the Trump administration initially appeared to be a negative turn of events for the SPM. Yet, the Trump administration had the opposite effect. During this period, the SPM experienced an upswing in not just grassroots opportunity but in political and

---

[73] I unfortunately did not have the space here to discuss the significant role that Ady Barkan—who is a progressive activist and organizer for the Center for Popular Democracy and the co-founder of the Be a Hero Political Action Committee—has played in the last few years of the SPM. When Barkan was diagnosed with ALS in 2016, he put much of his focus and energy in supporting Medicare for ALL and became an influential public face of the SPM.

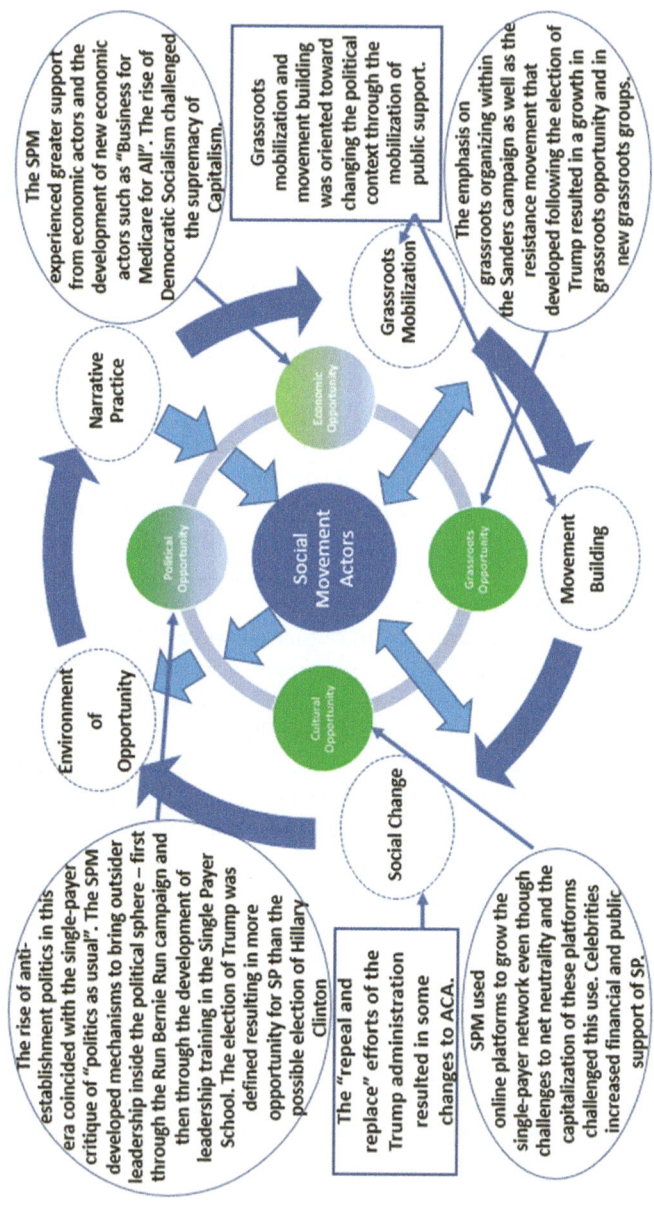

Fig. 7.2 The anti-establishment era narrative practice

economic opportunity as well. Although still an alternative position during the 2016 election season, by the start of the 2020 election season, Medicare for All became a "litmus test" within the Democratic party—with all major presidential candidates taking a position on single-payer for the first time. The story of how this happened started several decades before, but during this period this process would reach a zenith at which the successful progress toward a just society that included a single-payer healthcare system for all, would either become inevitable or materially impossible. As the movement gains traction, the opposition is also mounting a significant counter-offensive which is spearheaded by the Partnership for America's Health Care Future (PAHCF). This counter-offensive can especially be seen in the discourse and debates surrounding the 2020 election season in which two of the most popularly supported candidates—Bernie Sanders and Elizabeth Warren—have Medicare for All as part of their platforms and several others have co-sponsored single-payer legislation in the past. While the SPM had been "a fringe element—quickly dismissed" prior to the 2016 election cycle, the efforts of the SPM and the 2016 Sanders campaign had "elevated the concept of Medicare for all to public consciousness—and it's here to stay."[74] The SPM continues to mobilize with the hope that the 2020 election cycle may build the "political revolution" that will result in the creation of a political sphere that is transformed and supportive of a Medicare for All system in the United States.

---

[74] Fieldnotes: Paul Song Single Payer Leadership Meeting Las Vegas NV October 2017.

CHAPTER 8

"Everybody In! Nobody Out!": Achieving Success with Grit and Resilience

The historical process discussed in the previous chapters, which occurred over three decades, resulted in the current political moment leading into the 2020 election cycle in which single-payer is on the table and Medicare for All is "receiving more serious consideration from presidential candidates and lawmakers than at any time since the program's enactment over five decades ago."[1] A narrow definition of success that limits success to the achievement of primary policy goals would require one to conclude that the Single Payer Movement (SPM) has failed. However, if we understand that final success typically only occurs after decades of grassroots work that results in more minor accomplishments that facilitate movement toward that goal, then we can open the conceptualization of success to more measurable outcomes that go beyond specific policy change. Activists often tell stories about these victories that occur along the way, and these narratives of success produce hope that their efforts are moving them toward the final goal. While my analysis thus far has focused on the ways in which single-payer actors narratively defined success in order to encourage continued mobilization, I turn now to an analysis of trends in other indicators of success. While the core goal of the Single Payer Movement has not been

---

[1] Oberlander, Jonathon. 2019. Navigating the Shifting Terrain of US Health Care Reform: Medicare for All, Single Payer, and the Public Option, The Milbank Quarterly. 0 (00): 1–15 Published September 16, 2019. https://www.milbank.org/quarterly/articles/navigating-the-shifting-terrain-of-us-health-care-reform-medicare-for-all-single-payer-and-the-public-option/.

© The Author(s) 2020
L. S. F. Hern, *Single Payer Healthcare Reform*,
https://doi.org/10.1007/978-3-030-42764-1_8

achieved, there are additional measurable indications that there has been progress toward achieving this goal.

Political Success

The support of political actors is necessary for movements that have a primary goal that involves policy change. While the SPM has had the support of at least a small number of political actors throughout its evolution, its relationship with these political actors and the importance placed upon this relationship have shifted with perceived changes in the political context. Single-payer actors participated in the critique of and turn against establishment politics, concluding that "politics as usual" is the "enemy" of single-payer. Yet, this did not lessen the importance of political support. Instead it encouraged single-payer actors to change the political sphere by not only encouraging the co-sponsorship of single-payer bills but by supporting the candidacy of single-payer politicians. Political success can be measured in several ways.

The most often referenced marker of political success is the level of support for single-payer by current politicians. This is most easily measured by the number of original and final co-sponsors of single-payer bills during each legislative session.[2] Indeed, encouraging representatives to co-sponsor H.R. 676 was a central focus of single-payer actors during the second and third wave of the SPM. When a representative agreed to co-sponsor the bill, this was interpreted as a success. Figure 8.1 illustrates the trend in co-sponsorship over time. There was a peak in final co-sponsorship during the second wave of the SPM leading into the Obama era—with ninety-three total co-sponsors. The abeyance period following the Obama era and the enactment of the Affordable Care Act included less political support for single-payer legislation. In the 114th legislative session, there were just sixty-two final co-sponsors. While fewer than during the immediate pre-Obama period, it was still nearly twice as high as the count of final co-sponsors from the 108th legislative session in which the bill was first introduced. The third wave of the SPM, which is connected to the rise of Bernie Sanders to the center of American political discourse, resulted in a new high—with a total of 124 final co-sponsors in the 115th session (2017–2018). Even though that two-year period also included the loss of

---

[2] Original refers to the number of cosponsors at time of introduction. Final refers to the number of cosponsors at the end of the legislative session.

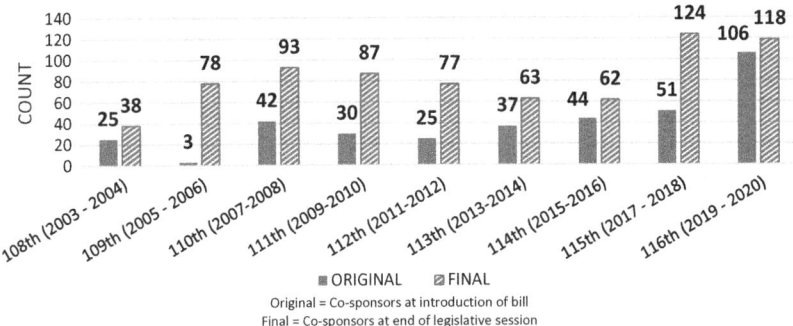

Fig. 8.1 Number of single-payer bill co-sponsors United States House of Representatives. (Source: congress.gov. Note: 116th Congress is H.R. 1384—Final Count as of 2/2020, all others are H.R. 676)

the original sponsor of the bill—Representative John Conyers (D-MI)—single-payer activists were able to mobilize more political support for H.R. 676 than ever before.[3]

The 2018 election cycle resulted in more political support for single-payer, especially in the House of Representatives. Not only did single-payer supporters run for office, but many of them won—at times first in primary challenges to "establishment" democrats. Single-payer activists celebrated the election of these candidates. Explaining that it was "another exciting outcome of last night: at least 11 more districts are now represented by single-payer reps! Please welcome these new cosponsors into our movement on Twitter!"[4] The resulting Democratic majority in the House of Representatives represented a significant shift in opportunity for all types of liberal or progressive reforms, including single-payer. Single-payer activists concluded that "Tuesday was a huge victory for so many reasons. With the Democrats now in the majority, we can move H.R. 676 to the House floor and pass it—but only if we continue to build the mass movement and step up the pressure on politicians."[5]

---

[3] Conyers resigned in December 2017 following accusations of sexual harassment. Representative Keith Ellison (D-MN) assumed sponsorship at that time.

[4] Healthcare NOW Email October 7th, 2018. This was a net gain of about six seats due to others who lost their seats or were redistricted out of office.

[5] Healthcare NOW Email November 8, 2018.

In the 116th Congress, Representative Pramila Jayapal (D-WA) took over sponsorship of the single-payer bill in the house. As part of the process of sponsorship, Jayapal worked with other single-payer supporters to create a new bill that included more details explaining how the proposed single-payer system would work and addressed a few unresolved issues[6] while still reflecting the principles of H.R. 676. Some single-payer activists were critical of the "abandonment" of H.R. 676, but others explained that rewriting the legislation was,

> a move that has become necessary as the social movement for Medicare for All has grown, and the details of how it can be accomplished come under growing scrutiny. Bernie Sanders learned this the hard way when, during the 2016 Presidential primaries, he floated the outline of a plan for single-payer healthcare that received intense criticism from his opponents—most of it dishonest and misleading, but made easier by the lack of some details in the original proposal. The new bill not only will be much more detailed, it will also add additional benefits and correct some major shortcomings in both HR 676 and the Senate Bill (S 1804).[7]

Notably, Jayapal responded to feedback from single-payer organizations while writing the bill because her "organizing approach impelled her to engage in extensive deliberations with single-payer advocates and to bring to the table voices that are often marginalized in the healthcare policy world, including advocates from the racial justice and disability rights communities."[8] Indeed, as a member of the Healthcare NOW board, I experienced this first hand when we were given the opportunity to give feedback on early drafts of the bill as part of the process. While the new bill, HR 1384, does not have as many final co-sponsors as the last iteration of H.R. 676,[9] it did start with a remarkable number of *original* co-sponsors—106—which is more than twice the next highest number (51 in the 115th Congress). This represents a significant shift in opportunity. While single-payer actors had previously spent a significant amount of

---

[6] Such as long-term care and the Hyde Amendment / reproductive choice within the new system.

[7] Day, Benjamin and Mark Dudzic. 2019. "Everybody In, Nobody Out: What We Know So Far About the Medicare for All Act of 2019" *Common Dreams* posted on February 7, 2019   https://www.commondreams.org/views/2019/02/07/everybody-nobody-out-what-we-know-so-far-about-medicare-all-act-2019.

[8] Ibid.

[9] As of 2/2/2020.

time encouraging even past co-sponsors to sign on again in support of H.R. 676 at the start of each new congressional session, during the 116th Congress this was much less necessary. There are several factors related to this shift that built upon the accumulation of support from all of the previous years of grassroots movement building, such as endorsing the candidacy of single-payer supporters during the 2018 election cycle.

This shift facilitated a more targeted strategy for mobilizing political support because single-payer activists did not need to spend a significant amount of time resigning past co-sponsors. During the 116th Congress, organizations like National Nurses United developed a strategy that focused on mobilizing the support of politicians who were members or chairs of the key house committees through which HR 1384 would need to move in order to be considered on the floor of the House of Representatives because the "first step is committee hearings and then we move to floor of house."[10] This included a multi-stage effort stemming from the "grassroots power"[11] of the movement. Healthcare NOW, for example, focused on mobilizing Representative Joe Kennedy III (D-MA) who is on the influential Energy and Commerce Committee. Ben Day, Executive Director of Healthcare NOW, explained that they had "decided to adopt Representative Joseph Kennedy."[12] This adoption involved a series of escalating tactics that included coalition building with local organizations, a social media campaign targeting Kennedy, and crowd canvassing during which canvassers asked people to make a call to Kennedy immediately after discussing the issue with a canvasser. This generated about 300 phone calls to Kennedy within a two-week period and resulted in a (first) meeting with Kennedy. As Stephanie, the Communications Director for Healthcare NOW, explained, "After getting a meeting with him and addressing concerns about the bill, we got him on."[13] This was a great success within the leadership development agenda of the SPM. This hard work paid off when Kennedy not only signed as a co-sponsor of the bill but also pushed for a committee hearing that finally occurred in December of 2019. Kennedy also made it clear that this committee hearing was a successful outcome of the grassroots organizing of single-payer

[10] Legislative advocate with NNU, Medicare for All National Conference Call, Nov. 13, 2018.

[11] Medicare for All Conference call (with Bernie Sanders) 11/13/2018.

[12] Ben Day, Medicare for All Conference call (with Bernie Sanders) 11/13/2018.

[13] Stephanie Nakajima, Plenary Address, Association for Applied and Clinical Sociology Annual Conference, Portland Oregon, October 2019.

activists saying, "It is through your efforts that we have gotten to where we are today. Including having that historic hearing ... the relentlessness with which you attacked congress basically took away every single excuse from an elected official not to have a hearing on the bill."[14] Indeed, Kennedy became a "passionate advocate"[15] for single-payer, which includes continued interactions with single-payer activists, such as participation in webinars with grassroots activists.[16] Earlier committee hearings in the Rules, Budget, and Ways and Means committees indicated to single-payer actors that their targeted political strategy had successfully moved them closer to the finish line.

Another indicator that single-payer activism had successfully built political support came in the form of a new caucus in the House of Representatives. In July 2018, Representatives Pramila Jayapal (D-WA), Keith Ellison (D-MN), and Debbie Dingell (D-MI) launched the Medicare for All Caucus through which they intended to

> help build the evidence base for Medicare for All. It will sponsor briefings on topics ranging from the basics of Medicare for All to financing to universal health care systems around the world. In development it is also a clearinghouse of resources for members of Congress and their staff. Additionally, the caucus will provide an opportunity for members and their staff to interact with partners and providers across the country to gain a practical understanding of how a Medicare for All system would work.[17]

The creation of this caucus represented the institutionalization of the SPM inside the halls of Congress. Whereas, previously, support for single-payer in congress was fluid and dependent upon individual political supporters, the caucus transitioned this to more concrete support for single-payer that was not dependent upon any one person. In addition to this, the caucus represented to single-payer actors the opportunity to "increase commitment level of cosponsors—deep—and ask them to step up and do some

[14] Representative Joseph Kennedy III, Medicare for All Resolutions Webinar on January 9, 2020. Available at https://www.medicare4allresolutions.org/past-webinars/.

[15] Ibid.

[16] Other hearings also occurred in the house such as the Rules Committee (April 2019), Budget Committee (May 2019), and Ways and Means (June 2019).

[17] Pramila, Jayapal. "Rep. Jayapal, Rep. Ellison, Rep. Dingell and Members of Congress Launch Medicare for All Congressional Caucus" Press Release. Posted on 7/19/2018 Available at: https://jayapal.house.gov/2018/07/19/rep-jayapal-rep-ellison-rep-dingell-and-members-congress-launch-medicare-all/.

work for our movement to advance the movement."[18] According to single-payer actors, this was necessary because "in order to win, we need not only wide but deep commitment to single-payer. It's not enough for our reps to sign on—they need to be actively advocating for the bill, on the hill and off, and taking the lead on educating the public."[19] The caucus was symbol of both success and the opportunity to encourage the seventy or so members of the caucus to support Medicare for All in action.

While single-payer activists focused on increasing support within the House of Representatives for many years, the centralization of Bernie Sanders within movement discourse, as detailed in Chap. 7, encouraged single-payer actors to pay closer attention to support for single-payer within the Senate. While Sanders had introduced single-payer legislation in the Senate for several years, the bill had never had co-sponsors at the time of introduction. This changed when he introduced S.1804 in September of 2017 with sixteen co-sponsors, many of whom spoke passionately in favor of Medicare for All at the bill's introduction. When Sanders reintroduced the revised legislation as S. 1129 in the 116th congress, most of the sixteen co-sponsors continued in that role.[20] In addition to Sanders, four of those co-sponsors went on to be significant contenders in the 2020 election cycle as candidates for the presidency of the United States.[21]

The emphasis on single-payer during elections for higher office, such as the presidency, is also an indicator of success for single-payer actors. While there had been single-payer candidates in past presidential elections—most notably Representative Dennis Kucinich (D-OH) in the 2008 election and Senator Bernie Sanders (I–VT) in the 2016 election—the existence of multiple single-payer candidates in the 2020 election indicated that there has been a "sea change" in attitudes toward single-payer. In addition to the five senate sponsors,[22] other politicians recognized as single-payer supporters in the past, such as Tulsi Gabbard, Bill de Blasio, and Julian Castro, also launched campaigns for the presidency.

---

[18] Ben, HCN Conference Call, September 2018.

[19] Healthcare NOW email: July 11, 2018.

[20] One of the sixteen co-sponsors in the 115th Congress—Al Franken (D-MN)—had previously resigned due to accusations of sexual harassment.

[21] Senator Cory Booker (D-NJ), Senator Kirsten Gillibrand (D-NY), Senator Kamala Harris (D-CA), and Senator Elizabeth Warren (D-MA).

[22] Sen. Bernie Sanders (I-VT), Sen. Cory Booker (D-NJ), Sen. Kirsten Gillibrand (D-NY), Sen. Kamala Harris (D-CA), Sen. Elizabeth Warren (D-MA).

Support at the highest level of American politics can also be better understood through an examination of the discourse within election-related events such as debates. Medicare for All was a central policy discussion in the 2019 Democratic presidential primary debates. Even though some of the debate participants did not support single-payer, just the fact that it was a policy up for debate represented a shift from years before,

> Let's take a minute to appreciate the magnitude of this moment. At almost any time prior to 2019, it would take a petition, a rally, some grassroots effort to possibly get a question about single-payer on the debate floor *at all*. Last night, the moderators didn't even bother asking about "defending the ACA" or a public option—they went straight to Medicare for All, and many candidates were interrupting each other to prove their commitment.[23]

In Fig. 8.2,[24] I illustrate the use of terms related to healthcare reform in the 2008 through 2020 Democratic presidential debates, namely, "Medicare for All, "Public Option," "Universal Health Care, and "Affordable Care Act." This allows for an examination not only of trends over time in the appearance of "single-payer" in the discourse but also a comparison of the use of different terms within each period. During the 2008 debates, candidates were more likely to talk in very general terms about healthcare reform using the term "universal healthcare" with the greatest frequency. Both "single-payer" and "Medicare for All" were used infrequently—early on by Dennis Kucinich who included single-payer in his presidential platform and later, after Kucinich had left the race, by Hillary Clinton when critiquing Barack Obama's past support of single-payer.[25] While Sanders was able to bring single-payer into the 2016 debates with greater frequency, discussion dealing with how to improve or protect the Affordable Care Act dominated during that election period. Although single-payer and Medicare for All had been used in the 2008 and 2016 period somewhat interchangeably, there was a noticeable decline in the use of "single-payer" and a significant increase in the use of "Medicare for

---

[23] Healthcare NOW email: June 29, 2019.

[24] To develop this analysis, I coded presidential primary debate transcripts from the 2008, 2016, and 2020 election cycles. The codes used were "Medicare for All" (M4H), "Single Payer" (SP), "Public Option" (PO), "Universal Health Care" (UHC), and "Affordable Care Act" (ACA).

[25] As the Affordable Care Act did not exist in 2008, it was not a code utilized during the 2008 period.

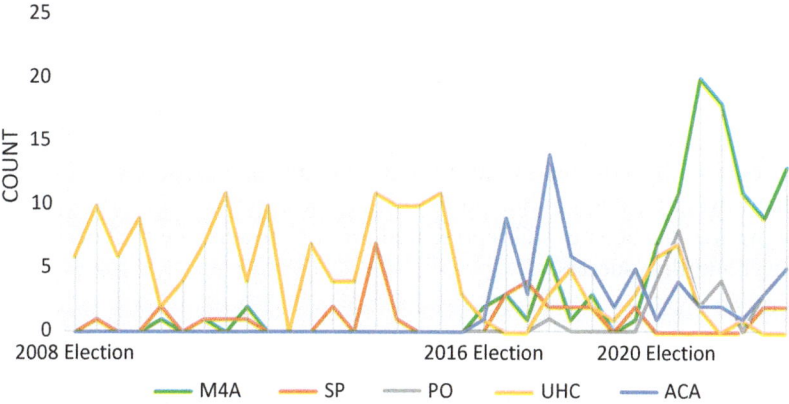

Fig. 8.2 Healthcare reform in democratic primary debates. (Source: Transcripts of democratic primary debates April 2007–January 2020. *M4A* Medicare for All, *SP* single payer, *PO* public option, *UHC* universal health care, *ACA* Affordable Care Act)

All" in the 2020 election period. This is tied to the transition to using the moniker of the "Medicare for All" movement following the 2016 election cycle and to the use of "Medicare for All" as a general term for a spectrum of policy proposals, including policies that allowed individuals to choose between a Medicare public option and private insurance. Single-payer activists were critical of this general use of the term,

> in response to Medicare for All, we've seen a number of proposals spring up that attempt to co-opt our movement, put forth by centrists unwilling to offend corporations. All of these proposals—from the Medicare for America Act to the various public option bills—preserve the existing, profit-driven healthcare system that every year costs more people their livelihoods and lives.[26]

In spite of this cooptation, the reality that all presidential candidates were forced to discuss the concept of Medicare for All at some point during the debates, as well as in the centralization of the idea in Democratic discourse, represented both success and opportunity. The term single-payer was no longer used interchangeably with Medicare for All, and indeed

[26] Healthcare NOW Email June 13, 2019.

single-payer was not used at all until later in the 2020 debate cycle. Sanders once again started using the term "single-payer Medicare for All" to differentiate his position from other candidates that began using the term Medicare for All to promote plans that were not quite single-payer. Although a few of the past single-payer supporters transitioned to "Medicare for those who want it" systems that would expand Medicare so that it would act as a public option within the current system, this period of presidential debates still represented progress toward the goal of single-payer and thus success.

Economic Success

Success within the economic sphere of influence is no less important to continued grassroots mobilization than successfully mobilizing support within the political sphere. Too often economic actors act as "resisters" that become oppositional forces inhibiting progressive reform efforts.[27] The economic actors that become "facilitators" contribute to grassroots mobilization efforts in a multiplicity of ways. They not only facilitate grassroots activity by contributing financial resources for these activities, but they also provide legitimacy to movements that support radical changes to established industries. The support of economic actors, such as groups of medical professionals, unions, and businesses, is an indicator to single-payer activists that they are making progress toward their primary goal.

In part because the primary goal of the Single Payer Movement would necessitate a radical change to the current medical industrial complex, the support of medical professionals is a crucial symbol of success for grassroots activists. Increasing the number of medical professionals, and especially physicians, that support single-payer is a core indication of this support and thus the legitimacy of the single-payer goal. The development of the grassroots arm of the SPM was supported by physicians. In 1987, Steffie Woolhandler and David Himmelstein began the work to increase the support of physicians for a single-payer type system through the formation of Physicians for a National Health Program (PNHP). While this organization started with only a handful of physicians participating at its conception in the late 1980s (around 400), it has steadily grown to a

---

[27] Luders, Joseph. (2006). The Economics of Movement Success: Business Responses to Civil Rights Mobilization. The American Journal of Sociology 111 (4): 963–998.

membership of around 23,000, which is significantly higher than their membership during the G.W. Bush era (8000 in 2003) or the Obama era (16000 in 2008). Figure 8.3 illustrates the upward trend in PNHP's total revenue.[28] This growth in financial support of the organization illustrates the increase in the strength of the organization to mobilize economic resources. PNHP continues to support grassroots organizations by sharing these economic resources, as well as through research and participation in grassroots activities.

While PNHP is an outwardly activist organization formed around one central goal, the increasing support of other types of professional organizations in the medical field is also a sign of success for the Single Payer Movement. While several medical professional organizations, such as the American Academy of Family Physicians and the American Association of Community Psychiatrists, had endorsed single-payer, or something like it, in the past, the endorsement of the largest medical specialty society and the second largest physician group in the United States—the American

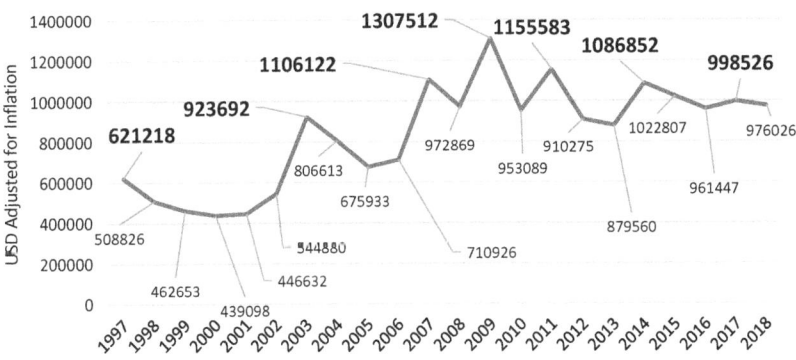

Data Source: IRS 990 Tax Forms for Physicians for a National Health Program
Includes all income: Membership Dues, Donations, Grants, Services, and Investments

Fig. 8.3 PNHP total revenue. (Data source: IRS 990 Tax Forms for Physicians for a National Health Program. Includes all income: Membership dues, donations, grants, services, and investments)

[28] Data was extracted from PNHP 990 tax forms and adjusted for inflation (to December 2019 numbers) using the Bureau of Labor Statistics inflation calculator. Investment income was typically minimal—around 2000 dollars. All other revenue was from membership dues, donations, grants, and services.

College of Physicians—in January of 2020 represented a new era of support for single-payer by medical professionals. This group, composed of 159,000 members, was only second in membership to the American Medical Association (AMA), which had long opposed any nationalized form of healthcare financing or provision.[29] A resolution at the AMA 2019 national meeting, which would have overturned the long-held opposition of the AMA to single-payer, was narrowly defeated with 47 percent voting in favor of the resolution. This resolution was supported by hundreds of physician activists who held a rally outside of the meeting before the vote. A few months later, after continued pressure from its membership, the AMA left the "Partnership for America's Health Care Future" which is a coalition of medical industry organizations that was formed specifically to oppose the Medicare for All movement. These events were viewed as a sign that there had been a "sea change"[30] in the support of physicians for single-payer. Steffie Woolhandler explained it this way,

> When we started PNHP, doctors who supported single-payer reform were considered radicals, and reporters likened us to 'furriers for animal rights'. Now we're squarely in the mainstream of the medical profession. More and more doctors have realized—often from talking to our Canadian colleagues—that single-payer is the only way to cut insurers' paperwork and profits that siphon hundreds of billions annually from care in the U.S.[31]

On top of these endorsements, the support for single-payer by medical student groups that have given the movement "incredible energy,"[32] such as the American Medical Student Association and Students for a National Health Program, indicates that the support of physicians will continue to grow. Indeed, the support of physicians transitioned from 58 percent

[29] See, Marmor, Theodore R. 1970. The Politics of Medicare. Aldine De Gruyter, New York. And Quadagno, Jill. 2005. One Nation Uninsured: Why the U.S. Has No National Health Insurance New York: Oxford University Press.

[30] Dr. Adam Gaffney, Executive Director of PNHP, quoted in FULL CITATION https://time.com/5709017/medicare-for-all-doctor-activists/.

[31] Steffie Woolhandler, PNHP co-founder, Distinguished Professor at the City University of New York at Hunter College, and Lecturer in Medicine at Harvard Medical School quoted in FULL CITATION https://www.commondreams.org/newswire/2020/01/20/doctors-prescribe-medicare-all-single-payer-reform-endorsed-americas-largest.

[32] Matthew Petty, Executive Director Physicians for a National Health Program—PNHP Fundraising email 2/5/2020.

being opposed to single-payer in 2008 to 56 percent being in favor of single-payer less than ten years later.[33]

Other medical professionals have also been important economic facilitators for grassroots single-payer activism. While some surveys have found other medical professionals, such as nurses, to be less supportive of single-payer,[34] these professionals have nevertheless supported the grassroots movement in many ways. In the previous chapters, I have discussed extensively the role that nurses have played in the movement through the organization—National Nurses United (NNU). Although NNU is now the largest nurses union in the country, when I first started my field research, it did not exist. I first began hearing about the development of a new national union of nurses at the 2007 Healthcare NOW annual meeting chaired by Michael Lighty, who was then the National Policy Director of the California Nurses Association (CNA). Just a few years later, in 2009, CNA joined forces with the United American Nurses and Massachusetts Nurses Association to form National Nurses United (NNU), which is now the largest union or professional association of nurses, with over 150,000 members. The role that NNU has played in the grassroots movement, including their ongoing work to mobilize grassroots activism in support of Medicare for All, is discussed throughout the previous chapters. I will add that the development of this organization and the growth of its supportive membership has been an indicator to grassroots activists that not only is the support of medical professionals growing but also the support of unions.

The Single Payer Movement has had a somewhat fluid relationship with unions as a whole—vacillating between alliance and opposition. While very early efforts for national health programs were supported by unions, increasing levels of employer sponsored insurance resulted in the reliance of unions on the use of healthcare coverage as an element of union power. This influenced their resistance to more state involvement in healthcare provision in the later half of the twentieth century.[35] In the context of this feature of the economic environment, single-payer actors worked to win

---

[33] These figures are based on surveys conducted by Merritt Hawkins, a physician recruitment firm. More information can be found about this survey at https://khn.org/news/doctors-warm-to-single-payer-health-care/.

[34] See Frellick, Marcia. 2019. "Healthcare Professionals Almost Equally Divided on Medicare for All, Poll Shows" Medscape Medical News. Published May 29, 2019.

[35] Quadagno, Jill. 2005. One Nation Uninsured: Why the U.S. Has No National Health Insurance New York: Oxford University Press.

the support of unions. Just a few years after forming "Unions for Single Payer," Kay Tillow was able to garner the support of 300 union organizations by 2007. Only ten years later, in 2017, this number had more than doubled to 637 labor organizations that had endorsed H.R. 676. While many of these were state and local organizations, twenty-two were unions with national or international membership. In 2009, Mark Dudzic—who is also a Healthcare NOW board member—worked with others to create the "Labor Campaign for Single Payer." This organization was designed to not only garner union support in theory through the passing of endorsement resolutions by union leaders but also in practice by encouraging the rank and file union members to put "boots on the ground" in support of single-payer. As of February 2020, "Nineteen unions representing nearly 10 million workers have stepped up to endorse HR 1384 The Medicare for All of 2019. This means that a majority of union members are now represented by unions that support Medicare for All."[36] This support of unions is a clear indicator of success for single-payer actors.

Members of the business community are also central actors within the economic sphere. Indeed, the most ardent opposition within the economic sphere is found within the insurance and pharmaceutical industry that would face significant costs with the implementation of a single-payer system. Yet, the single-payer narrative that I shared in the previous chapters also highlighted the role that individuals from even those industries have played in the movement. Wendel Potter, who is an insurance executive turned single-payer activist, has continued to mobilize the business community through the formation of "Business for Medicare for All," (B4M4A) of which he is the president. Members of this organization are business owners that believe

> a new system that guarantees health care coverage for Americans regardless of where they work is critically important to maintain our profits, grow wages for working families, spur entrepreneurship and compete globally. It is time to cut the middle man—health insurance companies—out of our health care system and pass those savings on to employers of all sizes and their workers.[37]

[36] Labor Campaign for Single Payer "Medicare for All: Is Your Union on Board?" https://www.laborforsinglepayer.org/medicare-for-all-is-your-union-on-board/ Retrieved on 2/3/2020.

[37] Business for Medicare for All "Who We Are" https://www.businessformedicareforall.org/who-we-are.html Retrieved on 2/3/2020.

This organization funded the creation of several single-payer-related documentaries discussed in previous chapters—*Fix It*, *Big Pharma Market Failure*, and *Big Money Agenda*. Grassroots single-payer activists continue to use these films to make the economic case for single-payer. I was asked by Dr. Ed Weisbart, PNHP (Missouri Chapter) Chair and Health Advisory Board Member of B4M4A, to be a discussant following a showing of *Big Pharma Market Failure* in Kansas City MO in the summer of 2017 at the Pharaoh Cinema in Independence, Missouri. The discussion with the full theater of attendees that followed the film was energetic and indicated to me that there was great interest in the issue in my hometown of Kansas City.[38] The production of these films, as well as their distribution, was facilitated by the opportunity presented within the cultural sphere by the rise of digital media technology.

CULTURAL SUCCESS

As discussed in earlier chapters, the development of internet-based technologies and their use by social movement actors facilitated the mobilization efforts and thus growth of the Single Payer Movement during the G.W. Bush era. The use of these technologies continued to develop during the Obama and Trump eras. Not only did single-payer actors create documentaries such as *Fix It*, but they also started using digital video technologies to include internet audiences in face-to-face movement events and in trainings as part of the single-payer school. In the current era, the use of webinars to engage with activists all around the country in real time has become an important tool used in newer mobilization efforts such as the Medicare for All Resolutions Campaign. In addition to this, the tactic of "birddogging"[39] elected officials or candidates at public events and then posting videos of their answers has become a way to activate grassroots supporters and share the single-payer solution with a wider audience.

In addition to media produced from within the movement, media produced outside of movement organizations that features single-payer or supporters of single-payer has also been influential. A primary example of

---

[38] Notably, on that same day there was a Medicare for All rally and march hosted by the Democratic Socialists of America happening just a few miles away in Kansas City MO.

[39] Birddogging is a tactic that involves attending public events, such as town halls or campaign rallies, and asking pointed questions about support for Medicare for All. The intention is for this to be recorded and shared on social media.

this is the documentary *Knock Down the House*, which "features Alexandria Ocasio-Cortez and 3 other rockstars who ran for Congress on progressive, grassroots platforms."[40] Central to this film is the story of Amy Vilela. I first met Vilela at a regional Single Payer Leadership Meeting that was held in Las Vegas, Nevada, in October of 2017. At this meeting Vilela explained that she had started the first Healthcare NOW chapter in Nevada for many reasons, but at the center of these reasons was the death of her daughter, Shaylynne, who had gone to the emergency room because of extreme pain in her leg. At the hospital the "first thing asked was do you have insurance,"[41] and Shaylynne, believing that she did not have insurance due to recent job change, said no. She was told that "If you leave now, it won't cost you anything" and "Go get insurance and see a specialist."[42] The pain in her leg was actually deep vein thrombosis and ultimately resulted in her death at the age of 22. Vilela explained that,

> The moment I decided to start becoming an activist was when my sister looked at me and started crying, "I've lost Shalynne, and now you're killing yourself." Because I was pretty much just isolated. My sister said, "Are you going to fight to help others or are you going to kill yourself?" So I decided to try and help others.[43]

Vilela went on to protest cuts to the ACA, start a Healthcare NOW chapter in Nevada, participate in one of the first classes of the Healthcare NOW leadership training project, and run for Congress as a progressive challenger to the establishment democrats. Although her primary challenge was ultimately unsuccessful, the coverage that Vilela's story received in both news media and in *Knock Down the House* was received as a sign of opportunity for single-payer activism because,

> Amy's story has the power to inspire a whole new wave of single payer activists and grow our local groups, but we need your help to make that happen. You can host a screening at home or at a public venue like a library or

---

[40] Healthcare NOW email April 24, 2019.

[41] Fieldnotes: Amy Vilela, Single Payer Leadership Meeting, Las Vegas Nevada, October 2017.

[42] Ganeva, Tana. 2017. "After Daughter's Tragic Death, Mother Begs for Single-Payer Health Care" Rolling Stone—published on May 16, 2017. https://www.rollingstone.com/politics/politics-features/after-daughters-tragic-death-mother-begs-for-single-payer-health-care-116295/.

[43] Ibid.

theatre. If you need help identifying a good place for your screening, or turning people out, please contact us. Knock Down the House is getting a lot of press coverage right now and has the potential to draw a young and excited crowd from outside the Medicare for All movement. Let's take advantage of this opportunity—sign up today to host a screening![44]

Much like SiCKO years before, *Knock Down the House* became a film around which to mobilize. Some individuals featured in *Knock Down the House* became "political influencers"[45] who adeptly navigate new media to promote particular causes. Both the campaign of and the subsequent actions post the election by Representative Alexandria Ocasio Cortez (D-NY) became an influential story within the single-payer narrative and within the narrative of mainstream American politics. These influencers, such as Ocasio Cortez, use media, including social media platforms, to inform the public and draw them into support of particular causes. This is understood as a signifier of successful progress and opportunity for mobilization by single-payer activists.

Media attention to single-payer has grown over time, another sign of success for the SPM. Figure 8.4 illustrates a general upward trend in the use of the term single-payer in print news media over the past thirty years.[46] While there are definite peaks during periods in which healthcare reform is "on the table" at the federal level, see the peaks during the 1992–1994 Clinton era, the 2008–2010 Obama era, and the 2016–2018 Trump era, there is also a trend of increasing coverage during periods in which healthcare reform is not at the center of American politics. In addition to the dips in coverage becoming less acute, the peaks become more pronounced as we move forward along the timeline. Following the last peak during the first year of the Trump era (2970 mentions), there was a dip (to 2361 mentions) during the following year. However, this dip was relatively minor and was likely due to the shift from talking about single-payer health insurance to Medicare for All.[47]

[44] Healthcare NOW Email April 24, 2019.

[45] Pérez-Curiel, Concha, and Pilar Limón Naharro. 2019. "Political Influencers. A Study of Donald Trump's Personal Brand on Twitter and Its Impact on the Media and Users." Communication & Society 32 (1): 57–75.

[46] For this analysis, news media was limited to newspapers available on the data bank Nexis Uni. This included all forms of articles—including news articles and opinion articles.

[47] To perform the analysis of news media presented throughout the text I used the data based Lexus Uni to search for and code articles using terms related to healthcare reform, including single-payer.

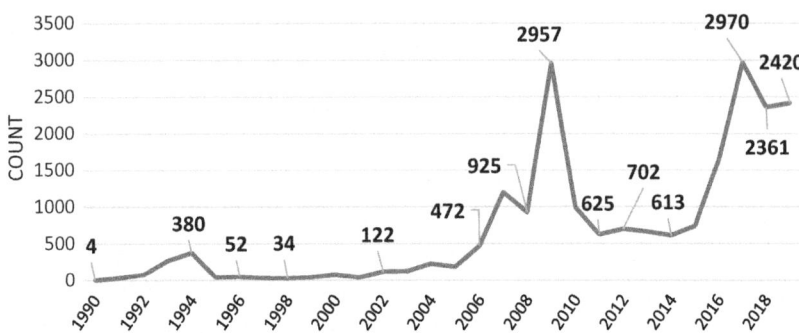

Fig. 8.4 Single payer in newspapers. (Sources: National, state, local—Nexis Uni database)

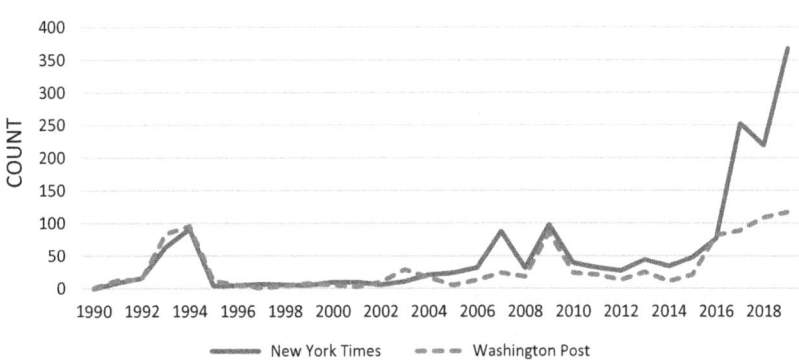

Fig. 8.5 Single payer in national newspapers

The most recent dip in the use of the term is also related to less use of the term in state and local news media, rather than in national media.[48] Figure 8.5 illustrates the trend in two national news media sources—*The New York Times* and *The Washington Post*. The trends for both outlets are similar, with peaks around the Clinton, Obama, and Trump eras. While the peaks before the Trump era look pretty similar, *The New York Times*

---

[48] An analysis of state vs. national newspapers showed a decline in the use of the term in specific states, such as Vermont, which affected the overall rates. I am only presenting the analysis of national news here due to space constraints.

has an additional peak during the SiCKO / G.W. Bush era and a more definite increase during the Trump era—indicating that *The New York Times* uses the term with greater frequency than *The Washington Post* beginning in the mid-2000s and especially during the Trump era. Overall, the increased use of the term single-payer in news media is a sign of success to single-payer supporters, indicating that their policy goal is becoming more mainstream and reaching a wider audience.

GRASSROOTS SUCCESS

Grassroots opportunity and the successful mobilization of support within the public sphere is tied to the ability to reach a wider audience with a narrative that counters the stories being told by those who oppose the goals of the SPM. This is also tied to the political and economic spheres as both economic and political actors can facilitate or inhibit the sharing of progressive positions with the wider public. Yet, any conclusion that grassroots mobilization is entirely an outcome of those forms of opportunity is far too simple of an explanation. Grassroots activists, as illustrated by the history of the SPM told throughout this book, also act on grassroots opportunity to encourage grassroots mobilization. Even in contexts in which there is very little chance of achieving policy-related success, activists mobilize in order to achieve success in form of more public support and more involvement in the movement.

The first measure of success in the grassroots sphere centers on public support for the goals of the movement. When I started this project, there was concern within the movement about whether or not the public even recognized or understood what single-payer is or how it operates. Now there is confidence within the movement that the public not only recognize the term but that a majority support it. More public support for single-payer indicates to activists that "we are at a tipping point in this movement."[49] Indeed, recent public opinion polls typically show that there is majority support for a single-payer/Medicare for All type of system. For example, the most recent Kaiser Family Foundation Poll found that about 56 percent of respondents in a sample representative of the United States were in favor of "a national health plan, sometimes called Medicare-for-all, in which all Americans would get their insurance from a

---

[49] Healthcare NOW email, November 8, 2018.

single government plan."[50] In Fig. 8.6, I use data from the Kaiser Family Foundation Health Tracking Poll to illustrate changes in public support over time.[51] This chart illustrates that there was a reversal in public opinion about single-payer sometime during the late Obama era. During the 2016 election cycle, a majority of Americans identified as being in favor of single-payer for the first time. Yes, this transition is tied to the campaign of Senator Bernie Sanders and the work that it accomplished to bring single-payer to center of public discourse, but it is also tied to the work that single-payer actors did for the twenty-five years preceding this period in order to increase public awareness and support of single-payer.

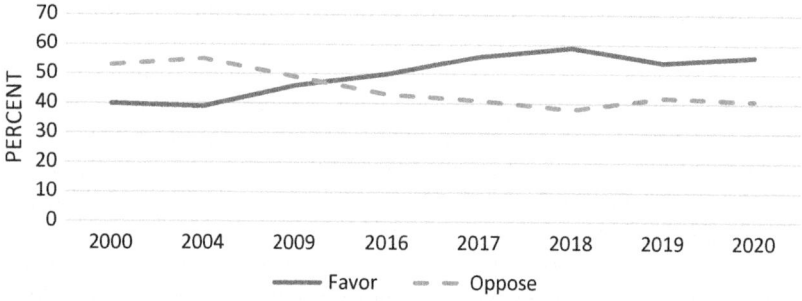

Fig. 8.6 Public support for single-payer/Medicare for All. (Source: Kaiser Family Foundation Polls)

[50] Lopes, Lunna, Liz Hamel, Audrey Kearney, and Mollyann Brodie. 2020. "KFF Health Tracking Poll—January 2020: Medicare-for-all, Public Option, Health Care Legislation and Court Actions" Kaiser Family Foundation Published on January 30, 2020 https://www.kff. org/health-reform/poll-finding/kff-health-tracking-poll-january-2020/.

[51] Note: The data for dates prior 2016 is also from KFF polling, but was collected before single-payer was consistently measured via the Health Tracking Poll. Only averages of polls from a range of years was available and the year represented on the chart represents a range of years. The 2016 and higher figures represent the average of the outcomes of all Health Tracking Polls in that year. Only one poll for 2020 was available at the completion of this book. You can find more data and information about this here, Lopes, Lunna, Liz Hamel, Audrey Kearney, and Mollyann Brodie. 2020. "KFF Health Tracking Poll—January 2020: Medicare-for-all, Public Option, Health Care Legislation and Court Actions" Kaiser Family Foundation Published on January 30, 2020 https://www.kff.org/health-reform/poll-find-ing/kff-health-tracking-poll-january-2020/ AND "Public Opinion of Single-Payer National Health Plans, and Expanding Access to Medicare Kaiser Family Foundation Published on Jan. 30, 2020 https://www.kff.org/slideshow/public-opinion-on-single-payer-national-health-plans-and-expanding-access-to-medicare-coverage/.

As expected, public opinion regarding single-payer is divided along party lines. I illustrate this, again using data from the KFF Health Tracking Poll, in Fig. 8.7. In January of 2020, a strong majority of democrats, 77 percent, indicated that they were in favor of a single-payer type system (either strongly or somewhat). Conversely, 72 percent of Republicans indicated that they oppose single-payer. It is also an important sign of success for single-payer activists that a majority of independents, 61 percent, also favored single-payer. This, in addition to the majority support from the whole, indicates that public opinion has successfully been shifted to favor single-payer.

In addition to public opinion, more participation in grassroots mobilization efforts is also a central indicator of both grassroots opportunity and grassroots success. As discussed in Chap. 7, there was an increase in both liberal and progressive grassroots mobilization efforts following the election of Trump in 2016. Single-payer activists began to work with progressive campaigns, such as the Women's March which "embraced Medicare for All as one of their priorities!"[52] The mobilization effort to stop Republican lead efforts to "repeal and replace" the Affordable Care Act also became an opportunity to grow participation in the SPM as single-payer actors worked to "build in all of the new people" so that the new-found interest in the movement was "not just a blip in the radar, not a surge and then phase out."[53] The emphasis within the Sander's campaign on creating a "political revolution" continued following the election cycle

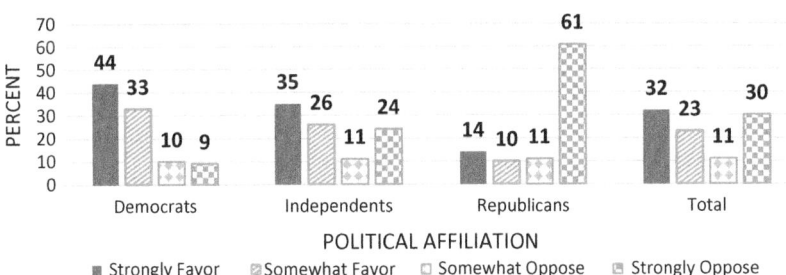

Fig. 8.7 Support for Medicare for All by political affiliation. (Source: Kaiser Family Foundation Health Tracking Poll Jan. 2020)

---

[52] Progressive Democrats of America Email Jan 14, 2019.
[53] Ben, Healthcare NOW Leadership Meeting, Las Vegas Nevada, October 2017.

with the creation of groups like Our Revolution and the reinvigoration of organizations like the Democratic Socialists of America. All of these changes brought new energy and participation into the SPM.

The Single Payer Movement also welcomed back several organizations that had previously shifted away from support of single-payer to support of incremental policy measures. A central example of this is the refocusing of the Universal Healthcare Action Network (UHCAN) onto the goal of single-payer. UHCAN's shift away from single-payer in the Contract with America era (1995–2000) had caused disruption within single-payer organizations at the state level and fragmentation within the national movement.[54] In the Trump era, UHCAN worked with other single-payer organizations, like Healthcare NOW, on the "Medicare for All Resolutions" campaign lead by Public Citizen. While the goal of this campaign was to pass resolutions in support of Medicare for All at the local level, an equally important goal was to use this campaign to "build local power."[55] Still other organizations that had worked with Health Care for America NOW during the Obama era (2008–2012), such as Social Security Works, became active supporters of and participants in the SPM during this era.

All of these factors facilitated the successful mobilization of a larger body of supporters for single-payer. Figure 8.8 illustrates the attendance record at the Single Payer National Strategy Conference that occurs about once a year. The attendance at these conferences increased during the

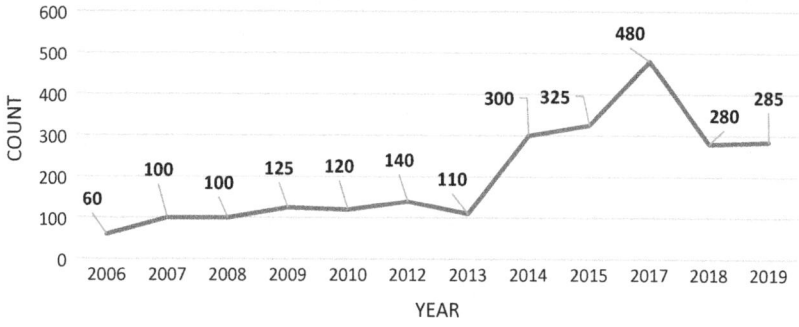

Fig. 8.8   Single-payer strategy conference attendance

[54] See Chap. 3.
[55] Healthcare NOW Email April 15, 2019.

ACA era (2010–2014)[56] when Healthcare NOW began organizing them with partners such as the Labor Campaign for Single Payer. This collaboration was a strategic decision to increase participation at the conference and in post-conference activities. Attendance at these meetings peaked directly following the election of Trump to the presidency, with almost 500 activists attending. Conference attendance is also affected by the participation of local- and state-based organizations in the conference location. So, some of that increase is also related to the fact that the 2017 conference was held in New York City, which has a large state-based movement. The discourse before, during, and after that meeting also indicated to activists that the Trump election had encouraged people to get involved. Following that peak, conference attendance leveled out to the previous norm of about 300 attendees, which was still almost three times higher than the average attendance, of 108 participants, prior to 2014.

Successful mobilization efforts in which there was more participation than expected, also indicated to single-payer organizations that they had successfully acted upon grassroots opportunity. For example, the Healthcare NOW "Street Team Campaign," which involved canvassing for single-payer and encouraging people to sign on in support of the Sander's single-payer bill in the Senate (S. 1804), started with a goal of collecting 10,000 signatures. Through a collaboration with other organizations, they collected over 40,000.[57] A barnstorm campaign lead by National Nurses United (NNU) following the 2018 midterm elections was also more successful than expected. Single-payer activists "had 151 barnstorms across the country, also Hawaii and Alaska, also Puerto Rico. There were 5000 attendees and 1500 canvases organized. Planned 150 a week, have had 800 so far."[58] All of this indicated to single-payer supporters that they had successfully grown the "grassroots power" of the movement.

[56] See Chap. 6.

[57] This was the result of a joint effort of Healthcare-NOW, Daily Kos, PDA, and many other national and state organizations.

[58] Kelly, National Nurses United Representative, Healthcare NOW Board Meeting March 2019.

Confronting Failure with Grit and Resilience

The Single Payer Movement has not achieved its primary goal of forcing Congress to enact and implement a single-payer system in the United States. However, this analysis shows that movement has indeed made progress toward this goal through minor successes that have increased support in the grassroots, cultural, economic, and political spheres of influence. It's important to highlight these successes, because they are necessary to the process of social change, especially if the desired social change is perceived as radical. Social change does not happen quickly, it is a slow process that builds toward the finish line. It is a process that requires grit and resilience in the face of failure.

CHAPTER 9

"Reality-Based Hope": Lessons Learned in the Single Payer Movement

Several key lessons can be learned from this accounting of the last three decades of the Single Payer Movement (SPM). Single-payer activists have learned some of these lessons through trial and error during the everyday practice of social movement mobilization. Other lessons are rooted in my analysis of the movement and can hopefully be helpful for continued movement activity. Each of these lessons is important to developing a holistic understanding of social movement success—which applies to both activists, scholars, and scholar-activists like myself.[1] Too often, there is a divide between scholarship and activism that limits both the conclusions developed in scholarship and the potential of that scholarship to be useful to social movement actors. If both scholars and activists are supportive of mobilization that is committed to the creation of a just and equitable society, then the lessons learned through both activism and scholarship should be mutually shared, respected, and valued. I'm sure there are other lessons that can be drawn from the experiences of the SPM, but here I will explain ten of what I find to be the most important lessons that are supported by the analysis presented in this text.

---

[1] For a more extensive discussion of scholar-activism, see Hern, Lindy. 2016. "From Stalker to Board Member: Navigating the Borderland of Scholar-Activism in the Movement for Single Payer Health Care Reform. Journal of Applied Social Science.

© The Author(s) 2020
L. S. F. Hern, *Single Payer Healthcare Reform*,
https://doi.org/10.1007/978-3-030-42764-1_9

LESSON 1: THE IMPORTANCE OF RECOGNIZING SUCCESS IN ALL ITS FORMS

Success is, of course, the desired outcome of any social movement. But defining success narrowly is not helpful as an exclusive definition can serve to hide the lesser successes that were needed along the way. In Chap. 8, I discussed extensively the many forms of success that the SPM had experienced within a context of failure to achieve the primary goal. It is imperative for social movement scholars to recognize the effect that the experience of failure, as well as success, can have on future mobilization. The stories told about social movements by those that study them must include an understanding of the low points as well as the high points within social movement activity if we are ever to develop an understanding of social movement success that is holistic and complete. Social movement actors must not only understand their failures in order to learn from them, they must also account for their successes, no matter how minor, in order to increase the hope that achieving their primary goal is possible.

LESSON 2: CREATING HOPE IS KEY—ESPECIALLY IN THE ABSENCE OF SUCCESS

In order to continue to mobilize, social movement actors must have hope that it is possible to achieve their goals. They must produce "reality-based hope"[2] through the interpretation of the conditions present within their environment of opportunity. Through this process, single-payer supporters are reminded that they "can and will get single-payer health care, improved Medicare for All, and that it will be the best Health Care for All system. Reality-based hope can help instill in you a realistic, firm belief that U.S. health care for all can and will happen."[3] This lesson involves an understanding that the process of social change is a slow race that builds over time and requires collective cooperation that empowers individuals. Nina Turner reminded activists of this saying,

---

[2] This concept arose through an email conversation that occurred in 2012 with Bob Haiducek who organized the Million Letters Campaign for several years. This concept later appeared in the organizational discourse via websites and other materials.

[3] Bob. Haiducek—organizer of the Million Letters for Healthcare Campaign—2012— retrieved from http://www.medicareforall.org/pages/Hope.

For every time that you are feeling weary in your well-doing—remember the four-forty relay we run as a team. And the first leg of the race sets the pace. The goal is to get distance between you and the team that you are running against so that you set up the next leg of the race, who gets more distance, then the next leg of the race who gets more distance, then the next leg of the race. That is what this fight is about. This is about us setting up the four forty relay generation after generation after generation. We gonna walk some folks down! Before they know it, we gonna be at the finish line baby![4]

In order to create hope in negative political contexts, activists must often direct their focus outside of the political sphere. While political opportunity may indeed be necessary to achieve the ultimate success of achieving the goals of a social movement—especially if those goals can best be achieved through the creation of public policy or programs—other forms of opportunity are no less important in the process of creating the path to reach that finish line. Social movement actors can focus on multiple forms of opportunity to create hope within social movements, even when the political sphere is lacking in the material conditions that can be used to produce hope or is openly hostile to the goals of the social movement. This hope can encourage social movement participants to continue to mobilize in contexts within which their goals seem impossible. Sustained efforts to mobilize can, at the very least, facilitate the retention of movement identity, process knowledge, and infrastructure and at the very best facilitate movement growth that can result in a collective mobilization effort that is large and powerful enough to successfully act on political opportunity when it next arises. Or, if it does not arise on its own, the movement can mobilize to change the political sphere into a context in which the goals of the social movement are not only possible but probable. This lesson should instruct those interested in successful social movements—whether activists or scholars—to not just include but to value forms of opportunity other than those specifically in the political sphere. Social movement participants in the SPM have learned this over time and have become quite adept at recognizing and adapting to multiple forms of opportunity. Creating hope that there is positive potential in social movement action even within negative contexts is perhaps the most important task for a social movement because without the hope that social change is

---

[4] Nina Turner—Keynote Address, Single Payer National Strategy Conference, January 2017, NYC NY.

possible, there is little reason to act in ways that make it probable by creating opportunities for change.

In the face of strong opposition, there is a need for resilience and true grit that is built by learning from failure without losing hope, giving in, and giving up. Success is made possible by cultivating a capacity for always failing forward in the knowledge that every great social innovation was built upon multiple failures from which leaders learned, and then, persevering, continued to move forward. Success for the SPM will require gritty people who refuse to succumb to failure, but instead adapt their methods and continue their work.[5] Throughout this book, I have examined how the political strategy of the SPM adapted to changes in the environment of opportunity in ways that produced hope that the movement could achieve some measure of success. While the political strategy during the Clinton era focused primarily on mobilizing the support of political actors within the existing political sphere, the lessons learned during the G.W. Bush and Obama era's encouraged single-payer actors to reorient their political strategy toward building a mass movement that would have the power to change the political sphere. This political strategy included tactics oriented toward increasing public support of single-payer as well as changing the meaning of single-payer within the larger cultural context in order to create future opportunities for mobilization, as well as hope that this mobilization would be successful.

Lesson 3: Sometimes Social Movements Must Create Opportunities, Not Just Act on Them

Rather than just acting on opportunities already present in their environments, social movement actors often must work to create opportunities to achieve their goals. Throughout this text, I have examined the ways in which the SPM adapted their political strategy in ways that would not only act on, but also create, new opportunities. In the Clinton era, the SPM was resolutely tied to acting on political opportunity out of necessity, because other forms of opportunity were more constrained by the larger material reality of the time, and also because the goal, and the strategy to achieve that goal, remained resolutely tied to the political sphere. Later, during the G.W. Bush administration, when the political context appeared

---

[5] A special thank you to my father—Kyle Hern—for discussing this idea with me and helping me figure out the words through which I could convey it.

so prohibitive in relation to progressive social change, single-payer activists were not only able to perceive through narrative practice other forms of opportunity and develop ways to act on this opportunity, they were also able to adapt these opportunities to their use. Single-payer organizations worked together to build an internet-based infrastructure that would continue to facilitate the growth of the movement during the digital age. They were able to act on the grassroots opportunity presented by left-leaning individuals who were affronted by the policies of the G.W. Bush administration by encouraging them to use that frustration in support of single-payer. Later, the Obama era appeared to be a time ripe with the opportunity for progressive healthcare reform, but it actually resulted in the alienation of the SPM as they were used as the straw man in juxtaposition with the Obama agenda for healthcare reform and firmly denied a "seat at the table." Yet, the SPM continued to act on narratives of grassroots, cultural, and economic opportunity by mobilizing the grassroots, cultural, and economic infrastructures or resources that they had been building for at least two decades. This allowed them to keep on keepin' on even within the new context of the Affordable Care Act, which was not open to challenges to this policy, regardless of whether those challenges were from the right or from the left. In order to create a political sphere with more opportunity to achieve their goal, they also encouraged single-payer supporters to run for office, most notably through the "Run Bernie Run" campaign that fed into the 2016 election season and by working with other social movements with problems to solve that intersected with the problem of healthcare reform. They found ways to act on the opportunities that were apparent within this context, and when it became obvious that the political sphere was constructed in such a way to prohibit the successful conclusion of their efforts, they focused on building an intersectional movement with the people power to change the political context through a political revolution.

Lesson 4: Social Movements Should Build Intersectional Alliances While Also Maintaining Focus

As the Single Payer Movement became oriented toward a movement building strategy focused on mobilizing public support for single-payer as part of a larger political revolution, it became more open to working with and supporting the goals of intersecting social movements. Yet, single-payer actors did not stray from the ultimate goal of single-payer. They had learned an important lesson following the death of healthcare reform in the Clinton era—that a shift to more general goals can result in fragmentation, conflict, and death within the movement. While the SPM did become more open to supporting other intersecting issues following the Obama era, they did not become more general in their goal. Instead of trying to unify with other healthcare reform supporters by taking a less specific or incremental approach to healthcare reform, they formed alliances with other progressive movements that were interested not only in achieving their goals but also in changing the context in which these goals would be achieved. This joining of forces pushed through changes in the political material context, even within a political sphere which had been shaped in negative ways by the rise of anti-establishment politics on the right. The rise of anti-establishment politics on the left, which included a definition of politics as usual as the enemy of progressive reform, worked to reshape the context while remaining committed to specific goals.

LESSON 5: WHEN DEFINING THE ENEMY, PROCEED WITH CAUTION

The effort to remain committed to a specific goal can shape the definition of the "enemy" within the narrative practice of a social movement. In each of the historical periods discussed throughout this text, the definition of the enemy was shaped by the environment of opportunity, and these differing definitions affected the movement building strategy of the SPM. For example, defining the enemy as "politics as usual" during the Obama era encouraged activists to focus on increasing public support in order to build a movement with the power to challenge the political establishment and thus change the political sphere into one that was more open to progressive goals. While it is important for movement actors to know who is working against the social movement and how they are enacting this counter-mobilization effort, it's also important not to limit movement building potential by concretizing these entities into intractable enemies with no positive potential in relation to the social movement. The opposition in one period may become an ally in a future period. While healthcare professionals and unions were some of the fiercest opponents of progressive healthcare reform in previous eras, they became significant supporters in later eras in part due to changes in the context and in part due to the efforts of social movement actors. Viewing individuals or organizations as permanent enemies can result in missed opportunities to turn these oppositional forces into allies. As the SPM grew, they learned to act on opportunities to create leaders from enemy forces. For example, as discussed in Chap. 4, Wendell Potter, who was an executive in the insurance industry that continues to create great opposition to progressive healthcare reform, became an enthusiastic supporter of single-payer and a leader within single-payer organizations. Recognizing potential allies within even oppositional forces can potentially facilitate the development of not only support but also leadership, within social movements.

LESSON 6: THE MAKING OF HEROES—LEADERSHIP IN THE MOVEMENT

Too often, the narrative of social change focuses on leadership in the political sphere and ignores the leadership that was mobilized in the grassroots sphere. When one hears about the creation of social security, the story often centers on the New Deal, FDR, and his "fireside" chats, while it ignores the extensive mobilization within the Townsend Movement that pushed FDR in that direction.[6] Discussions of the current focus on Medicare for All in American political discourse tend to focus on the role that Senator Bernie Sanders has played as a leader of that policy proposal.[7] While political leaders are indeed necessary to transition the goals of a social movement into the enactment and implementation of social policy or programs, grassroots leadership in the public sphere is often a precursor to the development of leadership in the political sphere. Smart political leaders have learned this lesson and recognize that they need grassroots action, and therefore grassroots leaders, in order to achieve progressive goals.

> They know, as we know, that this struggle will ultimately not be won here on capitol hill, but through the grassroots activism of millions of Americans

---

[6] For an extensive analysis of this, see Amenta, Edwin. 2006. When Movements Matter: The Townsend Plan & the Rise of Social Security Princeton University Press.

[7] See Oberlander, Jonathon. 2019. "Lessons From the Long and Winding Road to Medicare for All" American Journal of Public Health 109(11): 1497–1500 AND Levitt L. 2018. Single-Payer Health Care: Opportunities and Vulnerabilities. JAMA. 319(16): 1646–1647.

who are standing up and fighting back. Who are becoming more engaged politically. … And when we all stand together, we're going to be able to take on the insurance companies and pharmaceutical companies and Wall Street and everybody else.[8]

Social movement actors must act on this lesson, especially if they start from a position of dependence on political support or leadership.

The SPM learned this through trial and error and concluded that "legislators are not movement leaders—they will sacrifice principles if they think it's needed to pass the bill."[9] This lesson encouraged the SPM to focus more extensively on cultivating the grassroots leadership that could successfully build a social movement with enough people power to move political leadership to support the goal of single-payer. They also worked to encourage single-payer supporters to run for offices that they may not have considered before—examples of this can be found in the "Run Bernie Run" campaign and in the efforts of groups like Justice Democrats to support the outsider candidacies of contenders like Alexandria Ocasio Cortez. In addition to cultivating political leadership as part of their political strategy, social movement actors must recognize that in order to be successful, a social movement needs a core group of individuals who take on leadership roles within movement organizations and/or become the public face of the movement. The SPM recognized the need for multi-faceted leadership across geographic regions and social locations, and so developed mechanisms, such as the single-payer school, through which potential leaders could develop the skills and knowledge that would be necessary to lead the movement toward success. While public face leaders are of key importance during periods of extensive movement activity and public support, the most important leadership takes place within organizations and the everyday, often tedious, activities that are needed in order for a social movement to mobilize. These leaders sustain the social movement during periods of low support and create the mechanisms that allow mobilization during periods of increasing support. They are often the unsung heroes within a social movement. While the SPM recognized the value of political

[8] Senator Bernie Sanders: Speech Introducing S 1804 in September 13, 2017. Watch the full introduction here, https://www.c-span.org/video/?433998-1/senator-sanders-unveils-medicare-bill.

[9] Michael L., CNA organizer and HCN board member, Health Care NOW annual strategy conference, public address, Nov. 2009.

leadership and public face heroes, they did not center these heroes in the single-payer process or rely on these heroes to make social change happen.

Lesson 7: The Movement Needs Everyday On-the-Ground Warriors More Than Heroes

While heroic leaders are important to the success of a social movement, what is more needed are ordinary individuals who will be boots on the ground—taking on the everyday and sometimes tedious tasks of movement mobilization. Ben Day and Stephanie Nakajima, for example, are the current heart and soul of Healthcare NOW. They both started their work with the movement as activists having had experiences with the healthcare system as patients that left them adamant that a better way was possible. While they are both currently paid for the work that they do, they often work overtime and have at times of declining participation cut their own pay to keep the organization running.[10] Without the work that the on-the-ground warriors do—such as making fundraising calls, planning social movement activities, or paying the bills—a social movement organization cannot function or work to build the social movement. Heroes will arise within social movements at specific periods of increased attention and activity, but the work of on-the-ground warriors is continuous. Many of the activists who are currently core mobilizing forces in the SPM have been doing this work for decades. While reviewing historical documents, I was happy to find a statement in a newsletter from 1994 which was written by current Healthcare NOW board member—Rita Valenti. In that statement Rita said, "More efforts must be directed to stirring, exciting, and taking leadership from those for whom health care is a matter of survival."[11] Rita continues to be a powerful voice for mobilizing patients as leaders of the movement. The rise of anti-establishment politics during the Obama era resulted in the rise of anti-establishment heroes, such as Bernie Sanders, within the SPM. But, single-payer activists had learned their lesson from past disappointments and did not root their practice or their hope in single individuals. Rather—they rooted their practice and

---

[10] This was necessary at one point during the abeyance period following the enactment of the Affordable Care Act, but Healthcare NOW currently operates with a surplus due to significant fundraising from individuals that will protect the organization, and the staff, from financial hardship in the future.

[11] Action for Single Payer Newsletter, November 1994.

their hope in themselves, in their allies, and in the belief that their collective power could change the political context. While leaders did rise to the front of social movement mobilization and became key protagonists in the single-payer narrative, theses leaders were not immortalized but rather valued for their immediate and ongoing actions in support of the collective whole and the goals of the SPM. They were important protagonists in but not central to the single-payer narrative, which focuses on the everyday heroes who make social change happen.

Lesson 8: Recognizing the Importance of Narrative Strategy and Tactics

Social movement actors must learn not only how to craft their own narrative but also how to change the dominant narrative by using new cultural tools to reach a greater audience. Throughout this analysis of narrative practice, I have highlighted the ways in which activists have adapted to and utilized culture in order to seize the narrative of healthcare reform. Historical trends discussed in Chap. 8 suggest that the movement has been successful in the effort to make single-payer a central factor in the discourse of healthcare reform as the concept has more usage and support than ever before. Controlling the narrative of how this progress occurred is also an important task to which social movements must commit.

In part because dominant narratives of periods of progress tend to focus on social change heroes, the SPM recognized the need to create their own narrative explaining the process of social change. In this narrative, the movement does not focus on particular individuals but on the collective process that makes social change possible with a recognition that it is every day ordinary people, sometimes people who are the most hurt by current conditions, who are engaging in the everyday practices that can create a social movement with the potential to affect social change. Social change does not happen when a flash in the pan hero takes on the task, it happens through a slow burning fire that moves through ordinary individuals to create the hopeful passion necessary to take on the everyday tasks of social movement mobilization. It is through this slow burn that social movements create a context in which a flash in the pan can create the fire of social change that blazes so hot that it can burn down existing structures in order to create new systems that are grounded in collective solidarity and a shared respect for human rights. Social movement participants have recognized the need to tell detailed narratives of this slow burning process so that the story of social change is not incompletely told and thus misunderstood. If ordinary people think that social change only happens when there is a heroic leader who takes up the mantle of the social movement goal, then they will not understand that they too are needed. Social movements rely on ordinary individuals who are willing to take on the tedious tasks of activism in order to build the movement and to keep on keepin' on even within contexts in which heroes are few and far between.

LESSON 9: WHEN THE GOAL IS SOCIAL JUSTICE, WE NEED SOMEONE TO REACH FOR THE MOON

These are also lessons for organizations or individuals who do support healthcare justice but have decided that a more incremental approach is best. Sometimes incremental reform that is more immediately possible is needed, and society needs people who work to create those changes. But, those who focus on incremental change should cultivate an understanding that society also needs those who strive to "deliver the moon"[12] by working to make the impossible possible. The lesson for them is that even while focusing on incremental reform, they should value the work that activists mobilizing for progressive or radical change do because it is often this effort that works to create a context in which incremental changes seem less radical and thus more possible. This is illustrated in several past periods of social change in which more incremental changes were made in the context of a more radical movement. The Townsend Movement discussed in Chap. 1 is an example of this dynamic.[13] Within the story of healthcare reform, this process occurred when the Obama administration made arguments about the moderate characteristic of the Affordable Care Act by distancing it from single-payer. This was possible because there was a vocal SPM that was available as the straw man of this narrative. Indeed, I've

---

[12] Hillary Clinton quoted in: Kelly, Caroline. 2020. "Clinton doubles down on Sanders criticism, warns that he's promising 'the moon'" CNN Politics. Posted on February 6, 2020. https://www.cnn.com/2020/02/06/politics/hillary-clinton-bernie-sanders-ellen-moon/index.html.

[13] See Amenta, Edwin. 2008. When Movements Matter: The Townsend Plan and the Rise of Social Security Princeton University Press.

often wondered if the final thing that is needed to achieve single-payer in this country is a strong mobilization effort for a socialized healthcare system that entirely removes private entities from the process of health care delivery, as well as the financing. This could make single-payer appear to more people to be the moderate and conservative option for achieving universal health care that it actually is. Perhaps the challenge to the current political framework that a "political revolution" represents will also have this effect. In any case, it is important for all of those working to create socially just systems to refrain from denigrating the other for either "pie in the sky" or incremental goals. Reaching for the stars becomes more possible if we either work together or at the very least respect the grit and resilience of those who never give up on the moon.[14]

LESSON 10: ONWARD TO SINGLE PAYER?

Given the relative success of the Single Payer Movement in the last few years, the question becomes—what next? As I said in Chap. 1, as I finish the writing of this book, the country is at a crossroads leading into the 2020 election cycle. While the SPM is experiencing significant success and opportunity in all spheres of influence, the political context is still prohibitive of any form of progressive change due to the Trump administration and a Republican-controlled senate. The outcome of the 2020 election could have determinative power over the success or failure in relation to the primary goal of enacting single-payer legislation. Yet, even if a single-payer supporter, like Bernie Sanders, replaces Trump—creating a single-payer system will continue to be an uphill battle. If single-payer legislation is enacted, lessons from the states, as well as the recent challenges to the Affordable Care Act, inform us that enactment is not implementation and active support will still be needed to see the ultimate success of a fully functioning single-payer system in the United States.

One lesson is clear, any further movement toward progressive change in healthcare policy will take dedicated work, and this work will not be easy. Based on my analysis of thirty years of the SPM and my involvement within the movement for over fifteen years, I expect that single-payer activists will continue to fight and mobilize for single-payer. The dedication and fortitude of single-payer activists is not likely to be quelled any time soon, regardless of any shifts in the political context that might occur.

---

[14] A special thank you to Hillary Clinton for this analogy of promising the moon.

I hope that the history presented here will help activists involved in this process. It should be helpful for a social movement to have a detailed understanding of its history so that it can learn from both its successes and its failures. I was not able to include everything of importance in this book and plan to use my extensive amount of data to continue to write about the SPM. If you are a single-payer activist who has an important experience within the movement that has not been shared here, I'd be more than pleased to speak with you. The analysis presented here is based on the data that I have collected thus far, but I know that there is still much to learn. As a scholar-activist, I also plan to continue my work within the movement and use my limited expertise to inform and advise in any way that I can. Yet, the continued work of those currently involved might not be enough to push that heavy stone of progress over the top of that impossible hill.

If you have read this book for reasons beyond academic interest but are not yet involved in the movement, I also have some hopes to share with you. I hope that your reading of this text has helped you to not only understand the compassion that drives single-payer activists to work for a healthcare system in which everyone will have access to quality care with little to no costs at the point of service but also the extensive amount of labor that they have done so that we have reached this point in our collective national history at which a single-payer system seems more possible than ever—even with oppositional forces in the White House and Senate. I also hope that an understanding of this history encourages you to study further about this and other social movements working toward socially just systems. Finally, I hope that as you learn, you will also get involved in whatever way seems possible for you.

We are a community, and it is only through coming together as a community to fight collectively for progress that social change happens. When you do achieve success or experience failure, I hope that you are able to share those stories with others so that as a community we can learn and grow from experience. The story, relayed to you in Chap. 1, of how the tiny tired ant, who appeared to be too weak and too small, successfully ascended that impossible to climb path get to the tippy top of the tallest building, which was really just a table leg, is just as important as what happened when she reached her goal and finally experienced success. Others can learn from that process so that their success can support other mobilization efforts. Success along the path toward social justice has a cumulative effect. By working together we can push that heavy stone further along the path toward a socially just society that protects the rights of and ensures opportunity to all of its members. I know I'll be there on the path because, in the words of my dear friend Julia, gone but not forgotten, "I'm not sure if I'll see single-payer in my life time, but I sure as hell hope you see it in yours."

Index[1]

---

[1] Note: Page numbers followed by 'n' refer to notes.

© The Author(s) 2020

L. S. F. Hern, *Single Payer Healthcare Reform*,

https://doi.org/10.1007/978-3-030-42764-1

The manufacturer's authorised representative in the EU is Springer
Nature Customer Service Centre GmbH, Europaplatz 3, 69115 Heidelberg,
Germany. If you have any concerns regarding our products, please
contact ProductSafety@springernature.com

Printed and bound by CPI Group (UK) Ltd, Croydon, CR0 4YY
24/04/2026
02096333-0004